And God Created the Stars

A Masterpiece in the Study of Astropsychology

Dr. Louis Turi, M.D.S.

"He is wise who understands that the stars are luminaries, created as signs. He who will conquer the stars will hold the golden keys to God's mysterious universe."-----Nostradamus

"When will men stop killing other men in the name of God and their religions. When will men realize that the church is the Universe and acknowledge that the twelve apostles are the celestial laws written in light, in the stars. Most importantly when will men reach cosmic consciousness and perceive immortality and infinity. Ignorance is evil while cosmic consciousness the only path to self realization as to man's spirit becoming God"----Dr. Turi

Published by Re-evolution Press, LLC
19633 Ventura Boulevard, Suite B
Tarzana, CA 91356
www.reevolutionpress.com

ISBN: 0-9667312-7-1

Cover illustration & editing by
Madeline Rosenstein
www.madroseart.com

E-Mail Dr.Turi@cox.net

Web Page: http://www.drturi.com

Special 2004 Issue - Unlimited Edition

February 2004

Printed in the United States of America

Table of Contents

Acknowledgments

I would like to give a very special thanks to Jeff, Madeline, Melquida and my webmaster Gus. Without those brilliant old souls and their hard efforts to structure my work, mankind would have missed so much from the stars. Also, I want to give thanks to the numerous open-minded journalists and hosts of radio and television programs. I am grateful to all those spiritual men and women who have helped me enlighten their audience with the stars. I appreciate all those souls who have guided and supported my work in their efforts to further the truth. Lastly to all my readers, as they all are vital participants in the human experience. All have been invaluable in furthering the truth, and I am infinitely grateful to you for allowing me to share my celestial message to the world.

This work was transcribed from my audio-taped introductory Divine Astrology course album by Melquida Stephens. I upgraded all the information and Madeline Rosenstein produced the book cover and edited my work.

******

Letter from the Author

11/01/01

Dear Reader:

The golden key to wisdom can change one's life, simply because knowledge is power. Thus the possibility exists for each and every one of us to reach and enjoy the best of both the physical and spiritual worlds. Conventional disciplines such as traditional psychology, psychiatry and religious doctrines, will always fall short of tangible explanations for comprehending the complexity of the workings of the human mind. The purpose of this book is to enhance the understanding of what it means to be human and make good use of the tremendous spiritual dexterity available to each of us. Doing so can only help achieve peace, harmony, faith, love, health, emotional and financial security. Therefore, this stimulating reference work will act as a pathfinder to help you assimilate more knowledge and achieve true happiness. This "avant-garde" material is very controversial and can be quite offensive for some people. In no way would I purposely hurt anybody or try to convert anyone to my personal belief system. This book is simply a practical approach to any and all religions, and will test the reader's critical thinking to the extreme. The decision to accept these theories is solely yours and if, in the process of reading this book, you ascend to a much higher level of awareness, so be it. In the long run, this undertaking will undeniably help you to perceive the mechanics involving your Supraconscious in time and space, and dramatically help you to ascend to your own incredible Godly Power.

Once more, I thank you for your patronage and trust in my work.

--Dr. Turi

****

"Man is superior to the stars if he lives in the power of superior wisdom. Such a person being the master over heaven and earth by means of his will is a magus and magic is not sorcery but supreme wisdom."
--Paracelcus

INTRODUCTION

Divine Astrology and Astropsychology

In today's troubled times, man has sought answers to complex problems in medicine, politics, philosophy, science, religion and many other disciplines. All the while he is pondering the heavens and looking toward the stars as if to find answers, but not seeing as did the ancients, that the keys to life's mysteries are in front of his very eyes. As man has turned his vision toward the stars in space travel and technology, we have seen an unprecedented interest in Astrology and a renaissance of the oldest science in the world. Still, it is ironic that both the explosion of modern technology and centuries of religious dogma have produced more questions, death and trauma than real answers.

It is no wonder, then, that man's thirst for a more meaningful way of life has once again captured his interest in astrology. Sadly enough for mankind, astrology has been debased and maligned in modern times as a result of misunderstanding and commercial distortion. Thus, the old science has been deprived of its true spiritual values, transformed into confusing mathematical jargon by modern astrologers, and reduced to a punch line in your local newspaper horoscope column. I have made it my goal to return to you undistorted astrology, and through education and the dissemination of truth, future generations will join in a common search for true wisdom.

This tuition is my commitment to all the children of the world and to all people of all backgrounds, be they ethnic, educational, political or religious, who search for the truth. This work reflects my strong desire to rekindle the true meaning of the stars and the Divine Message of God from his celestial manifestation. I am also hoping that many teachers of modern science, and scientists alike, come to acknowledge the powerful meaning found in Astropsychology and Divine Astrology, rather than ignore its existence. Sadly enough, many of those young rational souls (mental snobs) cannot and will not be able to enter the intuitive domain of the stars. They are not aware of the fact that their limited, critical, scientifically oriented minds will quickly reject my work because they have been "computerized and programmed" by the Universal mind to accept only what is seen and proven physically. Well, what those scientists cannot see or understand just yet doesn't mean it doesn't exist, and they have all eternity in front of them to grow spiritually. Most of the time, scientists are protecting their academic accomplishments and their own ignorance from ridicule. There is still a significant difference between education and intelligence!

Divine Astrology, as practiced by the ancients, is a much-needed tool allowing spiritual regeneration in its purest form to all. Allowing the Divine Essence of the stars to clarify the human experience on this dense physical world, is a serious contribution to future generations' mental welfare and survival. I will work hard to reintegrate the old science of Astrology under the form of Astropsychology in our colleges and Universities to be accepted as a real discipline. The refusal to accept God's higher laws because of religious poisoning, skepticism or ignorance is not a valuable excuse and can only bring a serious penalty to mankind. Our children killing themselves in schools is an obvious message to the world that something is terribly wrong. Maybe its time for the educational administrations to realize the obvious failure and the deplorable situation they are in. The problem is not with the children, but with the system and the teachers. Restructuring the teacher's education, allowing them to look above their books to the stars, is the only valuable long-lasting solution. Those children are starving and dying because of the lack of spiritual regeneration, not knowing who they really are, where they come from and where they are going. They will not respond to dogmatic religious teachings, and as are the educational fields, both the psychological and religious fields are also at a loss, failing miserably to understand or remotely help those kids. Those young reincarnated spirits have been computerized by the celestial order of things, with a new and powerful set of dramatic stars. They can only survive on this dense physical world if they are fed a steady diet of undiluted truth coming from the spiritual teachings of the stars. There is no room for ignorance in both the physical and spiritual worlds, and anything less will bring a heavy penalty. It is now time to teach the children of the world, another set of spiritual laws that cannot be found in any of their schools' libraries, used by their assigned psychologists or taught in their local churches. They are a set of laws written in light, a set of spiritual laws coming from the stars which speak of God's glory and celestial manifestation. Lastly, for the purpose of happiness, peace and love for all, Divine Astrology will provide true spiritual guidance, stability and hope for all mankind.

As you make your way uncovering the secrets of the stars, you might feel overwhelmed and lost. Simply realize that you are not going to master the mysterious keys to the universe overnight. Dedication, perseverance and practice are the main ingredients you will need to bring forth your cosmic consciousness and become a confident and knowledgeable Astropsychologist. The idea is to be patient and the objective is to review this written material as many times as needed, so that you can grasp and assimilate all the information properly. Keep in mind that we are dealing with Divine Astrology, not Modern Astrology, and there is a big difference between the two disciplines. Divine Astrology is mostly intuitive and very symbolic in nature, whereas Modern Astrology is more mathematical and scientific. Like astronomy, mundane astrology seems to focus on details such as specific times and locations of births, trines, sextiles, risings, solar, Saturn returns and a myriad of other valuable astrological elements. However, at this early stage, an over concern with detail can also alter your objectivity and suffocate the intuitive message of the stars. In that respect, many valuable students tend to "miss the forest looking at the tree" and give up the study. Divine Astrology or Astropsychology deals with Nostradamus' 16th century method which was practiced at a time when many of today's tools were not available. Watches and computers had not been invented, and the calendars and methods of calculation were then very different. Thus I am going to teach you to focus mainly on the twelve symbolic Zodiac constellations and their inherent spiritual values. Later you may feel the need to expand to a more advanced type of Astrology, all the while maintaining your valuable intuition and objectivity. In that respect you can only improve your knowledge both rationally and spiritually to become a master Astropsychologist. When you advance to this level, you are ready to teach universal rules to the rest of the world. Again, realize that in Nostradamus' day, there were no computers or watches to specifically cut, separate or divide the universal energy.

As time progressed man became more rational in his insatiable request for knowledge. His newly invented tools began to appear and be used more commonly. For many specific reasons, calendars were also altered to improve the classification and categorization of all political and religious affairs. In the process, the true message of each zodiac sign, and its impact on the human psyche became distorted. I am still wondering to this day if it was really an accident of evolution, a scientific mistake, or a well-planned scheme by the politically oriented church. Was there any practical reason for the government, then the church, to cast aside the real purpose of the stars and their impact on humans? Why would they do that? Could it be that true knowledge is power? One thing, surely, is that power gives you the option to establish emotional, financial and spiritual stability. With this newfound independence, you become an outcast, denying the tax organization its power to manipulate you and tap your wallet to survive. Let's say it has been all disgustingly political, that the costly dance between the Presidential candidates Mr. Bush and Mr. Gore in the 2000 election was a hint of what has been really going on in our lives since day one. There is a valuable explanation pertaining to those two candidates, as far as the stars are concerned. For those who read "The Power of the Dragon," it is no mystery as to what really took place that election year. Both men were born with a hidden Dragon located in the sign of Gemini, predisposing and enforcing a duality in their lives, including all their political affairs. As a rule the numbers two, four, six, eight etc., will always be felt with them. The duality of counting and recounting the votes was a manifestation of the stars upon their lives. Of course, the uneducated American populace, including much of the rest of the world, scratched its head and wondered what really happened with the vote counting process.

To make it easy for you to assimilate, I will use the infamous murder trial of O.J. Simpson. I will be as objective as possible to point out the type of experiences (positive or negative) a soul has to endure when born dual. Much more is to be gained from my book "The Power Of The Dragon" of course, and your decision to expand on the matter is available to you.

O.J. Simpson was born with a Dragon's Head in Gemini, forcing duality in all he does. The symbol of Gemini is the twins, consisting of a male and a female, predisposing the soul to experience constant duality in all areas of his life.

O.J. has two (2) children (that we know of! But I am sure he has more out there).

Two (2) people died (killed identically)

Two (2) four (4) or more police cars chased him on the California highway.

Two (2) judgments were against him and he had to pay a dual number in millions.

Lastly, two (2) or four (4) attorneys or more were working on his case.

The list is endless if you dare to do some research, and I hope this little example will allow you to grasp my point. Much more can be read about O.J. and Nicole Simpson, and many other famous people, in “The Power of the Dragon”.

Realize also that disappeared civilizations such as the Incas, Sumerians, Atlantians, and also the Greeks, Arabs, and Turks, used the stars in their daily lives. So, my star student, like an old teacher of those long gone days, I am going to return you to a time when wise men used intuition and true wisdom. My goal is ultimately to teach you to recognize and use the symbolic power behind each sign of the zodiac. Unlike modern astrology, I will not harass you with mathematical jargon and long lifeless numeric tables. At this level you cannot afford to take a chance and spoil study. You may challenge me and say..."But Dr. Turi I've studied astrology for 20 years. Are you telling me that I've wasted my precious time?" In some ways my answer would be yes, indeed you took a chance and you certainly did not fulfill your need for true knowledge. Why would I say that? Simply because you are in my class, you're reading this book and you need more of the real stuff. Do I make sense to you? Of course! The problem is similar to a piano player whose rational teacher might have taught him to practice his keyboard scales the wrong way, and is now trying to play using a better technique. Similarly, this will make it all the more difficult for me to correct the problem of one who has practiced astrology another way. It is very common for the hardcore modern astrologer to "go by the book" and not challenge his own mental capacity or independent thought process. It's much like a religious fanatic who harasses everyone around him and cannot live life outside the codified thoughts or religious poisonings he suffered since childhood.

Still, never forget that astrology is a science and a valuable discipline where rules and numbers do play an important part. That's why it eventually became a science called Astronomy. This overly rational temperament is what I am so desperately trying to avoid. It is an attitude that breeds mental snobs who have long ago lost cosmic consciousness, dismissing the old science of Astrology. Meanwhile astrology is also an art in every sense of the word. Art involves inspiration, vision, revelation, prophecy, creativity, intuition, imagination, spirituality, symbolism, and all that deals with the subconscious or the spiritual world. Thus hardcore mathematics, rationale, basis, principle, reasoning, logic, and calculation must not take over the student's thinking-process. Sadly enough this is what usually happens, especially if the teacher himself was born with his natal Mercury (or assimilation of information, teaching, learning) into a rational earthy sign. Thus the fluidity of his perception is neutralized or badly hindered, shuts down, and puts a severe limitation to his domain. This scientifically oriented person should have learned and practiced astronomy in the first place.

If you are lucky enough, you were born with the natal tools for true and easy assimilation of hidden matters, as was Einstein or any famous soul who made history. Refer to "The Power Of The Dragon" to learn how and why the stars dictated many famous people's contribution to the world. This means a curious, open mind and powerful Mercury by house or Mercury in an advanced air or water sign. The beauty of being human is that regardless of your natal load, you can still reach cosmic consciousness and master the universal mind and use a wealth of information.

History: Now before going further, let me give you some information pertaining to a very important discovery made back home, in France, 1995.

Underwater Cave "Lascaux" Discovered

Near Marseilles

In January of 1995, at the base of a cliff in the region in southeastern France, just a few miles away from where I was born, Jean-Marie Chauvet discovered another complex of large caves. There, he found a "window of the Stone Age" that tells astonishing tales of prehistoric times. Interestingly enough, this discovery was very different from the one previously found near Marseille in 1991 by Mr. Cosquer and was immediately reported and broadcast all over the world including the United States. Jean-Marie Chauvet's discovery is recognized by the markings as "characteristic of the Stone Age," while the underwater cave discovered by Mr. Henri Cosquer involved a spiritual mythology and intriguing knowledge of cosmology!!

This incredible news-breaking story below was reported throughout Europe in September 1991. News writers Scott Collins, Denise Koptcho , Ellen Murphy and their editor, Laurent Aublin, reported as follows:

A prehistoric underwater grotto ornamented with carvings, charcoal and manganese dioxide drawings depicting dozens of animals as well as stenciled hand prints on the walls and ceiling, was discovered in Cassis, a town near Marseille, France. The discovery dates back to 27,000 B.C. and predates by about 20,000 years all other discoveries of prehistoric art in the southeast of France. To the puzzled scientists, the significance of the representations in the grotto remains a mystery.

Leroi-Gourhan's theory ascribes the Magdalene with refinement and claims that the cave paintings show that the animal depictions were placed on the wall in a determined order, their numbers and positions thereby revealing an established mythology and an evident cosmology.

In this view, the cave is regarded more as a sanctuary and place of worship. The entrance to the cave, currently situated approximately 120 feet below sea level, leads to a narrow passageway ascending 480 feet before opening into a vast space spanning 160 feet by 192 feet, and 9.6 to 12.8 feet in height from floor to ceiling. The center of the space is above the water level, although the sea touches the wall enough to hide the feet of some of the horse illustrations along the bottom. There are fissures in the walls, evident by the existence of modern-day bat cadavers that have allowed a steady stream of air from the outside to filter into the cave for roughly 14,000 years, permitting the art to remain intact. At the time of the Paleolithic Superior and the artistic activity in question, the sea level was about 35 feet lower, so that far from being submerged underwater, the grotto was actually elevated a good distance above sea level.

Thus, the southeast of France, once thought of as a "human desert" during this period, did, in fact, participate in the immense "cultural empire" that stretched from the Atlantic Ocean to the steppes of Central Asia. Recently categorized as a "Grotto of Paleolithic Cave Art" among historic monuments by Jack Lang, Minister of Culture, the cave has been baptized with the name of its discoverer, the "Grotte Cosquer." Its access has since been blocked to prevent all desecration to a discovery qualified by archaeologists as having "a unique and tremendous importance at the global level."

The cave beneath the sea: Paleolithic Images at Cosquer

In 1991, a professional diver named Henri Cosquer discovered a wealth of prehistoric art in a cave near Marseille, France. The opening to the cave, once several miles inland from the Mediterranean, became submerged when the sea began to rise at the end of the last ice age, about 12,000 years ago. Since that time, no human had entered this deep cavern or had seen the paintings and engravings of animals, human hands, and signs that cover the walls and ceilings until Cosquer swam cautiously up the flooded entrance passage.

News of Cosquer's extraordinary find flashed around the world. The French Ministry of Culture immediately sent two eminent archaeologists, Jean Clottes and Jean Courtin, to study the cave. Assisted by teams of specialists, they carried out two diving missions to the site, in 1991 and 1992. This book describes what they found and provides the first complete photographic documentation of this incredible site, one of the most decorated caves of Europe.

The explorers discovered not only the engravings and paintings in amazingly fresh earth colors, but also traces of the ancient humans who made the images. These included logs burned to illuminate the cave while the artists worked, flint blades — perhaps the very tools used to draw on the soft limestone walls and, on nearly every surface, thousands of the grooves archaeologists call "finger tracings." Among the earliest work done in probably intended to announce the presence of humans in the cave and establish their possession of it.

Because charcoal and charcoal pigments were found in such abundance at the site, and because the archaeological context was undisturbed, Cosquer is now one of the most thoroughly and firmly dated Paleolithic caves in the world. Thanks to a series of 12 radiocarbon dates, we know that the images at Cosquer were made during two different eras. The stenciled hands are extremely ancient, created about 27,000 years ago. The land animals — cold-loving plains horses, ibex, chamois, aurochs, and the huge ice-age deer called megaloceros — are some 18,500 years old. There are also marine animals, very unusual subjects in Paleolithic art: they include seals, great auks (penguin-like birds that are now extinct), and mysterious images that may represent fish and jellyfish.

Throughout this fascinating book, which includes notes, a full bibliography, and a glossary of 125 key terms, the Cosquer cave is discussed in relation to other prehistoric decorated caves in Europe. The authors judiciously speculate on the meaning of the ancient images and what they can tell us not only about the lost world of our remote ancestors but about the origins of myth making, symbolizing, and art making — in other words, of being truly human.

About the authors: Formerly in charge of prehistoric antiquities in the Midi-Pyrenees region of France, Jean Clottes is General Conservator of the National Heritage and Scientific Advisor on Prehistoric Art to the French Ministry of Culture and the French Community. He is the president of the International Committee on Monuments and Sites (ICOMAS). Currently the Director of Research for the National Center for Scientific Research (CNRS), Jean Courtin was previously in charge of antiquities in the Provence region of France and co-director of the Department of Underwater Archaeological Research (DRASM). Once more "it was determined that the drawings were made over 15,000 and in some instances, 35,000 years before the birth of Christ. To this day this is the oldest chronological report available to mankind. The cave paintings show that the animal depictions were placed on the wall in a determined order, their numbers and positions thereby revealing an established mythology and an evident cosmology." Again, with all facts in hand, there is nothing older than astrology!

I was as usual cruising through my friend Jeff Rense's website (www.rense.com) and this latest news from my country came to my attention:

Experts Rave Over French Prehistoric Cave Art Find By Crispian Balmer - 7-6-01 - PARIS (Reuters) - Stunning prehistoric engravings uncovered in a cave in western France could be just a foretaste of the treasures held in the dank interior, but the public will probably never get a glimpse, an archaeologist said on Thursday.

Art experts have hailed the find at Cussac in the Dordogne valley as a major discovery, with the grotto chamber covered in spectacular drawings of wild animals, hybrid beasts, birds and women and erotic imagery.

"This site is of world importance," said Dany Barraud, the Culture Ministry's head of archaeology in the Dordogne region.

Initial estimates have suggested the vivid engravings are between 22,000 and 28,000 years old — much earlier than famous wall paintings in the nearby Lascaux cave complex that are reputed to be more than 16,000 years old.

"We are talking about monumental engravings. We have found more than 100 engravings so far, but we think that there are many more. The trouble is that it is an extremely fragile site which is hindering our work," Barraud told Reuters.

The cave floor consists of unstable clay, while the limestone walls are flaky and susceptible to temperature changes, preventing large groups from visiting the chamber.

In addition, there is a high level of carbon gas in the underground passages, which means that archaeologists can only spend a maximum of three hours on site before having to return to the surface for fresh air.

REPLICA PLANNED FOR TOURISTS

“It will not be opened to the public, but the local authorities are considering creating a replica of the site in a nearby cave for tourists,” said Barraud.

The Cussac cave was uncovered by speleologist Marc Delluc last September, but the importance of the finding was only made public this week.

The engravings are dotted along a chamber 900 meters (yards) long, some 15 meters wide and more than 10 meters high.

Among the artwork is a picture of a bison some four meters long — one of the biggest single prehistoric engravings ever found — and one scene featuring up to 40 figures.

Among the line carvings are animals with deformed heads, a bison with a horse’s head, silhouettes of women and half a dozen representations of female erotica.

“There is undoubtedly a very special atmosphere at Cussac... There is an originality here,” said Jean Clottes, an adviser on Prehistoric Rock Art at the Culture Ministry.

Archaeologists have also found human remains in the cave, although they are not yet sure if the relatively well-preserved skeletons date from a later age than the artwork.

The Cussac discovery is the second major prehistoric art site found in France in less than a decade.

In 1994, potholers stumbled across a complex of galleries full of paintings in the Ardeche gorge. Experts believe the animal pictures there are some 32,000 years old and, as with Cussac, the public has been barred access to safeguard the site.

What really bothers me most is that those scientists are so totally uneducated as to not recognize anything that could be remotely involved with astrology, unless it becomes obvious. Even if they were evident drawings or astrological residues (as in the Cosquer caves), the government may not necessarily tell you all about it. In the Cosquer grotto, they somehow mentioned it as the Leroi-Gourhan's theory ascribes the Magdalene's with "refinement and claims that the cave paintings show that the animal depictions were placed on the wall in a determined order, their numbers and positions thereby revealing an established mythology and an evident cosmology." I am sure this much older cave is loaded with certain astrological paintings too, but as in the "secret Vatican library" only certain people can access the site. Meantime the huge and obvious astrological chart found at the entrance to the Vatican certainly tells more about the immensity of astrological work, and astrological secrets hidden away from the general populace for centuries.

I wish I myself had access to such marvels, as I am sure the French authorities do not tell all about the artwork they found. Especially since the infamous law of "exception" or the About/Picard bill was passed in France, on May 30th 2001 by the French Chamber. Showing it all would be sure proof as to the use of astrology in the old days and a certain disaster to the latest law against our common freedom. This would be a deadly blow against Christianity and the established status Quo. Thus, they found archeological excuses to insure that no one can see or investigate further all the "disturbing" findings. The same applies for the "Dead Sea Scrolls." Only those free of astrological references are available to the masses, the others are kept well hidden and perceived as "disturbing facts," by those in charge of our lives and wallets. You will find much of that jealously and dangerously guarded information under the Vatican's seven miles of secret library. Much of the work displayed there was confiscated by the Inquisition during the dark ages and brought back to the Vatican. This incredible amount of true knowledge does not belong to the Christians (enemies of mental progress) but to the many people who paid with their lives, the price of fear, ignorance and religious poisoning. The oblivious situation the French people are now under, infringing general freedom, could also affect the US unless we do something about it ASAP. I am also hoping for your understanding and your support.

Astrology is far from being dead, it continues to remain and flourish. It is growing and constantly gaining legions of new followers—mostly because it works! The new entourage is not just the common man in the street or your neighbor, but also involves famous people of all walks of life. Some examples are Presidents, such as Ronald Reagan and first lady Nancy, Kings and Queens (Lady Diana), and Heads of state, (both French Presidents Jacques and Francois Mitterrand, Saddam Hussein, and the list goes on).

(Note - Americans may laugh about Nancy Reagan's use of an astrologer. It seems that it may be common practice at the highest levels in other government as well.) PARIS (AFP) - Astrologist Elizabeth Teissier has decided to publish transcripts of taped conversations she had with former French President Francois Mitterrand between 1990 and 1995.

"I want to respond to all kinds of insinuations which have cast doubt over the purely professional discussions between Mitterrand and me, and to demonstrate the importance of astrology in politics," she told AFP.

Mitterrand's daughter Mazarine Pingeot said Saturday that her father, who served as president from 1981 to 1995, did not seek Teissier's advice to make important decisions. "It is all laughable and unimportant," she said.

The tapes reveal advising Mitterrand on such subjects as the government of former Prime Minister Edith Cresson and the date of the French referendum on the Maastricht Treaty. This was according to transcripts printed by pay-TV station Canal Plus, in the written version of one of its programs. Teissier claimed Mitterrand had called upon her often during the Gulf War, she said, adding that the former president was keen to seek her advice despite his skeptical and rational nature.

In one extract, Mitterrand asks for advice about the timing of a speech at the beginning of the conflict in January 1991: "I am going to have to intervene. Which, according to you, is the best day?" Mitterrand asks, "In the coming days?" Teissier replies, "Sunday, Monday, Tuesday; I will have to look into that, because I can't tell you point-blank like that," she says. "Come and see me," he finishes. Teissier said that she met Mitterrand in 1989 at his request, and that she recorded their conversations from 1990 onwards with his consent.

"The idea of recording came to me very quickly, but with his permission, of course. It was the only proof for me that it was all real," she said. "After several meetings, I went to see him with my recorder. He was taken aback. I told him it was for my grandchildren, and eventually to write a book." Teissier, who held her meetings with Mitterrand at the Elysees Palace except in 1995, when their conversations took place on the telephone, had already revealed the content of her interviews in a book published three years ago.

It was only after recent press speculation about their relationship that she decided to publish the transcripts, she said. The head of the Francois Mitterrand Institute, Jean-Louis Bianco, declined to comment on the revelations.

Again, put your self in the position of the French President, consulting an astrologer. What would other powerful leaders of the world would say about you? As President, I am supposed to make sensible judgments, and as the commander-in-chief of the country, I cannot afford to be thought incapable of making calculated decisions. This worry, all for fear of derision. Someone trustful like Mitterrand's own daughter, Mazarine Pingeot was "picked" to clean and clear the "laughable" situation about her dear daddy. I wonder how many death-threats Elizabeth Teissier endured, and most of all, how lucky she has been not end up victim of her rulers and another statistic as was Marilyn Monroe.

But do not be fooled, like many French Presidents, other powerful decision-makers (including Ronald Reagan, Hitler, Yeltsin and others) used the stars. Well, this letter was issued for a specific purpose, which is not to offend the status quo, mental snobs, or of course the religious lunatics of this world.

****

Disturbing news From France

With the Tail of the Dragon (negative) in the sign of Sagittarius (laws) since October 10th 2001, my worst fears related to religion and new laws became a reality.

Destruction, from suicidal bomb attacks to political turmoil, fueled the continuous deadly religious war in the Middle East. There is nothing new coming from this Neptunian part of the world, but I want to bring your attention to a different war taking place in my own homeland. The uneducated masses are not yet aware of the extreme power of organized institutions and their infiltration to the core of our lawmakers' offices, both in Europe and the US. Anything organized is Uncle Sam's deceiving attempts to control your mind and actions. All of these deceptive endeavors are hidden behind the good words of the Lord. Those operating in the open for Uncle Sam are also exempted of taxes, remember? So is your local church and much of its massive staffing we all support. The war against ignorance and fear (the Pisces age), and the future and its freedom of speech (Aquarius age), is doing battle right now. This battle has been going on since the dark ages and has taken the lives of millions.

I am so ashamed of what has transpired in my own country. And I sincerely hope for your support as I am far from being a cult or a religious leader for that matter. You do not have to be an affiliate or go to an expensive building to request my services. Your privacy is respected and no one will ever know you came to visit me, not even Uncle Sam. Once the About/Picard law is enforced, like a cancer, it will spread to the US and reach many other countries. In the name of God and your deceptive manipulative institutions, the New Age worker, the Light worker, the homeopathic doctor, and the hypnotherapy practitioner will end up burning on a modern stake. There are lunatics out there for sure, deceiving psychics and tarot readers on national television. There are cult leaders everywhere, and also the ruling parties want to clean up, monopolizing your belief system and your actions in the process. That's why the Bible and all other religious materials were "invented" by the rulers of the country of your birth. The result is a variety of deities and dogmatic teachings, a myriad of churches, temples and synagogues worldwide, all imposing their own dogmatic teachings. With no competition from the New Agers (seen by religious fanatics as pagans), or various dangerous cult leaders, there is much more power, money and control to be gained.

What is a cult leader?

Indeed the worst form of expression produced by Neptune is a "Neptunian," the best way to describe a cult leader. Based upon sensitive information one can make a good assessment of what a cult leader is all about. A strong and negative expression of the planet Neptune will plague the subject's personality, words, and behavior in various ways.

The subject believes he is Jesus or a religious entity such as the Virgin Mary etc. (David Koresh and Rev. Jones).

The subject believes he or she is a reincarnation of a religious entity or prominent religious leader.

The subject believes he or she has specific religious mission.

The subject thinks he or she is the only chosen one.

The subject has a definite purpose to save or change the world.

The subject hears voices (Joan of Arc).

The subject uses several, or foreign, long names.

The subject uses dignified words (great, master, grand order etc.)

The subject uses appearances (Jesus, long beard, long hair etc.)

The subject dresses magnificently or colorfully (long robs, hats, striking colors, gold, silver etc.)

The subject uses religious verses (Bible, archaic material etc.)

The subject uses lots of caring words (love, prosperity etc.)

The subject uses negative Plutonic energy, magnetic voice piercing eyes (Hitler etc.)

The subject uses and demands money for his cause (to build temples, statues, churches, etc.)

The subject uses physical strengths and abuses others (rapists, con men etc.)

The subject uses appearances (long beard, long hair etc.)

The subject is totally unaware of the working of the Universal Mind (religious oriented and skeptics alike)

In all honesty this type of endeavor is detrimental to a well balanced society and as much as I defend and support freedom of expression I am totally against any form of cult in any manner or shape. Here is a little test for you…

Would you or would you not support the following?

February 12, 2004

Castellane, France — Demolition workers have smashed the giant concrete statue built illegally by a cult leader in southern France. A controlled explosion toppled the 110-foot homage to Gilbert Bourdin, late founder of the Golden Lotus cult, and sent it sliding a few feet down a hill outside the village of Castellane in southeastern France.

Workers used heavy-duty jackhammers to hack away at the structure to weaken it after an attempt to demolish it on Wednesday was abandoned, when workers saw its base was reinforced with iron. French authorities said the monument to Bourdin, the focal point of the sect's "holy city of Mandarom" just outside Castellane, was built in 1990 without permission.

Cult followers compared the demolition of the statue, which shows the guru resplendent in white robes and a papal-style tiara, to the recent destruction in Afghanistan by the Taliban regime of colossal 1,500-year-old Buddhist statues. A small group watched from behind a security cordon with tears in their eyes as the statue wobbled under the loud explosion and then slowly fell backward down the hill. "It's a victory for law over the world of sects," he said, opening a bottle of sparkling wine. Bourdin, who also called himself the Cosmoplanetary Messiah of Synthesis, the Great Master of the Order of the Knights of the Triumphant Vajra, the Master of the Selection of Souls and the Great Pontiff of the Cosmic Diamond Order, claimed to be immortal. He died of heart disease in 1998 aged 74. He founded his "Aumism" movement in 1969 as a synthesis of all religions and created Mandarom, which is about 30 miles northwest of the Riviera resort of Cannes.

****

Biblical Cult leaders

Do you wonder why Leonardo Da Vinci carved Moses with a set of horns? Because Moses was a lunar cult leader and the horns are a representation of the crescent moon. During those ancient days, he was preaching his own moon's beliefs passed on to him, while a much older cult called the "Stellar" cult was worshiping the Sun God.

With the passage of time, various religious cults have disappeared who used animals to mobilize the Neptunian energy, especially the bull. The most successfully acclaimed, approved and followed religious cult leaders (in their own respective reincarnation time-in-space and geographical location world wide) are Jesus, Allah, and Buddha. Subsequently, an explosion of religious cults of all sorts have infested the world, producing a myriad of Neptunian reasons to destroy their neighbors (religious wars). Temples, churches, synagogues and a multitude of man-made buildings have been built, and doctrines taught, to reinforce Neptune's deceptive impact on this world.

The same positive or negative qualities of each and every planet is at work but not yet fully understood, or even recognized by the young-soul community (scientists, mental snobs, atheists or uneducated imbeciles). This crowd operates in a more rational, mundane way, and expresses its mental limitations on a more formal and practical level. You will find these people performing at a stadiums (sports figures, announcers), in labs (scientists), in churches (religious lunatics), or in the construction field just to name a few. Anything goes, as long as they do not have to extend their minds and refine their spirits outside of society's norms.

Now, there is a big difference between a New Age worker and a cult leader.

Let's take one single example, of perhaps millions. Just imagine this scenario: no more homeopathic medicines as of today, that's now a true and enforced law in the U.S. Now all the medical institutions and insurance companies will make more money from you, and will keep detailed records of all your health secrets to sell to other manipulative organizations. Uncle Sam will have an obvious record as to your whereabouts. Most of all, right now much of this natural medicine is either free or quite cheap, and Uncle Sam cannot grab the records and cannot tax you, or involve powerful insurance companies. So when it comes down to it, it's Evil Money, and a total waste of time, and Sam cannot survive without our tax dollars. Organized institutions bring mental discipline and solid records. Religions are also part of the hidden scheme of things and secret agendas are fully supported by governments all over the world.

The uneducated masses, falls victim to its ruling party and pays a heavy price in so many ways. But when freedom is at stake we should all fight and we have the right to do so. Hitler tried to take this freedom from us, he also ordered the burning of all astrological books and would punish with death, those found with such materials. Why? Hitler was a fanatic of Astrology and surrounded himself with many astrologers. What happened at the end with the Nazis? Knowledge is power, and the greedy Nazi leader was not about to share this valuable astrological knowledge with anyone. Realize again that knowledge is power, and power means your given options to establish emotional, financial and spiritual stability.

If this were so, then why would you need any organized institutions to control you? Because they are like a bunch of leeches or fleas on a dog and cannot exist without your blood. The repression in France against New Age, alternative and holistic people (including natural medicine, oriental medicine, herbs and homeopathy) started in 1995. Since then, with a system of denunciation similar to the one used during Nazi occupation of France in WWII, thousands of French people have been investigated, and their files are "ready" in police and justice structures. French citizens were asked by police to denounce their neighbors and members of their own family if they would find "subversive activities" such as:

* Making new friends * receiving many phone calls * going to meetings * reading a lot of books * burning incense at home * meditating at home * changing eating habits * becoming vegetarians * stop watching TV...

A law is necessary to prosecute all these people who are a danger to society, considered the "new heretics". The bill has been in progress for some time and has now become a fully-enforced LAW. See below.

Now French people displaying the behavior and "subversive activities" listed above will face 3 years imprisonment and heavy fines, as well as having their groups dissolved under "criminal activities". Again, if you think that this will never happen in other countries including in the "land of the free", well think again. We are not in Disneyland anymore...The days ahead will see how many "patriots" are left in the "home of the brave"...The "free Press" has been eliminated in France. In the USA, no more that 8 trusts/corporations own all the media today, ranging from radio/TV channels to magazines and newspapers, and the same multinational trusts also own oil companies, chemical companies, laboratories, everything, worldwide...

It is confirmed that the infamous law of "exception" had been passed in France, on May 30th by the French Chamber. The only resort now is a claim to the"Conseil Constitutionnel" (Constitution Council) that would prove that the law is non-constitutional, and a claim to the European humans' rights organizations. This procedure has rarely succeeded in the past.... The About/Picard bill is now a FRENCH LAW. France has now become officially a dictatorship, censuring its citizens and controlling their lives and beliefs. Since it is now a LAW, it could be used - and will be - to prosecute the 172 spiritual groups on the black list of the Chamber, and the many thousands of French people that have been investigated since the beginning of the repression in 1995 against spiritual, freethinking, alternative and holistic people.

Note: Native American speakers such as Wallace Black Elk (one of the pioneers of the American Indian movement) have been forecasting for about two years now in their public speeches, that the same dictatorship will happen in America... (Video available at: cptnlyur@wnclink.com) So what is happening in France may simply be a test for Europe and the world, since the "rulers of the planet" are not limited to one particular country. The new petition could also be sent by email to the CAP coordination in France: coordiap@libertysurf.fr

Check this internet list in English of support for France:

http://groups.yahoo.com/group/FreedomForFrance

****

A PETITION AGAINST THE ABOUT/PICARD LAW

The Coordination of Associations and People for Freedom of Conscience (CAP) is an association that was formed after the first hearing of victims of religious discrimination in France. It is open to people of all religions who have in common a deep attachment to freedom of religion and freedom of conscience. CAP has put on the Net, the text of a petition to be signed by all those who oppose this law originated by French senator Nicolas About and French MP Catherine Picard. The petition can be found at the following address:

www.petitiononline.com/CAP01/petition.html

Since its start, the petition has collected over 8000 signatures from various people. Numerous ages, jobs and countries are represented: France, Germany, Great Britain, the United States and also Mexico, Australia, Hungary, Russia, etc. CAP has received by E-mail numerous encouraging messages. Some have even sent prayers and poems! Various associations distribute the message amongst their members. As the mobilization against the law starts to grow, CAP will soon file the petition with its list of signatures to the main international bodies protecting human rights. For all those who do not have access to Internet, here is the text of the petition:

On June 22nd, 2000, the French parliament voted a new bill against "cults" proposed by senator Nicolas About and parliament member Catherine Picard. A final vote by the French parliament took place on May 30th 2001, in spite of strong reservations by mainstream religions. The law: gives for the first time the legal definition of a "cult," in contradiction with the French law of separation between religions and State and the French Constitution, which guarantees religious neutrality from the State. It creates a crime of "mental manipulation," punished by a 3 year jail indictment and a fine of 300 000 FRF. The law punishes the fraudulent abuse of a person in a state of psychological or physical subjection resulting from the exercise of serious or repeated pressures or techniques meant to alter one's judgment. As there are no objective criteria in this definition, it will open the door to all kinds of abusive interpretations.

The same act, a spiritual guidance or the practice of a confession, will be considered as normal if done within a mainstream religion, or be considered criminal if done within a group labeled as "cult". It is the first time that a democracy has created such a crime. Its formulation is very close to the crime of "plagio" (creating a state of suggestion) made in fascist Italy by Mussolini, to repress communist propaganda. The crime of "plagio" had been later removed from the penal code by the Italian constitutional court after it had been applied to catholic priests and homosexuals.

About/Picard modifies the French penal code by authorizing judges to punish legal entities such as associations, for a wide variety of minor offenses, whereas this possibility was formerly reserved to serious offenses. For instance, forgetting to put a fire extinguisher in a precinct that belongs to an association will give a judge the possibility to condemn the association itself.

It creates a new accelerated procedure to facilitate the dissolution of groups labeled as "cults", which does not guarantee adequately the rights of the defense, whereas dissolution is an extreme punishment, the equivalent to the death penalty for physical persons. It gives, in order to facilitate the dissolution of groups labeled as "cults", a new definition to a group considered a legal entity, in contradiction with the judicial principle that only those who commit an illegal act should be punished. Thus, associations, which are legally separate, could be dissolved in the same procedure, as long as they pursue similar objectives. Two minor offenses will be enough to make the dissolution possible, a fact that greatly endangers freedom of association. It limits the promotional activities of groups labeled as "cults", and gives mayors the possibility to refuse a building permit to those groups as long as they have been condemned twice, even for minor offenses.

With that law in France, the new religions such as minority religions, and groups promoting personal development, are easily labeled as "cults", a very arbitrary label as everyone knows. They are condemned to barely survive, with this permanent menace over their heads. It will suffice that if one of their leaders or the group itself be condemned twice for a minor offense after a quick trial, the group will be disbanded with an interdiction to reestablish itself. If such a law were applied to members of the French parliament, the parliament would be immediately dissolved as justice has condemned many of its members! There is indeed a real danger of this law being applied to mainstream religions or to any non-conformist spiritual group.

If the About/Picard bill makes it into law, France will be ranked among the worst dictatorships of THOSE WHO ENDEAVOR, FOR THE SAKE OF THE STATE, OR FOR GENERAL INTEREST, TO PERVADE INDIVIDUAL CONSCIENCE.

I think that the French penal code is sufficient to repress offenses and crimes committed within a group, whatever the label given to that group, for law must be the same for everyone, and I demand that this law proposal be rejected, considering the fundamental liberties that it threatens. If you do not have access to Internet, CAP can sign the petition for you. In that case, please indicate your name and nationality. And send to: coordiap@libertysurf.fr

It is part of my mission not only to teach you the secret of the Universal Mind, but also to educate you about laws or customs in the US or anywhere that infringe upon our research for truth and freedom. I just wonder where the meaning of those well acclaimed French words have gone… "Liberty - Equality - Fraternity". So many people died for our freedom, but did they die in vain?

As we proceed in this tuition, you the reader will learn to decipher every day, the manifestation of the Cosmic Mind in every person and all things with which you deal, see, and touch. We are all but vibrations, and this particular dense physical world vibrates at a very low frequency. We all vibrate differently at a certain speeds or levels, and that is our only reality. The more superior the vibrations, the higher, more valuable the knowledge the soul will inherit. We will all undergo positive or negative, and sometimes dramatic experiences. Thus a magnet will not attract a piece of wood. Similar people will attract specialized crowds of unique interests. It is through this constant battle between ignorance and wisdom that one can expect to be challenged, and with it the option for spiritual growth.

Truth and knowledge therefore, are not a part of your soul. Thus, experiences are forced upon you and others, and by this interaction you can learn, sometimes very painfully. Consequently, you only know what you know, and you may be thinking that you know better than others but chances are you don't. You simply cannot know better just yet, unless you "walk in the shoes of that person". With fanatics, you will have to deal with people who have total reluctance to enter someone else's views and values. In the process, a world of incredible information is avoided, and the soul stagnates. In most cases, this phenomenon is due to fear of ridicule, induced religious poisoning, or mental snobbery. This is often the result of an earthy Mercury afflicting the soul at birth. They haven't yet realized that what is not seen or touched by rationally educated scientists or what has been cast aside by religious groups does not mean it does not exist. The fact is, simply by looking into someone else's world, you will expand your own world and in the process, your own cosmic consciousness.

Each one of us has chosen a very specific time of the year to be born. You also selected a specific location. For instance, you could have been born in Africa, Russia, etc., for that matter. You have picked your precise place of birth and even your parents, and all this for a very good karmic reason.

Before you entered this dense physical world, higher spirits helped and protected your arrival. At the specific time-in-space, your chosen world and location, and your parents and conditions, the pattern of the stars froze in a fixed position. This complex celestial signature impregnated your psyche. This is commonly called an astrological chart, natal chart, a wheel etc. You somehow "waited" in time and space for the "right time" to reincarnate into this highly sophisticated spiritual design or celestial configuration. All was set, and perfectly in place, to "submerge" your spirit, so to speak, to make you the truly unique person you are. Contrary to what has been said by some famous people, MAN IS NOT born equal. Some children are born sick, some are born healthy, some have musical gifts or are adept in drawing, speaking, writing etc. Some, no matter how they educate themselves, can never excel at these things. Some children will grow to become very tall, and some will be small. Some will be smart by birth, intuitive, and sensitive, and some will have difficulty in comprehending or accepting certain information. Some children will be overloaded as was I, by Mercury (the planet regulating the nervous system). They will be handful, and will be classified as having ADD by the educated "mental snobs". As were Einstein and President Clinton by the way! If any one of us had to, or was forced by our concerned parents (following the advice of the school psychologist) to ingest this poison, there might not be an Einstein, a Clinton, or a Dr. Turi, operating in this world. Thanks to a lack of destructive prescriptions such as of Ritalin or Prozac then, we have all made our contributions. But who stands to lose tons of money? The doctors and the well-established but unconcerned pharmaceutical companies producing those harmful drugs, they would lose money.

Incidentally, there is a big difference between education and intelligence. A well-educated person who makes large amounts of money doesn't mean he is more intelligent than you. Especially that irresponsible scientist prescribing volatile drugs to our children! He is simply educated in handling numbers or different types of information. Most of the time; he was born with a rational, shrew, business mind. He is the professional student and "mental snob." Most important, our unaware society (you the parent) always rewards his professional talents (or death sentences). This same person may also have problems relating to a much higher type of information, and simply denies or refuses to expand on spiritual matters. The soul is just not yet ready to dig into the divine or intuitive domain of the world so to speak (the outside world, stars, UFOs, etc). What would the established institutions say if they were to find that I am a student of Dr. Turi and the stars? Would they take my license away? Would they ridicule me? Would I make or lose more money? Can I work as a child psychologist (psychiatrist) without drug prescriptions? Are there alternate ways and more uses of homeopathic medicines for me? Will my government do what was done in France, and impose new laws against homeopathic medicine practitioners or spiritual groups? How much do I have to relearn? All of those questions are about themselves, but what about the children? Would they feel better? Would I screw up their minds? What about the secondary affects of their lives, in the long run ? Those very last questions might not even enter their minds.

So, by realizing and accepting this reality, all of us have our own (advanced or not) spiritual gifts. However, our will is much stronger than a set of rational stars, thus by keeping an open mind, the option to grow spiritually is offered to the young soul. In certain cases, many reincarnations are needed to reach a higher level of spirituality.

IMPORTANT: The stars cannot be controlled (mutual reception). The stars are set. The stars just do. The stars do not think. The stars do not feel. The stars are not emotional. The stars impose their subtle vibrational functions, and we will feel or act upon their higher jurisdictions. The stars have a specific and a divine purpose. But the beauty of being human is that you can apply your will to use those stars. However, without cosmic consciousness your will becomes useless, and like the millions of people around you, you are nothing more than a physical robot, spiritually and remotely manipulated by those stars.

Our challenge here is to decode the message of the stars for the well being of mankind. Slowly but surely, and with my guidance, you will understand my message and become a master in handling and understanding others through Divine Astrology or Astropsychology. Also, during the course of this study you will be building what I call a "reflex," to aid in understanding and assimilating this information.

"Oh, say, can you see through the starry night, are those twelve signs still in sight..."

Are You a Genius?

Witelson and her team acquired Einstein's brain after its keeper, scientist John Harvey, who had read about the university's brain research, contacted them. Harvey was a pathologist working at a small hospital in Princeton, NJ, when Einstein died in 1955 at the age of 76. Harvey performed the autopsy; determined Einstein died of natural causes and took the brain home with him. Some parts of the brain were given to scientists, but no major study was ever conducted, until now.

Sue Nelson -BBC News, June 19, 1999: The secret of Einstein's immense intellect may finally have been uncovered -one area of his brain was significantly different than most people. "Within seven hours of his death his brain was removed and preserved" Albert Einstein, who discovered the theory of relativity, died in 1955, aged 76. His brain was then removed and preserved for scientific research. Scientists at McMaster University, Ontario, Canada, compared the shape and size Einstein's brain with those of 35 men and 56 women with average intelligence. They think their findings may well explain his genius for mathematical and spatial thinking.

Dr. Turi's rebuttal: There is not much physical distinction between your brain, the one of a killer, or Einstein. This sophisticated human computer has general functional characteristics, and very little difference in size, density, weight and wiring. However the purposes, responses, desires, fate, health, vices, gifts and virtues, are pre-programmed by the universal mind very differently. The only difference is the "program" Einstein was blessed at birth by the omnipresent mind. Any plausible answer pertaining to the mind is to be found in the universal mind! Dropping the scalpel and looking above the head of Einstein will bring the answer scientists are looking for. His genius originates from the location of the Dragon' Head (exploration) in Aquarius (universe) in his 12th. house (or the subconscious). But hell, what does this astrological jargon mean to any of those scientists? That is were the problem is, those researchers are totally unaware of the direct relationship with the universal mind and its interaction upon the human psyche. My book "The Power of the Dragon" is an excellent choice for them to start reaching cosmic consciousness.

Continued - In general, Einstein's brain was the same as all the others except in one particular area - the region responsible for mathematical thought and the ability to think in terms of space and movement. Extensive development of this region meant that Einstein's brain was 15% wider than the other brains studied. Uniquely, Einstein's brain also lacked a groove that normally runs through part of this area. The researchers suggest that its absence may have allowed the neurons to communicate much more easily. "This unusual brain anatomy may explain why Einstein thought the way he did," said Professor Sandra Whitelson, who led the research published in the Lancet. "Einstein's own description of his scientific thinking was that words did not seem to play a role. Instead he saw more or less clear images of a visual kind," she said.

Dr. Turi's rebuttal: Einstein was born on Friday March 14, 1879 with both Jupiter (learning/teaching) in Aquarius (the sign of genius) in his 12th house (the subconscious). That was the only reason why; Einstein was programmed by the universal mind to explore and dwell comfortably in time and space, which ultimately brought him to the conception of the law of relativity. Incidentally, Pluto (investigation) and Neptune (Lord of visualization) affected Einstein's 3rd house (the thinking process). But again what good can this information do for researchers? Unless they respect the word "science," and investigate outside conventional studies, the golden key of what it means to be human will never be offered to them. Most of all, can the scientist enter the intuitive domain of astrology? Chances are that they inherited Mercury (learning) or a strong Saturn (structure) in the rational "scholarship" 9th house. Thus the opportunity to reach the universal mind is not yet available to these young, discriminating souls. Understanding the dynamics of the universal mind is where the answer lies.

Continued - Einstein allowed his brain to be studied after his death. The idea that various abilities are determined by physical differences in the structure of the brain, is currently of great interest to scientists. "To say there is a definite link is one bridge too far, at the moment," said Professor Laurie Hall, a brain-imaging expert from the University of Cambridge. "So far the case isn't proven. But magnetic resonance and other new technologies are allowing us to start to probe those very questions." The researchers hope that the study will encourage the donation of brain specimens from other gifted individuals.

Dr. Turi's rebuttal: Let's try another approach. If I understand this ridiculous theory, the brain is larger in some area, so one has the potential for genius. Then, I proclaim that whales are geniuses, and pigeons aren't! Why? Because a whale has a much larger brain than a pigeon. But I am still facing a dilemma here because both use their inborn computers to navigate the earth! Uh! Thus, if a whale can do this with his enormous brain and a pigeon with his pea brain, obviously the brain size is not and has never been a factor. What about ants, bees, etc. Like humans, they all have inborn programs, and they are reacting to electromagnetic fields coming from those far distant stars. In that respect one of the scientists, that is Ms Whitelson, seems to be more perceptive.

Continued - Other researchers found that, overall, Einstein's brain was the same weight and had the same measurements from front to back as all the other men. Whitelson said and confirms the belief of many perceptive scientists that focusing on overall brain size, as an indicator of intelligence, is not the way to go.

The researchers compared the founder of the theory of relativity's brain with the preserved brains of 35 men and 56 women known to have normal intelligence when they died. "That kind of shape was not observed in any one of our brains and is not depicted in any atlas of the human brain," said Sandra Whitelson , a neuroscientist who led another study, published in this week's issue of The Lancet, a British medical journal. "But it shouldn't be seen as anatomy is destiny," she added. "We also know that environment has a very important role to play in learning and brain development. But what this is telling us is that environment isn't the only factor." The findings may point to the importance of the inferior parietal region, Witelson said.

The next paragraph gives me more hope when this intuitive woman researcher mentioned: "While the differences may be extraordinary between Einstein and everyone else, there may be subtle, even microscopic, differences when the anatomies of the brains of people who don't fall into the genius category are compared with each other," she said.

Note: She is approaching the truth when she subconsciously describes her lack of awareness of the function of the universal mind on the brain by using the word "subtle". This word "subtle" sounds like astrology or mysticism or spirit and is not a normal part of their vocabulary. Many of them are reluctant to explore the meaning behind those "spiritual" words. She said it is likely that the groove, known as the sulcus, was always absent in that part of Einstein's brain, rather than shrinking away as a result of his intelligence, because, as one of the two or three landmarks in the human brain, it appears very early in life. "We don't know if every brilliant physicist and mathematician will have this same anatomy," Witelson said.

Dr. Turi's rebuttal: I can assure you that a brilliant physicist or a mathematician will have inherited at birth very strong Mercury (the mind) in earthy Capricorn (structure), while his brain may not have the same physical anatomy. This research is physically oriented only and no exploration has been done on a more "subtle" or spiritual basis. It is like trying to repair a sophisticated computer with a hammer or paint with a shovel. The tools used to try to perceive the dilemma (the mind) are too rational. However, raising the awareness of a scientist to the workings of celestial mechanics is a serious challenge in itself. Making this researcher aware of the subtle force of the universe and prove its interaction with our own computer (our mind) is still feasible. That is of course, if the "programmed" soul himself is not limited in his perception of the "unknown" and is willing to explore and conceive things that he can not see or comprehend just yet.

Continued - "It fits and it makes a compelling story, but it requires further proof" said John , an associate professor of psychology at Stanford University. "We don't have a clue, so anything that is suggested is interesting," he said. "There must have been something about his brain that made him so brilliant. "Brilliance of the kind Einstein possessed is so extreme, however, that although the findings may give a clue to the neurology of genius, whether they could apply to normal differences in intelligence is more doubtful," Gabrieli said.

Dr. Turi's rebuttal: Again, they simply don't have a clue, and it is "that something" that made Einstein so brilliant.

Those powerful celestial bodies located and operating in his subconscious produced his incredible findings. He was set like anyone who made history in his own way, to do so in that fashion. He was equipped at birth with his own abilities, like a gifted musician who plays his part in this world. That's why we humans are so different to each other and so unique in so many ways. But how can any scientist or researcher relate to me if they don't speak the universal language. This type of "subtle" information might not be available to them because of a religious belief or a nefarious location of their natal mercury (the mind). Most of all, common sense dictates that if they made it all the way to Stanford, Cambridge or McMaster Universities and graduated as neurosurgeons, psychologists, psychiatrists, brain-imaging specialists, etc., chances are those "educated" souls had been overloaded with a strong rationale at birth. These souls may not necessarily be ready to explore anything deeper other than with their eyes, scalpels and hands. The very essence of their study is the mind, and the answers they so desperately seek is in the Universal Mind.

We are children of this universe, a part of a much larger scheme that our dedicated scientists can not begin to comprehend. Especially if they do not have the spiritual tools needed to explore the universal mind, as Einstein or even myself were endowed at birth. The universal mind dictates, affects, and controls all of the minds under its jurisdiction, animals included. The complex celestial program created our sins, virtues, gifts, mental conceptions, sexual drives, creativeness, aggressiveness, and all that makes us human. Again and again, those stars above us are more than dead rocks, and do have spiritual values. How can scientists and astronomers perceive only the physical manifestation of those stars is not a mystery to me. This world needs people to build gearboxes, bridges, cities, but also needs people to dwell with the spirit, create beautiful pieces of art, sing and dance. In time and space, you chose your world, your country, and your parents as you reincarnated on this dense physical world. You must now perform and grow, physically and spiritually. As incredible as it may sound, all you will ever be or accomplish is already pre-determined by the universal mind. Luckily for us, our will is much stronger than those stars, and with education you can apply your will. But first you must understand the working of the universal mind and its impact upon your psyche. You are simply a reflection of all your psychological and physical gifts, and the full manifestation of this principle is yourself in thought and action.

Keep in mind also that those large organizations survive through your tax dollars, and at this rate of exploration, they are pretty secure for the next few thousands years. They have kids to send to college, payments for their living expenses, car, insurance etc. They need your financial support to be able to do so. Like any other governmental and educational businesses, they desperately need your taxes. Thus they need more cadavers, so that they can experiment and waste more of your precious dollars. In a few years, Astropsychology will be reintegrated into our colleges and universities and accepted as a solid discipline. Then, this nonsense and waste of time and money will cease, finally offering mankind the real answer to what it means to be a human and what it takes to be a genius. What you do not know is that, behind the research lies a strong desire for the government (the sponsor) to create a genius and, in the process, use his ingenious LEGACY to gain more control and power over the rest of the world. You may call it a hidden National security endeavor. In that respect, once the truth is finally available, Astropsychologists of the future will be able to tap onto the universal mind and accurately plan the birth of a genius. With the understanding of the celestial order, they will tackle the best of the stars and plan the exact arrival of the superman. Is that, in biblical terms, what the "Kings following a star" knew and planned for, when Jesus arrived on earth? It makes you think.

****

"And God created man in His image...."

So what can we do about religion, and what is the answer? Well let's try to clarify the long established dilemma that plagues the world. What a pretentious person Dr. Turi is, you may think; centuries of religious dogmas can not and will not be fixed! Yes it can and will in the future, and education is the key.

What one must realize is that if you were born, raised and induced by Oriental disciplines, the imposed religious teachings would be quite different than someone born in the Middle East or those following Occidental disciplines. Thus your religious education would be totally different than someone born elsewhere in the world. To make the situation even more difficult, over the centuries and under the nomination of Neptune, many more and different religious denominations have been created. To save the reader's feelings, I will not specify them but the various choices are yours. The battle to own your soul (and your wallet) has been going on for centuries. An army of soul saviors will knock your door on a daily basis, insisting of freeing you from a sure trip to hell if you convert to their specific religious convictions. The human preservation instinct is usually a perfect spot to tap. Most of the time, those lost souls are trying to prove to themselves that, if they do manage to convince you, they have the real "truth". Sadly enough, hundreds if not thousands of lost souls have followed fanatic religious leaders like David Koresh and Rev. Jones, and think about those deceived souls dying for Osama Bin Laden. In the name of fear, ignorance and God, those poor souls, in search of the truth, have lost their precious lives.

Those "pagans or infidels" refusing to follow the particular imposed deity or his specific written commandments, will be beset by a myriad of eternal punishments. Deceiving promises of outlandish kingdoms are also offered to the God fearing souls. Mostly those young souls are simply trying to convince themselves by convincing you, of their own righteousness.

This is where it might become difficult for you to assimilate my message. Let's use common sense. If you have been created in the image of God, then you are God too! Why is that? Well if I take a picture of God and a picture of you, I will have the exact same image, is that true? Of course it is.

Scientists want you to believe that you came from a monkey! Religious fanatics believe otherwise. For example, if you are a woman, you came from the rib of a man. This is pure nonsense. Keep in mind that nearly 2000 years ago, in absence of paper and pen, and dealing with illiterate suffering peasants (the prime targets), much of the knowledge was passed by word-of-mouth. Through centuries of religious training (poisoning), it became easy to accept myth as fact. The problem is, now we have grown, and the rules have changed; we are no longer stupid peasants, but educated souls in search of the real truth. I also doubt that the church wanted to pass along real knowledge, mostly because knowledge means power, and power means freedom. In that respect, mankind will sooner or later meet with his own creativity (his future) and literally melt with infinity.

If man is an "animal," he is incontestably of a superior nature to other animals. He can think, discern, and judge good from bad. With man in past times, Lucifer the "Prince of Intellectuals," a fallen angel from the sky, challenged the order of God. In this respect, man identifies himself with Lucifer and has the potential to control, for good or worse, the fate of the world. Incidentally, in Greek mythology, the word Luci means Venus, the shiniest "star" in our solar system. God ordered Adam and Eve to stay clear of the tree-of-knowledge and not to eat the apple! Of course Eve convinced Adam to eat the forbidden fruit. Evidently, the trap was set and impossible to avoid. The all-knowing God knew it all, and as with the rebellion of

Lucifer, (and the different light he brings!) intended from the very beginning for it to unfold this way. In doing so, God willingly allowed Adam and Eve to gain a form of consciousness and a free will in order to create their own reality and their own future. Purposely, God gave a portion of his mighty power to man, and this seems to be the greatest gift to humanity.

Common sense also must apply to the following: Why would God give us the stars, the heavens, the world at large and everything of his own creation if man could not govern it himself? What direction would the world have taken if human evolution (by the subtle order of God) did not gain the Creator's awesome power? What if God's plan did not come true? What if Adam and Eve did not eat the apple? What would our world be like now? This mythology has a direct impact in the context of human evolution as we perceive it, since we all had a taste of the "forbidden" apple. Well this world was set for a specific purpose, and that is to burn karma, learn to feel, and learn to create with thought power. And if there is a hell, it is here on earth, and it was set this way by the Eternal. You can still, as many souls do, make it a fantastic place to operate. That is, if you "ask and you shall receive" more knowledge to allow you to gain power, recognition, wealth, and health.

"Organized religion is a deadly trap! Once you fall in it, your free spirit sinks."

--Dr. Turi

Some people will ask, what is astrology?

Astrology is a science and an art. It is a science because it has discipline and a solid structure. It is an art because the practitioner will need feeling, lots of practice and a good spiritual ear to perceive the twelve celestial sounds. Incidentally a musical scale is made of twelve notes! Thus, like a pianist, a painter or a singer, one must be born with "the gift" to grasp and translate the subtle symbolic meanings of the stars through the twelve signs of the Zodiac. Incidentally, entering the intuitive domain of the stars is somehow difficult or impossible for some. Thus I will refer to this crowd as "Young Souls," instead of; naïve, skeptics, professional students, religious fanatics, unperceptive, educated mental snobs, ignorant, stupid or imbeciles. These people are mostly victims of society, or the fruit of the combination of science and religion. They are totally uninformed or incapable of grasping higher vibrations and will refer to astrology as a pure waste of time and a pseudo-science. "Psuedo" is a Greek prefix, signifying false or bogus. Sadly enough, 99% of the people in charge of your life, from the law makers, local school teachers, to those in position of power in government, are young souls. They are the "educated," the skeptics, and the deity suckers. They will refer to me or perceive me as a guru, a dreamer, a dangerous con man and a nuisance to society. I am, in their badly informed world, a disturbing and hazardous factor against society and the Status Quo. In the dark ages and in the name of God, the same young souls burnt me over and over again (and many of you reading this book) on the stake. They will also classify my work and my mission as “the work of the devil.” This has been the eternal struggle between fear and faith, stupidity and intelligence. The battle in astrological terms is between the decaying age of Pisces (restriction/past) and the burgeoning Age of Aquarius (freedom/future).

Since the dawn of time, Astrology has been used by every civilization including the Incas with their temple of the Moon and temple of the Sun, the Sumerians, the Atlantians, and many other long gone cultures. Astrology is simply a map of the universal mind depicting the reincarnated soul’s legacy, strengths and weaknesses. Sir Isaac Newton said, “For every action there is an equal but opposite reaction.” Thus the accumulated experiences of the soul from its previous incarnations becomes its dues, in terms of gifts or sins, of karma. The inherited set of stars through the souls’s relationship with the Universal mind, produces all its sins and virtues, fate, health, habits, opportunities, etc. All of its life’s drama will unfold as imposed by the stars, right here on this dense physical world. To really understand the dynamics of the universal mind and its subtle impact upon man’s psyche, one must simply keep an open mind and educate himself to the phenomenon. Until then, in the name of ignorance, he will remain a robot and victim of his own stars.

I firmly believe that God created the stars and heavens for more than the sake of beauty; he gave them to us to interpret, so that we may live a more productive life. Never forget what Paracelcus wrote. He said, “Man is superior to the stars if he lives in the power of superior wisdom. Such a person, being the master over heaven and earth by means of his will, is a magus, and magic is not sorcery but supreme wisdom." This great philosopher knew that God's higher truths are cloaked in his creation and that, as he speaks to us through the light, his real message is in the stars. Knowledge of both the physical and spiritual laws can only bring power, and power in many ways means freedom.

They are great truths, which are taught from the position, symbols, and names of the heavenly bodies. When God created and set them in the firmament of heaven, he said, in Gen. i. 14, "Let them be for signs and for seasons."

Genesis i. 14 is very clear and therefore, "They (heavenly bodies, Moon, sun and the stars) were conceived by the Creator to be used as signs (that is things to come/predictions) and for specific cycles (periodicity). "Nothing can be more articulated in reference to this biblical passage from God. The heavenly bodies contain not only specific Revelations (predictions) involving "the things to come" to be learned in the "signs" of the Zodiac, but also in reference to the "appointed" times in his unyielding celestial will.

The bearing of the sun, moon and distant stars are so organized that towards the end of a specific period in time they "divinely" proceed, almost exactly in the same position, in harmony with each other around the earth. Consequently, we have seasons and Eclipse Cycles on a regular basis.

Gen. xviii. 21: "At this set time in the next year..."

Gen. xviii. 14: "At the time appointed I will return."

Gen. xvii. 2: "At the set time of which God has spoken."

In the old days, Astronomy co-mingled with Astrology, and this rational science of the stars was at its infant stage. The Babylonian libraries refer to the following - Isaiah, xlvii. 13, "Thou art wearied in the multitude of thy counsels. Let now thy astrologers (wise men), the star-gazers, the monthly prognosticators, stand up." The tremendous astrological works of the Babylonians accommodate seventy tablets, and were gathered by the command of Sargon of Agade, thirty-eight hundred years BC. This is referred as the "Illumination of Bel."

This celestial memorandum was made daily in high towers called "Ziggurats." Those cleverly built lookouts were erected in all large cities, and their "celestial" narration was sent regularly to their Masters for further explanation before reaching the King. Well before we were able to do so, the "wise men" calculated eclipses and heavenly motions. They also knew about the sunspots and all known comets. Incredibly, my friend Zacharia Sitchin, one of the rare scholars able to accurately translate Babylonian tablets, reported finding a full scale of our solar system. This included Uranus, Neptune, and Pluto, well before the first telescope was ever invented. The Babylonians were the creators of the Zodiac, and in the British Museum, (Fifth Creation Tablets) there are clay tablet fragments of two planispheres with incredible figures and astrological calculations impressed on them. Incidentally, the months were named after the signs of the Zodiac.

It reads as follows:

"Anu (God), made excellent the mansion (the celestial houses) of the great gods (twelve Greek mythological gods) in number (the twelve signs or mansions of the sun)." "The stars he placed in them. The lumasi (groups of stars or figures) he fixed."

Note: Babylonian Life and History - Fragments of these colored glazed bricks are to be seen in the British Museum.

"It must never be forgotten that the Babylonians were a nation of stargazers, and that they kept a body of men to do nothing else but report eclipses, appearances of the moon, sun-spots, etc., etc."

~ Dr. Budge

Letter to the Pope

Even the American Indians in the United States of America suffered the power of the church. The Pope himself and his very important signature are also responsible for many Indian demises. But how many people know this fact? When you control someone's source of information and education, you control that person's entire destiny. This type of "mental" control was performed by the politically oriented churches of the 15th century, upon many native Indian tribes found living in the "new world". Thus, entire nations and countries suffered this type of mental manipulation and many people, their cultures, ways of life and traditions were altered and changed forever. In the name of ignorance, greed, fear and control, the good words of the Lord were used and abused to benefit a privileged section of a far away controlling society and its rigid agenda. I think one of the hardest things to leave behind is religious upbringing and guilt. It is hard because so many are herded into that corral, and it feels a bit strange and uncertain leaving it behind. It takes courage to explore a new region, but just like an explorer, you will see many new and beautiful lands and experience a rich spiritual life.

In 1999 I was at the AFA (American Federation of Astrologers) in Florida lecturing on Nostradamus' astrology and doing readings. A well-dressed gentleman asked for his Astro-Tarot reading. I began to "read" him and I noticed that he was born with a Dragon's Head (luck) in Sagittarius (foreigners/law/Indians etc.) We talked for a while and in the reading, I mentioned many of his Indian past lives and his natural flair for the law. Incidentally, as predisposed by the stars, and I did not know this fact just yet; he was a law practitioner and a very interesting and educated person. He was pretty astonished of my ability to pick up on his subconscious and mentioned to me that he was involved in the Indigenous Law Institute. We talked for a while and to my surprise, a few hours later he came back to my booth and presented me with this letter issued on May 4th 1993, to Pope John Paul II. Because of the deeply concerned message involving this letter, I decided to share its content with you in this book.

His Eminence, Pope John Paul II

Vatican Rome, Italy

May 4, 1993

His Holiness, Pope John Paul II,

In a special message to American Indians in Santa Domingo on October 13, 1992, you observed that it is impossible to forget "the enormous suffering" of the Indian people during the "conquest and colonization" of the Americas. You also pledged that the church would work to defend Indian's rights. We applaud your statement, for it was an important step towards healing and the restoration of Native spiritual traditions. Five Hundred years ago, your predecessor, Pope Alexander VI, issued the now famous Inter Cetera bull. That papal decree expressed the pope's desire that "barbarous nations," those "discovered" and yet to be "discovered," be "subjugated" and reduced to the Catholic faith and Christian religion. He said that in this way, the "Christian empire" would be propagated. The Inter Cetera bull was in direct line with an earlier bull issued in 1452 by Pope Nicholas V. to King Alfonso V. of Portugal, which called upon the king, "to invade, search out, capture, vanquish, and subdue all Saracens and pagans, whatsoever, and other enemies of Christ." Pope Nicholas also directed Alfonso to take away and convert the non-Christians' possessions and property, "and to reduce their persons to perpetual slavery."

Now in 1993, the "International Year of the World's Indigenous People," as declared by the United Nations, our spiritual elders tell us that it is time for the Age of Subjugation to end. During that age, the Traditional Nations and Peoples of the Western Hemisphere have endured what historian David Stannard has referred to as the worst holocaust in the history of humanity. For many of us it still continues. It is now time to acknowledge that the papal documents mentioned above directly contributed to our suffering, misery, and to the genocide committed against us.

We therefore call upon you, with all the respect that you deserve as the head of the Vatican City State, and as the Supreme Head of the Roman Catholic Church, to formally revoke—in a bilateral ceremony with our spiritual elders and representatives—the Inter Cetera bull of May 4, 1493. By doing so, you will thereby demonstrate your solidarity with Indigenous Nations and Peoples throughout the world.

The revocation will not only show your love and affection, but also your willingness to honor and respect our inherent rights to liberty, justice, and peace. Your action will also show that the Catholic Church supports and defends the territorial ownership and integrity of our Nations, and our desire to be free of all forms of subjugation. You will thereby align yourself with our efforts to revitalize and to restore our own Spiritual Ways of Life, in keeping with the Natural Laws given to each of our respective Nations by the Creator.

Also, because they are vitally necessary to our healing and spiritual restoration, we respectfully offer the following points:

For generations now, the Church has taught our people that our own ceremonial traditions are "heathen" and "pagan". Many of us have been taught to fear, ridicule, and even deny our own family members who follow traditional ceremonial practices. Your revocation of the papal bull will begin to remove this legacy of fear and judgment from the ears and minds of our people.

Scores of our Nations perished. Many of our languages have been completely destroyed. In parochial boarding schools the Church forbid our children from speaking their own language, often inflicting abusive punishments on those children "caught" doing one of the most natural things of all: speaking their own mother tongue. It is now time for the Vatican to support the restoration of the Native languages that the Church worked so hard to destroy, before it is too late and those languages vanish.

It is time for the Vatican to support the healing of the deep and lasting emotional and spiritual scars that it has inflicted on our Nations and Peoples. We call upon the Church to provide practical support for "unresolved historical grief" work.

Does the Vatican hold the human remains of Indigenous people in its archives? Does it possess any of our sacred objects? We call upon the Vatican to return all such skeletal remains to our communities, so that they may be given proper traditional burials. We also call upon the Vatican to immediately return any of our sacred objects that it has in its possession.

We call upon the Catholic Church to open the Vatican archives to us so that our scholars may study what those records reveal about our past.

The Church is now holding portions of our lands, which nation-state governments "gave" to the Church. It is now time to restore those lands to their rightful indigenous owners.

The revocation will support the restoration of our sacred lands which at present are being unjustly and unlawfully occupied, lands such as the Black Hills of the Lakota and their Allied Nations, Newe Segobia of the Western Shoshone Nation, and Mt. Graham of the Apache Nation, to name just a few.

History also reveals that the Church persecuted women of earth-centered spiritual traditions though the Inquisition and other repressive campaigns in Europe as well as in the Western Hemisphere. Untold women and children suffered and died from this unspeakable mistreatment. The revocation will enable the Church to deal honestly, candidly, and openly with these shadows of its history. Such disclosure is a difficult yet necessary step toward the healing that now needs to occur for the sake of all beings.

We hereby invite you and your official representatives to meet with us for an International Summit of Indigenous Nations, so that we may discuss these and other issues face-to-face, heart-to-heart, and mind-to-mind. For the sake of our healing, the healing of Mother Earth, and the benefit of the future generations, we ask you not to turn your heart away from us.

In conclusion, we are writing you this letter because you have demonstrated to the world community that you are a person of great vision. We invite you to walk with us on the Sacred Path toward the healing of historical guilt, grief, and shame. With the ceremonial revocation, we will honor the Indigenous principle: "Respect the Earth as our Mother, and have a Sacred Regard for All Living Things."

All Our Relations,

Birgil Kills Straight The Indigenous Law Institute

Steven T. Newcomb VIA: P.O. Box 907

Maria Brave Heart Marcola, Oregon 97454

****

Another apology from the Pope

A few years ago the Pope, in the name of his predecessors and Christianity, apologized to the world for condemning Galileo and sending him to decay in jail. The astrologer knew then, that the earth was not the center of the universe, but revolved around the sun. What good can an apology do to this departed soul? Think about the hell the "erudite" men had to go through until the end of their lives. However, in 1999, the Pope felt once again the need to apologize to the world and to another astrologer, Nicholas Copernicus.

Update: 6/8/99

Torun, Poland (CNN)— Nearly 400 years after the Roman Catholic church condemned Nicholas Copernicus's discovery that the Earth revolved around the sun as heresy, Pope John Paul II visited the astronomer's birthplace and praised his scientific achievements. "The discovery made by Copernicus, and its importance for history and science, remind us of the ever-present tension between reason and faith," the pope told officials of the university in Torun named after the astronomer. The pontiff is on the third day of 13-day trip to his homeland. The church condemned Copernicus' theory in 1616 and later condemned Galileo for supporting his findings. Copernicus' book "De Revolutionibus Orbium Coelestium" was banned by the Church until 1822. In 1992, John Paul proclaimed that the Vatican had erred when it condemned Galileo. In praising Copernicus' achievements, the pope noted that new scientific breakthroughs were "growing at a dizzying rate." "This progress gives rise to both wonderment and fear," he said. "Man is becoming ever more fearful of the products of his own intelligence and freedom ... Concern for the moral conscience and the sense of moral responsibility has today become a fundamental imperative for men and women of science." The pope has warned of moral dangers associated with recent breakthroughs in cloning and artificial fertilization.

In the audience, modern Polish astronomer Alexander Wolszczan. praised the pope's call for defining the relationship between faith and science. "They complement each other, though it is not always evident," said Wolszczan. "They are both directed at man and especially now ...we are absorbed with so many problems, their cooperation is necessary." In 1992, Wolszczan discovered the existence of planets outside our solar system.

Note: What is even more astonishing is that, the astronomer mentioned not a single word pertaining to astrology. Incidentally, both Copernicus and Galileo before being astronomers, were astrologers, and it is from the work of those wise men, that astronomy was born. It is important for the readers to be aware of this fact.

"It must never be forgotten that the Babylonians were a nation of stargazers, and that they kept a body of men to do nothing else but report eclipses, appearances of the moon, sun-spots, etc., etc." —-Dr. Budge

The Fishes

Why did Christianity "subconsciously" select the fish for its symbol from the astrological work of the ancients? First let's try to clarify and understand the meaning behind some of the zodiac symbols. Pisces is the sign chosen subliminally by Christians. Now keep in mind this is not a direct attack on Christians or anybody else, just a rational approach, based upon the work of the ancients, to any and all religions. Neptune or Poseidon governs the twelfth house (ruling the subconscious). A negative Neptune rules deception, illusion, drugs, alcohol, and places of confinement such as synagogues, churches, jails, asylums, hospitals etc.

To represent financial security (house #2 in Astrology), the ancients priests (astrologers) carved in clay tablets, the symbol of the Bull (Taurus). Incidentally this sign also rules Switzerland where all the major banks and savings of the world's wealthiest people are located! Keep in mind that every single country in this world is controlled by his respective zodiac symbol. (My book, "The Power of the Dragon," will teach you more).

The sign of Pisces (a karmic sign) is of the two fish swimming in opposite directions. This denotes the tremendous struggle the soul must generate to "swim" against centuries of dogma and deception. Like the salmon swimming towards his birthplace against a continuous treacherous current, the soul must return to his place of origin, the stars; where he comes from, as "a child of the Universe". No matter how hard the current gets and how many falls are ahead, the soul is enslaved to push upward to recognize its godly nature, and free itself from ignorance, fear and evil.

The fish swimming downstream along with the current represents the negative aspect of the planet Neptune. The soul refuses to accept his divine nature and follows a myriad of religious doctrines and deities. This type of undertaking ultimately produces relentless, ruthless religious wars, caused by classifying its God as preeminent, and following a specific doctrine, a particular building, or a distinct denomination. Sadly enough many victims of illusion have paid the ultimate price, and have wasted their precious lives by adopting the apocalyptic teachings of religious leaders such as David Koresh and Rev. Jones. Incidentally, Neptune rules all chemicals and poisons. Interestingly, the maniac Rev. Jim Jones, as induced by Neptune's deceptive power, poisoned his followers. The same applies for another lunatic, Marshall Applewhite who decided to bring to death his followers in the name of his UFO's "saving" legacy. To my knowledge, regardless of the police findings, the Neptunian leader poisoned the mind and body of those lost souls. Especially when I fully and unarguably predicted the infamous incident in Moon Power Starguide1997 to the exact day.

The following is a reprint from that 1997 Moon Power book.

WED., THU., FRI., SAT., SUN., MON. — MARCH 26th, 27th, 28th, 29th, 30th, 31st:

RULERS — Pluto (hidden things brought to light) and Jupiter (expansion):

Environment: All villains will be busy, so be careful out there and don't trust strangers. Avoid places overloaded with turbulent, crazy people. Pluto likes accidents and panic. As always, especially in a waning Moon (negative), expect dramatic and destructive news to plague the media. Earthquake, mass murderers, vicious killers, rapists and the worst of society will be active, led by the Lord of Hades.

Starting January 1st, 1997, Neptune's subtle power will begin its karmic work upon this world. Using Divine Astrology — Neptune will be operational as of January 1st, 1997 and will stay with us until October 25th, 1998. Neptune raises drug and alcohol consumption, which promotes greater incidence of sexually transmitted disease and elevated suicides. A negative Neptune rules fanaticism, illusion and desperation.

Events: This energy has the awful power for unity in discord. A form of death in anv form, the beginning of becoming born again is to be experienced soon. People around you will become their true selves and during this transforming cycle a new you may be rediscovered. All changes MUST BE accepted and some of us must be ready for the ugliest time of our lives. A few examples of Pluto at work: the Rodney King beating — the illegal aliens beating (1996) — I wished so many times for police executives to be aware of this fact and tip-off our police officers of the serious threat they do face when Pluto is in charge. Many police officers have lost their lives because of this lack of knowledge. Hopefully more of them will have the opportunity to read my work, as I know this fact could save their lives. Be ready for this type of mess during these days. Pluto rules the police force and all of these dramatic stories.

Following the religious doctrine imposed at birth by demanding pious organizations, the responsible souls (the parents) will pass on what seems to be the truth to their own children. Keep in mind that those teachings vary and change based upon the country of nativity. Thus, induced at an early age, it is natural for any child to respect and obey authority. Following what has been established and accepted by most, this sole truth is somehow easier to accept and requires no other spiritual challenge. Meantime, what is firmly accepted by the majority doesn't mean it is the fact. Precociously "poisoned", the contaminated souls later in life, act eccentrically and kill others who do not agree with their religious values or their externally shaped virtuous behaviors.

Simply explained, the positive fish needs more than dogma, and decides to aim for its higher-self. Thus against all odds, and usually against the early family's archaic teachings, the "pagan" soul begin to swim upstream, looking for its celestial identity and inborn godly nature. However, the biblical phrase "ask and you shall receive" becomes a necessity if your soul is to reach its creative powers. Then, when you have finally found yourself, you finally have found God, and that's you!

In doing so, you are aiming for an unlimited power that has always been in you! Rest assured that deceiving doctrines, promoted by organized religions, would not dare to educate you to this fact. Mostly because knowledge means power, and power means the spiritual freedom to unlock the strength in yourself. The plain truth about yourself has been distorted and hidden from you by those religious organizations. The negative fish swimming downstream represents 99% of the people living on earth, those who follow deities and are a part of any and all religions. Sadly enough most of the people living on this world today are totally unaware of their godly nature. The fact is that, in time and space you have created your sole reality. You may run the risk of becoming stuck and therefore refuse to ask; thus you may not receive the different light that increases your own vibrations. However, if the single thought to acquire more advanced knowledge is generated powerfully enough; you will read this progressive material. In the process, you will become "the black sheep" in the eyes of less advanced souls, and particularly, your own family. This work will help you gain more consciousness to the facts of your real relationship with God, and your inborn celestial creative forces. This awareness will turn your own very thoughts into laser beams, thereby intensifying your own creativity.

Because of the present traditional educational system, I tend to despair for future generations. The spiritual regeneration found in the investigation of any spiritual disciplines, is often taken away from them. Poisoned and limited by contemporary science or deceiving religious dogma, many generations may have to work even harder to grasp the answers for which God has enslaved us all to search. However, I have great hopes, as the age of dogmatic Pisces is slowly but surely deteriorating. In the last two thousands years, the world had to experience the deceiving pull of Neptune, the ruler of Pisces. Incidentally the fish were subconsciously chosen by Christianity, and marks the beginning of the era in Christianity when Jesus was born.

So if man is God, what is the practical reasoning behind my theory. Everything in time and space is interconnected. Imagine that! Your finger is attached to your hand, which in turn is attached to your arm and of course the rest of your body. While exploring the content of your pocket, your fingers (that area is a part of you) can only dwell within that small confined area. Your sense of touch will help you to visualize through feeling, what is in that pocket. You (God) are much too big to get in there. Thus, you can not go into your pocket as a whole being. But your fingers (man), a small part of you can, and they are attached to the rest of the body (God).

In time and space you and only you (as a whole or God) have decided to reincarnate on this dense world to perform, feel, create or burn off some karma. The senses, memories, purpose, and vibrations of this system are deliberately limited. For if you knew what is really going on (and you can not), you would not be able to function here in this world, and execute your specific purpose.

The story of the Cross

Many of my students have asked me, Dr. Turi where did the symbol of the cross come from? Using history and my rational mind, here is my personal explanation. You will be the sole judge of my theory and the following little story:

The Roman Empire was built with great determination, solid organization, and reached all the neighboring countries of Europe. Much of the Roman's time was spent perfecting warfare and recruiting soldiers. Another favorite pastime was to gather gladiators and watch them savagely kill themselves. Many outlaws or slaves were spared if their talents as warriors were consistent. Either they died in the arena or joined one of the proud Roman legions.

Centuries before the birth of Christ, a brave warrior named Spartacus became the leader of about 4,000 slaves, and began rebelling against the Romans. He escaped with his followers into the mountainous regions of Rome, and sustained a ferocious war against the Roman regime. Finally, upon the order of the Emperor, a well-trained legion was dispatched to exterminate or capture the rebels. After a few bloody battles, Spartacus knew the end was in sight. He wanted to save the lives of the remaining slaves, and ordered a mass surrender to the Romans. The long march back to Rome was humiliating and the enraged vindictive Romans killed hundreds of exhausted slaves who could not walk any longer. Spartacus was very aware of the fate and his followers and his own, but as a leader he had to keep walking with pride back to the city of Rome.

After a swift judgment from the Roman authorities, he and his followers were condemned to die. During these harsh times, food was scarce, and putting people in jail was out of the question. They all had to be discarded like pests, to avoid future confrontations and serve as examples to those opposing the Roman rules. Thus as they did for centuries before, the Romans ordered the slaves to build crosses, and they were nailed on them. For miles, and in all directions, the entire road system leading to Rome was encrusted with thousands of wooden crosses. Anyone going through the city was to acknowledge the deadly result and see the lifeless bodies of those who dared to challenge Rome's community or government. A few centuries later, another slave leader named Jesus met the exact same fate as Spartacus and died on a cross. The Roman political authorities of those long gone times, made sure that no one, slave or religious leader, would interfere with its infrastructure.

Note: The first documents ever written about Jesus took place over 400 years after his death. Incidentally in "The Dead Sea Scrolls" that pre-date Christianity for a few thousands years, not a single word pertaining to Jesus has ever been mentioned.

****

What the Christian Bible Never Teaches You!

The Slaughter Of The Incas In The Name of God

The church (which was the government in the past) always sponsored adventurous men and their ships, to proliferate the good words of God or Christianity to the new world. Of course behind this entire masquerade, the church aims have always been to own more real estate and to steal the gold from the indigenous Incan people and to destroy the "pagan" culture. The following has been reported by a Spanish soldier in his diary during Cortez's dramatic voyage to what is known nowadays as Peru.

The Spaniards hiding in the buildings around the courtyard became terrified when they looked outside. Holed-up in the Peruvian city of Cajamarca, they were surrounded by Inca warriors as far as the eye could see – an army of more than 50,000 men. Worse still, the Incas looked as if they were preparing an attack.

The Spaniards were under the command of conquistador Francisco Pizarro, who five years earlier had discovered the legendary gold-rich Incan Empire in Peru. After gaining permission from the King of Spain, Pizarro had returned to Peru with an invasion force of just 180 soldiers and a dozen muskets.

By the time Pizarro tracked down the Incan emperor Atahualpa in the city of Cajamarca, his men were hundreds of miles inland and outnumbered 500 to one. Now they were waiting in terror as the Incan emperor, preceded by a throng of warriors in brightly colored tunics and gold and silver headdresses, was carried into the square on a litter borne by his noblemen.

A Spanish high priest strode out to meet the emperor, his bible held high. "Accept Jesus and the rule of the Spaniards," he intoned. He handed the bible. Never having seen a book before, the emperor flung it to the ground. Enraged, the fanatically religious priest shouted,

"Come out Christians! Come at these enemy dogs that reject the things of God!"

Pizarro rushed out, brandishing a sword and a dagger, and screamed, "Santiago!" At the signal, hidden gunners unleashed a volley of deadly fire on the unsuspecting Incans. Pizarro and four other men slashed through the crowd of Incans, and grabbed Atahualpa while their cavalry and foot soldiers sprung from hiding and attacked from all sides. Many Incans fled in panic at their first sight of horses.

Filled with religious and murderous lust, the Spaniards cut into the mob, slicing off limbs, sending heads rolling from blood-spewing necks, and spearing the unarmed as they fled. Screams of dying men mingled with the whinnying of horses and gruesome sounds of steel cutting into flesh. In the hours of butchery that ensued, 7,000 Incas were slaughtered in the name of Christianity. "If night had not come on, few out of the more than 40.000 Indians troops would have been left alive," a Spaniard later attested.

Not single Spaniard lost his life. After the fight, Pizarro held Atahualpa hostage and promised that he would be released in exchange for several tons of gold and silver. When the loot was delivered, the Spaniards executed Atahualpa and ruled Peru for the next 260 years.

– from "The Greatest War Stories Never Told"
- By Jeff Wise.

Corporate $ for your church?

Yes, it is a fast growing business and it does bring about three million dollars a year to your local church! There are still no taxes imposed and millions of free hands and empty minds to promote this hidden and shameful business.

Signs your church has sold out to corporate sponsors:

Nike "swoosh" on the cross

Communion now sponsored by Welch's Grape Juice

Taco Bell's talking dog now reading announcements

In the Christmas play, Joseph is seen with a pack of Luckys

Greeters all dressed like Mr. Goodwrench

Personal pew licenses now sold

Baptismal includes a dolphin show from Sea World

Statue of Mary seen holding keys to a Jeep

Holy water spiked with Diet Pepsi

The 12 disciples replaced by Disney characters

Luxury pews with wet bar and satellite TV

Scripture verses brought to you by Windows '98

Pastor doing subliminal product messages during sermon

Bulletin has a coupon section

Choir members wear Dockers

The holy water font has Perrier

There is a twist of lemon in the holy water

In the restrooms, an attendant hands you a towel

There is a credit card swipe on the collection plate

Offering envelopes bearing Visa or MasterCard emblems on them

Handicap parking sponsored by the Family Medical Group, LLC

Wednesday night suppers sponsored by KFC

Sunday morning televised services sponsored by the FOX network

Church vans traded in for Ford Broncos

Church bell chimes to the tune of the NBC chimes

Choir robes with the Lands' End emblem on front

Sunday bulletins with the CNN logo

Free Perrier at all baptism

Church flag football team sponsored by the XFL

******

Selling the church and its products has been a business since day one.

Minister Charles (private) has the power to make you a LEGALLY ORDAINED MINISTER within 48 hours!!!!

BE ORDAINED NOW! As a minister, you will be authorized to perform the rites and ceremonies of the church!!

WEDDINGS, MARRY your BROTHER, SISTER, or your BEST FRIEND!! Don't settle for being the BEST MAN OR BRIDES' MAID, most states require that you register your certificate (THAT WE SEND YOU) with the state prior to conducting the ceremony. FUNERALS are a very hard time for you and your family. Don't settle for a minister you don't know!! Most states require that you register your certificate (THAT WE SEND YOU) with the state prior to conducting the ceremony. BAPTISMS you can say "WELCOME TO THE WORLD!!!! I AM YOUR MINISTER AND YOUR UNCLE!!" What a special way to welcome a child of God.

FORGIVENESS OF SINS The Catholic Church has practiced the forgiveness of sins for centuries. Forgiveness of Sins is granted to all who ask in sincerity and willingness to change for the better!! VISIT CORRECTIONAL FACILITIES. Since you will be a Certified Minister, you can visit others in need! Preach the Word of God to those who have strayed from the flock

WANT TO START YOUR OWN CHURCH?? After your LEGAL ORDINATION, you may start your own congregation!!

At this point you must be wondering how much the Certificate costs. Right? Well, let's talk about how much the program is worth. Considering the value of becoming a CERTIFIED MINISTER I'd say the program is easily worth $100. Wouldn't you agree? However, it won't cost that much. Not even close! My goal is to make this life changing program affordable so average folks can benefit from the power of it. Since I know how much you want to help others, you're going to receive your Minister Certification for under $100.00... Not even $50.00... You are going to receive the entire life-changing course for only $29.95.

For only $29.95 you will receive:

1. 8-inch by 10-inch certificate IN COLOR, WITH GOLD SEAL.

(CERTIFICATE IS PROFESSIONALLY PRINTED BY AN INK PRESS)

2. Proof of Minister Certification in YOUR NAME!!

3. SHIPPING IS FREE!!!

LIMITED TIME OFFER: ORDER TODAY! SEND Only $29.95 US - (CREDIT CARD, CASH, CHECK, OR MONEY ORDER) 'SHIPPING IS FREE!!! For Shipping OUTSIDE the US please add $11.00. To place your order merely fill out the following form and fax to 1-////6. If this line is busy, please try faxing to 1-4///63. Or mail to:

Internet Information Services PO Box ///2 Billings, MT 59104. (ALL ORDERS FILLED WITHIN 24 HOURS OF RECEIVING THEM). Please allow 8 days to receive your certificate by mail. If you do not receive your order within 10 days, please send us a fax letting us know of the late arrival. We will then contact you to figure out why you have not received your order. Credit Card Order Form - (Please print very clearly in dark ink) Name on Credit Card: Address: City/State/ZIP: Your email address: Your card will be charged $29.95 for your Ministers' Certificate.

For Shipping OUTSIDE the US please add $11.00. Type of Card, circle one (Visa, MasterCard, and American Express). Credit Card Number: Sorry, we do not accept Discover. Date Credit Card Expires: Please tell us your phone Number: Please tell us your fax Number: Fax to 1-775-667-7386. If this line is busy, please try faxing to 1-413-375-0063. This ad is produced and sent out by:

Universal Advertising Systems. To be removed from our mailing list please email us at ...

How the hell did they manage to get *both* of my email addresses? And if they can not reach me this way chances are they will try calling or faxing me, as other organizations sell email addresses. Is this business or what? WANT TO START YOUR OWN CHURCH?? Do we really need more churches? There are so far well over 875 different denominations and who really cares as long as they make money and poison more children with hell and evil. Breeding more religions can only fuel future religious wars. When will man learn that he is himself a God and does not need a church, a deity or a doctrine to create his own fate and success in life?

What's next? I received this bit of humor from a friend. Imagine hearing the following:

Most of us have now learned to live with "voice mail," as a necessary part of our daily lives. But have you ever wondered what it would be like, if God decided to install voice mail? Here is some food for thought to tickle your funny bone regardless of your faith.

"I am sorry; all of our angels and saints are busy helping other sinners right now. However, your prayer is important to us and we will answer it in the order it was received. Please stay on the line.

If you would like to hear King David sing a Psalm while you are holding, press 4.

To find a loved one that has been assigned to Heaven, press 5, and then enter his or her social security number, followed by the "pound" sign. (If you receive a negative response, please hang up and try area code 666.)

For answers to nagging questions about dinosaurs, the age of the earth, life on other planets and where Noah's Ark is, please wait until you come for a personal office visit.

The office is now closed for the weekend to observe a religious holiday.

****

Religious poisoning

Some people may wonder what the meaning behind those harsh but real words are.

Well, here is a full example directly from Mother Teresa herself!

Priest Performed Exorcism on Mother Teresa by Kamil Zaheer 9-6-1.

CALCUTTA, India - An exorcism was performed on Mother Teresa a few months before she died because of fears that she was being attacked by the devil, the Archbishop of Calcutta said on Thursday. The half-hour exorcism took place while Mother Teresa, who devoted her life to caring for the ``poorest of the poor,'' was in a Calcutta hospital for treatment of heart problems and was unable to sleep.

Note: Astropsychology at work. This great Lady was born in August in the constellation of Leo. On the medical aspect of my work Leo rules the heart, love, romance, children and youth. Souls born in August carry with them a subconscious fear of death and diseases. One of the reasons's why Mother Teresa became a nun, nurturing a deep subconscious fear of death and disease. Thus serving God would allow her to live forever in paradise!

The 8th house of death for a Leo is located in the sign of Pisces; this sign was chosen subconsciously by Christians responding to the power of the stars (astrology). On a negative note, Pisces rules the subconscious, dreams, drugs, alcohol, religion, escape, jail, asylum, hospitals, temples churches etc.

What they will not tell you about Mother Teresa's death:

Modern science is not yet aware of the incredible impact of the stars upon mankind and its direct relationship with the Universal Mind (stars). Thus they did accelerate her mental decay by prescribing drugs to the famous nun. In the name of science (ignorance in many cases) a succession of prescriptions was the last thing to extend the life of the old lady. The negative reaction and her death is simply the accumulation of foreign Neptunian agents in her tired body and a very nefarious impact on her very vulnerable psyche. Alzheimers and schizophrenic diseases are solid manifestations of Neptune's out-of this-world, and illusory negative powers altering the good function of the brain.

Exorcism is the casting out of an evil spirit through prayer.

"When doctors said they could not find a medical reason for her sleeplessness, I thought she might be getting attacked by the devil,'' Archbishop Henry Sebastian D'Souza told Reuters. "I wanted her to calm down and asked a priest, in the name of the church, to perform an exorcism prayer on her. She happily agreed. After he performed these prayers, she slept very well that night,'' he said.

Another calculated way was to use Mother's Teresa's notoriety to sell their services against "the devil" to the God fearing masses. The old Lady was a sure investment for the Vatican's army of well paid doctors who certainly prescribed her with relaxing drugs weeks or months before the damage on her psyche started to manifest itself. The diagnostic was an early stage of madness due to Alzheimers disease and schizophrenia.

``I did nothing special. In the history (of the Catholic Church), hundreds of saints have gone through such things (as exorcism),'' Stroscio said. The 79-year-old Sicilian-born priest, Rosario Stroscio, who performed the exorcism, told Reuters she had been "behaving strangely'' just before the special prayers.

"HARASSED BY SATAN''

"She was a little dazed and behaved strangely. Maybe Mother Teresa was under harassment from Satan. But after the prayers, she was quite calm,'' Stroscio, who has lived in Calcutta for 62 years, said. The archbishop who oversaw preparation of a 35,000-page report on the nun's life that was sent to the Vatican last month as part of her canonization process said, "since she was such a holy person, the devil could (have been) tempted to attack her.''

Again this is another clever way to sell the church against "Satan". Well thousands of pious souls bought it, and will end up the same way or schizophrenics; like Mother Teresa, if not worse. Nurturing a constant fear of the devil is very detrimental in the long run, to the fragile human psyche. Neptune's deceiving illusive powers target not only the religious community. Saints, nuns, ministers, priests, cult leaders, drug addicts, lunatics, imbeciles along with normal people like you and I, can easily become Neptune's next victim. Modern science's fear-of-ridicule is an active participant in the prescriptions of Neptune's tools. Slowly but surely millions have sunk in the deep, deceiving quicksand of his madness. But ultimately, the real victims are the children who suffer ignorance through religious poisoning induced at an early age by the unenlightened family.

Mother Teresa, who was born in Macedonia, came to India in 1937. She founded the India-based worldwide order of the Missionaries of Charity 52 years ago with 12 members. Beatification, in which a person is declared as blessed, is a major step toward canonization or sainthood. Mother Teresa is already popularly known as the "saint of the gutters'' for her work among the poor and sick. The Nobel prize-winning nun, who founded the Missionaries of Charity, was put by Pope John Paul on the fast-track to sainthood soon after her death in 1997 at the age of 87.

The same Pope gave sainthood to all gypsies in Europe after centuries of persecution from the church! The failing age of Pisces has taken away many followers and their financial support. The New Age of Aquarius continually stimulates more critical thinking and challenges the structured power of organized religions. A fresh, curious, and advanced attitudes promoted by Uranus (God of the Skies), is slowly taking over the dogmatic and deceiving teachings of the dying age of Pisces.

The Observer - London

9-9-01

Cardinal Murphy O'Connor, the Archbishop of Westminster, admitted last week that Christianity is being 'vanquished' from government and people's lives in Britain. The Archbishop of Canterbury says he agrees with his Roman Catholic counterpart. We congratulate both men on their candor. And while we fully respect the Christianity that many Britons still practice today, we welcome the dramatic change that clerics are belatedly acknowledging.

"For far too long, religion has been a pre-condition to morality. Too often, elites have bemoaned the decline in religious faith without being able to summon any great conviction themselves. It has been thought vitally important for the credulous 'lower orders' to believe in heaven and hell if they were to have any moral compass.

It is hardly surprising that younger people are ever less interested in organized religion with its often intransigent positions on issues such as women's rights, contraception and gays. Taught to challenge deference to shibboleths, they are simply unprepared to wait the customary couple of hundred years that some bishops admit privately it will take to execute a change in approach. But if new generations are abandoning the churches, it does not mean for one moment that they are abandoning spirituality. There is, as we know, a plethora of spiritual beliefs shared by Britons today.

All societies, from the most primitive, have had rules that bind them together, rules, for example, of ownership and partnership. The whole cannot function without reciprocity of obligation. Christianity once performed that role, too, but no longer. The watershed acknowledged by the archbishops is an opportunity to consider what sort of morality is appropriate for Britain in the twenty-first century.

A child brought up without religion can certainly be a moral human being. And in a multi cultural society, we need to develop a secular morality - of equality, honesty, fairness - which can unify, rather than divide, as religions have done so often in the past and still do, as last week's nauseating events outside a Northern Ireland school have shown. But championing this secular morality requires confidence and bravery. It will mean that faith will become a wholly private matter, not subject to either state interference or sponsorship.

It is regrettable that, just as society recognizes this, politicians are showing themselves as keen as ever to kowtow to some religious groups. It is ludicrous that Ministers should be considering more, not fewer, faith-based schools. It is similarly ridiculous that they should be contemplating the introduction of more, not fewer, clerics to our legislature. But this is hardly the first time that politics has dragged far behind public reality."

****

The same poisoned and abusive law makers will be seen at church at every Sunday service, and will also use the system to their advantage. You will also see some of those sharks' friends proudly advertising their new-found buildings, along with options for expansion in the future. This is because of the land they manage to steal legally from the pious-but dead-person. How thankful they are to those who are willing to give them even more properties and office space, so that they can poison even more people and children in the long run. Those "advertisements" won't be broadcasted in the late, less-expensive hours of the night, but right during peak day-time slots. Jesus' promoters and psychics alike must mislead and suck your money, advertising their own godly ways or their false psychic powers, on national television. Simply stated these are different pipes but the same old stinky sewer. Why can't people see through these manipulative and deceiving endeavors is still a mystery to me.

What a job! And talk about religion, manipulation, financial and social security!

Our Senators and Congressmen do not pay into Social Security, and, therefore they do not collect from it. Social Security benefits were not suitable for them. They felt they should have a special plan. Many years ago they voted in their benefit plan. In more recent years, no congressman has felt the need to change it. After all, it is a great plan.

For all practical purposes, their plan works like this: When they retire, no matter how long they have been in office, they continue to draw their same pay until they die, except it may be increased from time to time by the cost-of-living adjustments.

For example, former Senator Bill Bradley (New Jersey) and his wife may be expected to draw $7,900,000.00 over an average life span, with Mrs. Bradley drawing $275,000.00 during the last year of her life. Their cost for this excellent plan is "0", nada, zilch. This little perk they voted in for themselves is free to them. You and I pick up the tab for this plan. Our tax dollars at work!

With Social Security, which you and I pay into every payday for our own retirement, plus an equal amount matched by our employer, we can expect to collect an average of $1,000 per month or less. Or, we would have to collect our benefits for 68 years and 1 month to equal the Bradley's benefits. Imagine for a moment that you could structure a retirement plan so desirable, a retirement plan that worked so well, that Railroad Employees, Postal Workers, and others who were not in the plan would clamor to be included. This is how good Social Security could be, if only one small change was made.

That change would be to jerk the "Golden Fleece Retirement Plan," out from under the Senators and Congressmen. Put them into the Social Security plan with the rest of us. Watch how fast they fix it!!! If enough people receive this maybe a seed will be planted and maybe good changes will evolve.

Don't forget, our girl, Hillary Rodham Clinton, thanks to the infinite wisdom of New York State voters, now comes under this Congressional Retirement Plan. Don't forget also that each so-called retired president also collects over $200,000 per year. Don't forget, they lost their jobs and are still getting paid for them. Do you? Will you? Can you?

Talking about the Clintons, it's common knowledge that, in order for them to establish New York State residency, they purchased a million+ house in upscale Chappaqua, NY. Makes sense doesn't it? Now, they are entitled to Secret Service protection for life. Still makes sense. Here is where it becomes interesting. A residency had to be built in order to house the Secret Service agents. The Clinton's now charge the Secret Service rent for the use of said residence and that rent is just about equal to their mortgage payment, meaning that we, the tax payers, are paying the Clinton's mortgage and it's all perfectly legal. You gotta love it!

But the beauty of knowing, understanding, and using the system, is NOT against the law. There are laws, and as much as the religious and political abusers in position of power do, so can you! First you need to gain that knowledge and the power it brings, and with it your option to establish emotional, financial and spiritual stability. Well what are your chances to become the next Pope or the United States first Lady? This possibility is quite remote, if at all practical. Well you too can use men's and star's laws; they are reachable and available.

Since the dawn of time, the Creator has shown his truth to the humble, a truth that is hidden from the vain, blinded by worldly pleasures, but which is written in the skies, which nightly speaks of the glory of God.

—*Nostradamus*

There is no room for ignorance if you are to make significant progress in life. Both the physical and spiritual worlds have rigid laws. Those who master those laws and use the system will advance, and that is the reality of things as seen in many branches of the government. Let's take a simple example, you decide to drive through China and you do not know that the laws of the road are different there. You never took a Chinese class and you do not understand the language. Thus you will not know your real options for safety or getting to places of power.

Chances are that you will not respect the signs, and as you drive through ignoring the "rules," you are bound to be hurt very soon. Other people more curious or "educated" use those laws for safety or position in life. Again, there is no room for ignorance, in anything else you are wasting time, and time is also money. For your own protection you must know and respect the laws of man. This produces a myriad of law enforcers, starting with judges, lawyers, leading ultimately to an opening for the Presidency (Clinton is a lawyer, so is his wife). Other smart rational souls, will also use men's abundant laws to perform all sorts of legal abuses, covering their frugal and selfish endeavors behind the good words of God. Thus no matter how you use those laws, they are there for many valuable reasons and you must stop at the red light in the street, the stop sign, respect the DMV and the IRS laws. The same rules apply with another set of laws found in our universe. These are the laws written in light via the stars. You must learn, and respect these celestial laws, and that's what astrology was designed to accomplish by the wise men. Doing so will allow you to be more knowledgeable if not more powerful than many Kings, Queens and Presidents of this world.

Now realize also that those wise men, regardless of religious doctrine, were not kings or priests per se. You need to cast aside what has been forced upon your psyche as a child (religious poisoning) and challenge all biblical assumptions. You must ask in order to receive, and most of all use your critical thinking. My question to you is

"How can you follow a star?"

OK, let me use sarcasm now, as you all know me well; Dr. Turi has a problem with stupidity!

Unless turbo-charged camels (or space donkeys) were available to travelers in the Middle East two thousand years ago, there was no way for anyone to follow a star. Even nowadays with our entire incredible technological arsenal, we are still incapable of following a star. The only plausible answer is that; anyone can follow a star but it has to be plotted on a map or through the long metallic body and eye of a telescope. Thus, those wise men can only have been astrologers...and were guided by a certain astrological configuration involving Neptune and Jupiter. That configuration happened to be the birth of Christianity, a new religion, a Neptunian deceiving doctrine, and not a child. What a perfect story! Realize that other stories and their respective icons were also created in a different time and part of the world. There were then a wide variety of political and religious rulers all over in need of control and discipline.

The age of Pisces and its relatively young Christian religion was born about 2000 years ago, and Jesus became the icon. The "wise men" were simply announcing the approaching dark age of the 2000 deceiving years to be governed by Neptune, the ruler of Pisces. On the negative physical representation (the fish swimming downstream) Neptune's worse traits are illusion, deception, suffering, pain, remorse, sorrow, hidden enemies, all places of confinement, churches, synagogues, temples, jails, asylums, hospitals, etc. Indeed, it is one of the most difficult energies to grasp in Astropsychology, due to the very principle of deception itself.

The perfect symbol chosen and carved on clay tablets over 35,000 years ago by the Sumerians was the fish, to represent Neptune's (Lord of the oceans) best or worse powers. Three quarters of this world is submerged under water and this also represents Neptune's illusive and deceptive grasp over the masses, plus the creation of deities and multitudes of religions worldwide.

Incidentally the Christians subconsciously chose Neptune's symbol, the fish swimming in opposite directions. They certainly hate Dr. Turi and would love to see him rot in a jail or burnt at the stake for writing such words against their belief system. However, they all advertise astrology with a fish glued on the back of their cars driving around town! Of course elsewhere, before and after Jesus, in other governmental "offices" or synagogues and temples; more religious icons such as Allah and Buddha were born, and with them serious conflicts and destructive religious wars. Neptune rules also the Middle East, and this is where the Christians, Jews, and Muslims continue to kill each other in the name of their respective Gods, religions, or dogmatic teachings. Again, each and every planet is both positive and negative in its own right, and Neptune happens to be the most difficult planet with which to deal and rationalize. Wherever this deceiving planet is located in your chart (by house and sign) you are most certainly prone to delude yourself.

That is Neptune's job, as represented by the Fish swimming downstream following the general trends and established religious belief systems. Anyone born with a moon, a Dragon's Tail in Pisces or a very strong and badly aspected Neptune can only become the worst of this planet's manifestation, and its victim. The negative Neptunian will drink like a fish! They will become hooked to any varieties of drugs such as cocaine, speed, magic mushrooms, acid, opium, pot, Prozac, alcohol, cigarettes smoking, etc. The desire to "escape" reality is so strong that it fuels a constant spiritual need which becomes a deep seated purpose. The soul then is sucked into Neptune's deceiving, illusive, and treacherous waters, and sinks into anything ranging from cults, to any of the 875 organized religious institutions out there.

The negative fish slowly but surely follows a very destructive current and will end up attracting a nefarious Neptunian crowd along with its Neptunian leader. David Koresh and Reverend Jones are good examples. They were the "avant-garde" and the deceiving Captains of Neptune. In the name of Jesus (or anyone), thousands of innocent God fearing young souls have lost their precious lives by swimming downstream. Incidentally, Neptune rules also exotic places and islands, not to forget drugs. This is exactly where Rev. Jones chose (as dictated by Neptune), an island, away from any genuine help, and he used a powerful drug to kill over a thousand people.

Neptune rules Pisces and the 12th house or the subconscious. A negative Neptune (fueled by drugs) often induces uncontrolled imagination. Schizophrenia and all actual mental problems come from the depths of the subconscious. Then the soul sinks into the deepest and ugliest parts of Neptune's destructive power, into the confusing world of illusion. Infamous and seriously disturbed criminal minds such as John Wayne Gacy Jr. and Jeffrey Dahmer were instruments of a Dagon's Tail in Pisces, or the worst of Neptune's power. (Read this in "The Power of the Dragon").

Where ever Pisces or Neptune is located in your chart, the most incredible effort will be needed to keep your "head out of the water". Millions of people are right now at this very second, victims of Neptune's incredible deceiving influence. You will find them injecting powerful drugs in their veins, drinking themselves silly to forget their dramatic experiences, abusing Prozac, or joining cults or new religions, looking for God or Jesus, Fatima, Allah or Buddha, Hare Krishna, Mother Mary, or a new rising guru in Peru. Neptune leads the people of this earth in a dangerous illusive dance to the sound of a myriad of illusory chimeras and doctrines. Since the dawn of time, man's folly has created religions and their appropriate icons, and they are feared and venerated until the deadly poison of their own imagination condemns and contaminates the young souls to their own self-destruction (religious wars).

The ancients really knew Neptune's strength, and carving the two fish swimming in opposite directions was the perfect symbolism. Since day one, God has enslaved every one of us to swim upstream towards himself. Like a salmon, against all odds, poisoning fears and ignorance, the soul must swim upstream towards its birthplace or the stars. As a child of the universe this is where we all came from. Sadly enough, the powerful current of the river will never stop or change direction and the poor fish (soul) must fight endlessly to reach the true waters of peace, knowledge, cosmic consciousness and himself or God. It is not surprising then to realize why so many people give up the fight. Many lack either the opportunity or curiosity to exit the relentless river. They can only follow the illusional current, as nothing else has been made available to them. But even if a helping hand is presented to the sinking young souls, they were taught (poisoned) either not to take the chance or violently reject it. Their elders, parents, organized religions, churches and governments, took control of their psyches at an early age and established the rules centuries ago. The tremendous amount of religious dogma through the codification of thoughts, is piled against the soul as soon as he or she can learn. This is commonly called "religious poisoning" and takes away any form of spiritual criticism at a very early age. Unless the soul is advanced, he will only swallow the spiritual food available to him without any questions what so ever. Anytime the word "organized" is used; it is most certainly produced by the government's hidden agenda, to control the masses' psyches. This is especially true when the organization itself is exempt from taxation and its budget is over a million dollars a year!

There are a bounty of beautiful souls out there willing to offer their services to God for free. Manpower to support and promote abusive organizations is not only cheap but also inexhaustible. An incredible amount of wealth is also recovered this way, and a good example is the pious widow nearing death, giving her expired husband life's savings and real estate properties to the church. It's like buying a place in paradise as she approaches the judgment day. Perfect mental manipulation started when both husband and wife arrived in this world, to collect all the free goodies after their deaths. How many god-fearing people have suffered this manipulation? It usually starts when one of the numerous recruiters suckers-knocks the door of your vulnerable grandma or mother, and convinces them to follow the "right" God in their church. It's only a small fee to start with, but ultimately Neptune sucks the soul in and later on with it; all the wealth that belongs to the family and their children. The deceiving plan has worked for centuries and is still working miracles. By watching them simultaneously on two or three televised channels during peak hours, or loud and clear on the radio in the middle of the desert where reception should be impossible is nearly a miracle in itself! Your resources are well used, and affords them with the best and most expensive technological tools to broadcast their message to every corner of the world.

Like a vicious circle, this immeasurable wealth is well accounted for by the church authorities, and is redistributed and used within powerful real estate endeavors, and translates into building multitudes of churches on every city block. Not knowing better, the young God-fearing souls first become and then play very active parts in the promotion of fear, ignorance, and mental control, through a hidden, deceptive and controlled political agenda.

Imagine what I would do with such wealth? But again, you are not afraid of me, and I am teaching that you are in charge, and you yourself are god! So why should you give me your financial support if there is no hell and punishment in my teachings? Why would you be a participant for the light, for freedom, for true knowledge that would benefit all the children of the world? Promoting the truth is free, and those suckers need you. I just cannot understand why people cannot think and see things as they are really happening. It amazes me to see such obvious manipulation in action, and the majority of people's reluctance to make change for the better.

Investing sums to promote the truth is honorable and really priceless for mankind's progress, but no one has ever done it for my very message or me so far. Without asking, your church at this very moment is sealing incredible deals and legally stealing invaluable resources from those ignorant souls and their children. I wish I could tell you the incredible stories experienced by some of my clients in the name of god, and what the preacher, the religious leader, and churches did to them. But it might be too much for the sensitive reader to acknowledge. Some of those stories are simply unbelievably deceptive and abusive in nature and would make you puke of disgust.

In some cases, unless you paid the specific religious organization a fee or a substantial percentage of your earnings, you are not allowed to enter or pray in that man made building called a church. You will have to go elsewhere; you're not a part of that specific Neptunian grouping. These religious buildings will be found in the most expensive locations of any city. For example look in the most famous areas of the city of Sedona in Arizona. But do not look for hidden places as you would expect any church to be. Instead they are in plain view against the red rocky mountainsides, and in the extraordinarily unapproachable, unthinkable expensive real estate areas. The power displays itself conspicuously and starts right inside the city board decision based upon the American capitalist money-making machine. Some other religious denominations will have the white, majestic monuments built less than five feet away from the busiest and noisiest highway 5 in the most expensive La Jolla area, or any US city, sometimes becoming a landmark. If that is not an in-your-face combination of spiritual pride and rewarding business then I do not know anything about spiritual pride and enterprises.

The current goes in one direction only and is accepted by all as true, and over the years has become the only truth. In a time when there was no paper or pen available to a bunch of god fearing and ignorant peasants, knowledge was passed by word of mouth. Over the centuries these stories became a reality, as the true message and true manifestation of God through the heavens was lost. With Neptune in charge, all celestial knowledge was to be replaced by man's folly and overactive physical and spiritual imagination.

The challenge is somehow too difficult to handle and the powerful current much too strong to fight. How is it then possible for the soul to free itself from Neptune? Too many years of religious teaching turns into mental poisoning. The assimilation of multi-sided and archaic principles is much too deep and strongly established within the psyche, and it becomes intolerable or unacceptable for the young soul to see, believe or conceive anything else. Your reality has become your induced specific deity, denomination, church or basic religious culture. You can trace its source coming from one of your parents, opening the door to one of the fleas (Neptune's soldiers), and convincing them to 'follow" the right path to Jesus and God. They are still operational and multitudes of them keep trying to convince (by successfully convincing you) that they are right and have the right God for you.

But when will mankind realize that; to mention the word of a deity or "Jesus" for instance, in some parts of the world would cost your precious life? People from this part of the world were "trained and forced" by their government for many centuries to accept, assimilate, and believe, a very different creed, and their deity has a different name.

The 9th house in the astrological housing system regulates religion and how the soul will respond to the codification of thought. Thus any aspect to Neptune and this house could turn anyone into a religious fanatic willing to sacrifice or kill others for his own belief system. Realize also that the church has killed millions of erudite people and astrologers alike, while no astrological group has ever killed a single religious person.

Only one religion taught astrology in the old days and that is the Jewish religion... Nostradamus was Jew and was taught the secrets of the universal mind and the Cabala by both his grandfathers. Fleeing many persecutors, his family arrived in the South of France and in order to stay alive, they had to convert to Christianity. You will learn much more on Nostradamus' stars etc. in "The Power Of The Dragon".

No long ago and in every part of the world, the established local church was the only government, so common sense applies!

It's time to use your imagination. You and your wife are responsible for the well being of your tribe designated kingdom on this earth. We all know how difficult it to deal with others, as everyone's stars are so different, so subtle, and affects every one of us in such complex ways.

Back then you knew that in order to operate harmoniously, your society needed to establish rules and make the people beneath you understand and respect those rules. Thus your first challenge was to make those laws and pass them on without any opposition from anyone. Being just a man or a woman, even a King or a Queen, will not necessarily cut it. Neptune's effective trickery and power of imagination needs much more than common sense to be operational. So you, the rulers decide to use that "energy," and now you have a profound need to "create" something more powerful than man himself. This entity, or the deity (as a God) had to be created to produce the expected results. The new godly rules have been created, enforced, and so with them, why not add some fears (evil, Satan etc.), and use the preservation instinct to accomplish your aims?

Most certainly the people then, behaved more like animals, than the refined and educated humans found in our society today. Thus killing and eating their enemy was probably very common, especially when food was scarce. Two thousand years ago, mankind was not as sharp as he is today and would not be able to challenge anything. There were no books, paper, pens or basic education available to these people. Chances are they were very different mentally, if not plain stupid. But what I still find quite amazing nowadays is that some young souls without any mental challenge, embrace and accept the possibility that a "man" could walk on water.

The desire and need for Neptune's vibrational belief system in our human experience is obviously very strong.

Thus a much higher "entity" was needed, and simply created directly from a powerful but well organized imagination (Neptune rules imagination). The man-made stories and holy names began to flourish and exploded from different parts of the world. Responsible rulers (anywhere in the world) had the same aim, to control the minds of their subjects. Barraged at an early age by Neptunian data, as the subject ages it becomes the rules. The mind can then be easily disciplined and with it, the hidden desire of control by your rulers. Simply stated, by assimilating a set of laws (bible, Ten Commandments etc.), the possibility for order, harmony and peace becomes a real possibility.

The first challenge of course was to use the human preservation instinct and tap into the fear principle. This always works, and you end up in hell if you challenge God and break his divine rules! The point I am trying to make here is that man wrote those rules, not God! Parts of the bible are so real and totally unarguable, but one must read between the lines and not lose the spirit for the printed words. This is evident with such a phrase as, "men have ears, but they do not hear. Men have eyes, but they do not see."

Man has written everything under the stars, but God never wrote any books. However, God made the stars and unless one raises his cosmic consciousness, he will never be able to perceive, hear, and heed the divine message written in light, via the stars. I personally believe that ignorance is pure evil and I do understand now, why Nostradamus made such a remark to a stone carver creating the body of the Virgin Mary. He said, "You're making stone evils". This statement could have cost the great Prophet's life when the church worker (then the government!) denounced him to the Inquisition. You see, Nostradamus had full cosmic consciousness and knew how the stars worked on the human psyche. He was also smart enough to realize the manipulation principle behind the church and its power to kill anyone challenging its rigid governmental rules using religion. Most of all, Nostradamus was aware of the damage produced by ignorance. He also felt helpless to talk, teach or promote the stars and what he deeply knew to be God's real manifestation throughout the universe.

He saw the stars in action then, and also knew how to read their hidden message. He was very aware of how they would affect mankind's fate. He knew that the age of Pisces (or dark ages) was then in full action. This Neptunian, illusive, restrictive, religious-oriented energy would take a heavy toll on humans but had to run its full course. He also knew that until the Age of Aquarius came along and took over mankind's general psyche over 400 years in the future (that was in 1945), that many people would perish in the name of God, ignorance and fear.

Terrorism Predicted

The worst case of Neptune's (ruler of Pisces) illusive and destructive power ever experienced by mankind, took place on September 11, 2001 in New York in the United States.

Note - In 1991, I was invited by famous radio talk show host Art Bell, to be a guest on his program "Kingdom of the Night." I told him that "In a few years from today, a religious war would take place in Europe (Kosovo) and (then) the United States." He was quite astonished by this prediction. The war in Europe (Kosovo) eventually came to pass. And, a few years later, on September 11, 2001, the dramatic WTC/Pentagon attacks took place and my full prediction came true. The tape of this show should be available to anyone upon request.

Early in 1997, I also sent him a letter and told him that he would experience, in 1998, serious stress and drama involving his career. On October 13th, 1998 my prediction came true with his announcement to quit broadcasting because of serious supposed 'threats' to his family. I immediately photocopied page 209 of my 1998 Moon Power book and faxed it to his office to remind him of my prediction. As usual, the printing process makes my prediction totally unarguable, and HIS name and predictions were fully spelled out and printed a year earlier. Sadly enough for Mr. Art Bell, like many pious people, he can not dwell with true predictions and he never invited me again on his show. See the re-print following this page.

Luckily, my dear friend, radio host Jeff Rense, not only can discern and accept the truth, but also realizes the good, caring work and tremendous response my efforts generate on the air. He offered me a regular monthly guest appearance on his nationally syndicated, worldwide radio show, the Jeff Rense Program, so that I could educate the masses about the cosmic will and Divine Astrology. His interview guests are quite impressive. I strongly advise you to visit his website and worldwide news service site at: http://www.rense.com/ and educate yourself to the realities of our world...from

Chapter 12
Celebrity Predictions

Increase in celebrity divorces: 75% of all actors/actress/entertainers who have appeared in movies will have sought an emotional or business-like divorce before the end of 1998. Loss of eminent actors, singers and painters is also high on my list. Due to the Dragon's Tail in Pisces (drugs, alcohol) many of those listed below will be forced to a full restructure. The following names will be directly affected by the Dragon's Tail and should be cautious in all they say, sign or do.

Stress/drama in partnerships is foreseen for some famous names below: Michael Douglas — Gloria Estefan — Lily Tomlin — Raquel Welch — Larry Hagman.

Stress/drama in the area of Work and Health is foreseen for some famous names below: Tony Braxton — Bill Wyman — Tracy Nelson — Maria Maples — Dale Evans.

Stress/drama in the area of Children and Love is foreseen for some famous names below: Tracy Nelson — Roseanne — Julia Roberts — Richard Burton — Prince Charles.

Stress/drama in the area of Family Members is foreseen for some famous names below: Don Johnson — Janine Turner — Amy Grant — Gerard Depardieu — Rush Limbaugh.

Stress/drama in the area of Career is foreseen for some famous names below: Art Bell — Will Smith — Juliette Lewis — Jo Piscopo — Marky Mark.

Noticeable career growth is foreseen for some famous names below: Larry King — Tonia Harding — Ken Griffey Jr. — Meg Ryan — Sally Field.

Children and Love are foreseen for some famous names below: Jennie Garth — Andy Garcia — Shannen Doherty — Connan O'Brien — Julian Lennon.

the UFO/Alien issue to the most revealing geopolitical conspiracies.

My prediction of what to expect with the Dragon's Tail (negative) in Sagittarius (foreigners/religion) led me to predict the energies surrounding the dramatic September 11 destruction of the towers in New York. Those predictions were written almost 2 years previously, and long before Sept 11 2001, in my yearly 2001 Moon Power publication http://www.drturi.com/MP2001.html and in my other book "2001 Nostradamus Dragon Forecast" http://www.drturi.com/nost2001.html. Those predictions were also posted on September 2nd, 2001 on my site www.drturi.com.

Again realize that I am not trying to gain from this drama, I am simply making you aware of the power of Real Predictions. Unlike "Mrs.Cleo," and those so-called famous psychics and so-called famous astrologer newspaper horoscope writers, I AM REAL!

What about the higher Papal or Tibetan Lama spiritual leaders? They represent God's will on earth, don't they? Where is their knowledge of the highest forces affecting the affairs of mankind and why did they NOT tell us about it? Guess what! "THEY DON'T KNOW as much as one would have you believe, and THAT'S WHY!" But who the hell does Dr. Turi think he is, some may ask?

I am not bragging or assuming to put myself above those respected "wise" ecclesiastic men, but I certainly KNOW more about God's will through the stars and the fact is there, right in front of your eyes, just read it.

This is where I am asking the American population to acknowledge this fact, and join me in my prayers for all the victims of terrorism world-wide, and all the while help me to pass on my VERY IMPORTANT MESSAGE to the rest of the world.

The printing process, in regard to my books and predictions, makes my work UNARGUABLE to ALL the dramatic major news stories that have taken place the last few years. Radio and television programs and certified letters are available to prove all my claims!

Let people know about this site and make good use of it with the daily and monthly forecasts.

http://www.drturi.com/daily.html

http://www.drturi.com/monthly.html

May God bless America and the souls of all the victims.

--Dr. Turi

At 8:45 a.m. EDT, the first of two airliners crashed into the World Trade Center, opening a horrifying and apparently coordinated terrorist attack on the United States, which saw the collapse of the two 110-story towers into surrounding Manhattan streets and a later attack on the Pentagon. The following is the prediction pertaining to the WTC/Pentagon attacks written almost two years earlier, from "2001 Moon Power Starguide."

"Full Moon - September 2, 2001 in the sign of Pisces: Because of the Uranus/Neptune and Saturn impact these days, expect some surprising developments to take place in the near future. Pisces rules the Middle East, religion, drugs, alcohol, deception, the difficult abortion dilemma, the Pope, the church, oil, etc. This energy can affect sophisticated electronic equipment and produce bad aeronautic accidents. Just be ready to provide as much help as needed and do not lose faith in the future. More devastating forces producing destructive weather and flooding in the very near future. Expect a general feeling of hopelessness plaguing the media and the church authorities. Deceiving news will take place and affect many of us; some desperate souls will fall for Neptune's suicidal tendency and some will end up in jail or a mental institution. This trend will be very difficult for some, but do not lose faith in yourself and trust the Universe; get all the help you can to fight Neptune's depressive tendencies; keep busy and let go of the past. Life must go on. Expect shocking news with volcanoes, earthquakes, tornadoes etc. *Expect anything surprising, even incredible to take place soon and see the real power of both Uranus, the planet of sudden release of energy in action and Saturn forcing the government to take drastic actions."*

==========================

Here is an excerpt from Dr. Turi's "2002 Nostradamus Dragon Forecast For All Signs".

June 7, 2001 - Printed in the United States of America

NOSTRADAMUS 2002 DRAGON FORECAST

Pluto in Sagittarius: Pluto moved from Scorpio to Sagittarius on November 11th, 1995 and will stay in this sign until January 26, 2008. Constrained to face the horrible consequences of his own destructive power, and pay the heavy consequences of mass destruction, man turns to religion for comfort. In Sagittarius (religion) Pluto (regeneration) will promote a disturbing wave of religious fanaticism that will plague the world. In the US, the impact of Pluto in Sagittarius has already spoken with some religious fanatics, committing serious crimes, and many will have to pay the ultimate price for their destructive behavior. Some Middle Eastern residents have also shocked the world, and will keep spawning suicidal bomb attacks, on major European and US cities. The "contract" they sign with their manipulators, before blowing themselves up, surrounded by the highest possible number of innocent victims, promises "the martyrs" twenty or more virgins after an immediate entrance to paradise!

After the painful passage of Pluto (expiration) in Sagittarius (codification of thought), the world will be ready for wiser, new age and religious leaders. Those well-adjusted souls will teach all the higher expressions of all the religions of the past. They will introduce a new image of a God free of fear, full of love and attention. Those futuristic religious leaders will combine their teachings with a more comprehensive scientific understanding of the manifestation of the Creator throughout the Universe. With Neptune still in the down-to-earth sign of Aquarius, this planet of illusion will advocate a form of positive (arts) or negative (deception) energy.

"Ignorance is evil; when you control someone's source of information or education, chances are that you will control that person's entire life."

— *Dr. Turi*

Important note:

Never forget that the future of mankind depends on the reincarnation of common thought. For every action you will gain an equal reaction. Mankind was made in the image of God. In the eternal fight between good and evil mankind has always succeeded.

It is important that all of you join me in constant massive prayer on a daily basis in order to go against evil itself. You do not need a special day or special time for prayer. It is an intrinsic part of the human psyche promoting hope, love, and peace to the world, happening at all times with your help.

Ignorance is evil. The true evil in any terrorist endeavor is ignorance and the world must grow with the true knowledge written by God in the light through the stars.

Astropsychology Personality Profile of:

Osama Bin Laden "The Anti-Christ"

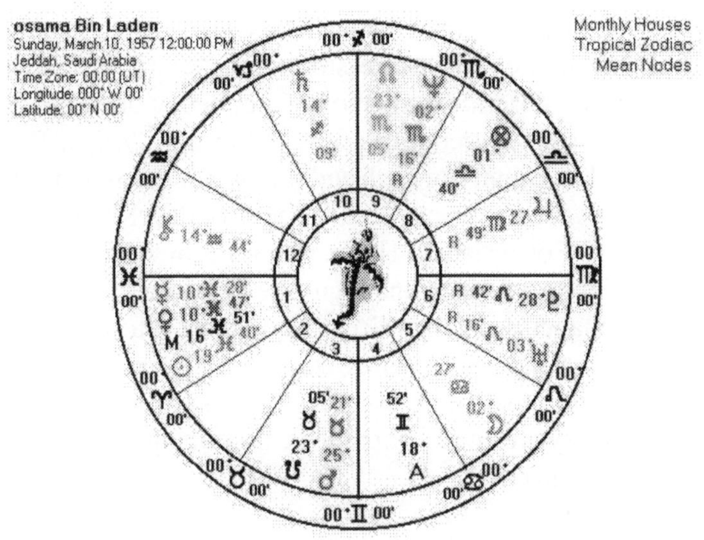

The Breeding of a Terrorist

Astropsychology can reveal many things about Osama Bin Laden's life and true personality. The descriptions that follow will give you a full understanding of his nefarious relationship with the Universal Mind. The spiritual essence coming from the stars is both positive and negative, and the entire world and all mankind are under its jurisdiction. The stars may indicate the hand you were dealt at birth, but it is up to the soul to play that hand well, to achieve its positive or negative goals. How it is expressed is really up to you and involves personal karma. We tend to work at expressing ourselves more positively most of the time and only lapse into negative behavior when depressed, angry or scared. It is possible that some of the worst expressions of the "stars," depicted as symbols, describe the personality or behavior earlier in life with such extreme cases as Hitler and Osama Bin Laden. The country of birth and ruling planet will play an important part of the positive or negative development of the soul. For instance, Hitler was born in April, in the constellation of Aries, the sign ruled by Mars. The red bloody planet is called in Greek Mythology "the planet of war." Germany is an Aries country and expressed the worst, most destructive essence of Mars, by stimulating Hitler's psyche in an attempt at producing a superior (Aries/Aryan) race.

According to Interpol, Osama Bin Laden was born on March 10, 1957 under the pious sign of Pisces in Saudi Arabia. Neptune rules all religions. Note also that the entire Middle East is under Neptune's jurisdiction, and confirms the development of three major religions stemming from this part of the world. With the character and location combined, the stars produced the most evil energy of Neptune, ruler of Pisces, creating this mad man. Note also that the symbol of the fish is also used as a representation of the Christian religion, subconsciously responding to the deceiving pull of Neptune. The location of the Dragon's Head and Tail reinforce positively or negatively each sign, house and planet's description. The higher the Strength, the more you are likely to feel its aspect, and to act it out in your life.

Osama Ben Laden's Sun in Pisces (1st house):

Pisces are well known for being sensitive, emotional and artistic. Their moods change like a chameleon to blend with those around them. At times it may be difficult for Ben Laden to separate fact from fantasy. He lives in a semi-dream world, and retreats into his illusory and religious nature whenever the pressures of real life become unbearable. He is prone to daydreaming (especially as a child). Pisces are usually very shy, and this limits the ability to make friends easily. The soul must learn to be less concerned about what others think, and concentrate on improving the self-image. Because of its genuine desire to help others, it is an easy victim to those who would abuse its kindness. In this case the desire becomes a "religion" and breeds fanaticism. The soul is often cheated, and should be careful to surround itself with people it can trust. The worst of Neptune's deceiving pull is to turn a religious mission of serving others, into a mission of martyrdom. If the soul swims upstream, a positive Pisces will be attracted to the arts and the mystical. The soul can also have inherited highly developed intuitive and psychic abilities. If the soul swims downstream, religious poisoning is often the result, as this sign naturally nurtures deep religious commitments, to the point of suicide. Feelings of greed and competition are foreign to Pisces, who find such energies irritating to their sensitive natures. They are usually not found in the dog-eat-dog corporate world—unless other factors in their charts give them this competitive edge. Consequently, they will use all their assets and wealth to promote and support their rigid religious principles. In this case, Bin Laden's choosing to destroy the WTC towers in New York was an obvious confirmation of Astropsychology at work.

In affairs of the heart, a positive Pisces is devoted, tender, gentle and affectionate. Since an advanced Pisces has so much love to give, others often misunderstand their motives and consider them to be "coming on" to them. The truth is that Pisces is sympathetic and understanding to all others needs—not just their inner circle of loved ones. Pisces is also known for being evasive with others, but rarely purposefully deceptive unless under the powerful and deceptive grasp of its ruler, Neptune. The key word here is "purposefully." A fish swimming downstream will often deceive itself without inward analysis, and therefore consider itself to be quite truthful when others recognize the deception. This is what is happening with Osama Bin Laden through the eyes of the world and the United States. He is so self-deluded that his rational senses and critical thinking do not apply any longer in judgments and course of action.

Sun in the First House (the will)

This house placement indicates a very forceful personality. The issue of power will keep recurring in his relationships with others. However, Osama Bin Laden would prefer to dominate his partners, simply because he is quicker to act than they. He certainly monopolizes conversation and makes plans without asking their opinions first. He is a person who stands out in a crowd and attracts others easily and usually makes a good first impression. His devout Muslim attire and personal natural charm take over, and he easily wins friends and influences people.

He is very direct in his speech (sometimes brutally). He also believes in getting to the point, and is not inclined to indulge in elaborate rituals, other than the religiously oriented ones. This house placement also indicates a generally healthy physical body and a strong desire to lead (or rule) others for a specific often violent religious purpose.

Moon in Cancer (emotional response to life) 5th house

The Moon is quite comfortable in this sign, since it rules Cancer. Osama Ben Laden is truly a "Moonchild," and he is subject to serious mood changes, which accompany the fluctuations in the moon's phases. The word "lunatic/crabby/moody would apply to his personality. His home life is very important and he will do all he can to make it as comfortable and pleasant as possible. In this case, the comfort for which he strives, is to eliminate the US influence and power in the region of his birth. The Moon also rules habits and memories from our past. He may be quite possessive of cherished objects (or persons) from his natal country, as seen by his offer to help against Iraq's invasion of Saudi Arabia a few years ago. Osama Ben Laden's fight against the West is an investment in the future of the Muslim religion and the Middle East. He also has a shrewd way of making money easily, and real estate or the Middle East itself is a chosen area for him to invest in. This is more because of his inability to cut ties with the past than the need for money and variety. Although he may not actively seek the spotlight in life, he doesn't mind the publicity he gets to promote his goals every now and then. (Read Moon Power) http://www.drturi.com/MP2002.html

Mercury in Pisces (thinking process) 1st house

Pisces is the most difficult sign for Mercury, as the dreamy, foggy nature of Pisces interferes with Mercury's rational and logical thinking processes. Since Mercury rules communication and reasoning, it also indicates problems in this area. He may find it difficult to express his ideas with clarity and precision, and at times it may seem as though he is trying to talk under water. This position of the "thinking" planet, Mercury in Pisces predisposes the soul to excessive worrying, negative thinking, religious fanaticism, use of drugs and regrets over the past. So far, his escape of death and the many traps he has avoided is due to his strong intuition He may follow it even more than his logical reasoning. As a matter of fact, he surely is annoyed by people who continually demand that everything be logical. His strong, deceiving, uncontrolled imagination contributes to his love of religious fantasy and such subjects. He could also be classified as a "visionary" and display a talent for poetry and creative writing, as well as music.

Osama Ben Laden is an extremely sensitive man and his emotional states have an overwhelming influence on his thought processes. This sometimes prevents clear thinking and makes it more difficult for him to cope with the challenges of day-to-day practical life. This stimulates suicidal thoughts as he strives hard to maintain a positive attitude towards life. This Mercurial position breeds a constant flow of negative thoughts leading to depression and worry to the point of immobilization or religious refuge. These celestial afflictions of mercury make it even harder for the crazy man to solve his real-world problems. I would counsel the soul to avoid tendencies to see things the way he wants, rather than the way they really are. This obfuscation can only result in a rude awakening to reality, and in his case a probable suicide when cornered in the future.

The serious problem of Mercury (reason) in Pisces (dreams) is that the subject's mind can be chameleon-like, and readily adopt different ideas. This would depend on the country's established religious system, along with the people whom the soul trusted and was brought up with. Mercury in Pisces is prone to serious deception and makes judgments based on emotional reactions rather than logic and reasoning. The psyche of Osama Ben Laden is set to make judgments for religious and personal reasons and finds it impossible to imagine anything beautiful being produced by a country like the US he so dislikes and wants to eliminate.

Mercury in the First House (the self)

Osama Ben Laden has a keen sense of humor and a sharp and curious mind in relation to the affairs controlled by Pisces (religious code). He cannot tolerate boredom, and may become restless and high-strung. This speedy position helps the regeneration of the atomic structure of the body and he will maintain a youthful look. With his burning desire to express his religious agenda and ideas, he can be an eloquent speaker.

Venus in Pisces in the 1st house (the self)

Osama Ben Laden is highly emotional and likes to be "tuned in" to others' needs. His expression of love and sex is repressed in search of purity and chastity and he seeks to impose this cleansing, perfectionist attitude to others. He seeks spiritual not sexual union with anyone and will work hard to establish this subconscious desire. With Venus in Pisces, he tends to be attracted to "stray puppies"—people who need to be loved and saved from their sorry lot in life. In this case he took on the problems of others to the point that they became his own. Since he tends to idealize others by not seeing their bad qualities as well as their good, he sets himself up for disappointment in love by expecting people and partners to be perfect Muslims, as he thinks he is. Venus in Pisces often commits to a deceiving purpose, dedication or suicide is usually the ultimate end. This position breeds martyrdom. Osama Ben Laden carries karmic baggage from other lives into this lifetime. This placement again has produced many martyrs and sacrificial lambs. His natural charm and magnetic personality provide him with a way of winning people over. He could also be somehow mystically attractive and will maintain this quality well into his later years, but I seriously doubt that he will be long-lived.

Mars in Taurus in the 3rd house (war/the mind)

Osama Ben Laden is very persistent and patient when striving toward his financial and spiritual goals. This reluctance to give up, is largely due to his natal Dragon's Tail's (the past) location in the incredibly stubborn sign of Taurus. Incidentally, the Tail of the Dragon resides in the 3rd house of communication and affects in some way his thinking process. On the Tail, money and other material possessions are important to him as a means of control over others. One of the positive lessons of this placement is to learn to share the great bounty he inherited, and to promote love and peace, as Venus (the Goddess of love) rules Taurus. He shows his lust for power by lavishing his partners with gifts of extraordinarily expensive weaponry, especially those he can use to support his evil aims.

Mars in the Third House (Communications/traveling)

Osama Ben Laden is very assertive intellectually, and may have many disagreements with others. Mars (Lord of War) induces impulsive and aggressive thinking and does not deal well with opposition. The mind is constantly racing and colored with aggressiveness and war and this makes him nervous and high-strung. Where ever Mars is located in a chart is a sure indication of danger entering the life of the subject and in this case a violent death to the head or suicide is highly probable. His religious daily meditations may help him to slow the mind to allow his intuition to guide him accordingly.

Jupiter in Virgo (partnerships/associates)

Jupiter rules the codification of thoughts, laws, and all religious books and their rigid regulations. Virgo rules purification, chastity and perfection, making Osama Ben Laden overly practical, even methodical, to bring about the purity of his religious endeavors. He does so cautiously and takes his responsibilities very seriously. Since he is a born fanatic and willing to work hard in the Virgo "cleansing" process, he will go to extremes as an expert in his chosen field of terrorism. He was born overly cynical, and critical of others not supporting his "cleansing" efforts.

Jupiter in the Seventh House (partnerships/contracts)

Jupiter (Lord of Luck) makes him friendly, good-natured and tolerant of other terrorists from different countries. Many of his most valuable lessons and support will be learnt and gained through those relationships. Traditionally, Jupiter in the Seventh indicates a protection, and growth with foreigners.

Saturn in Sagittarius (religion/study/foreigners)

On a negative note, Saturn rules the "fear and restriction" principle. Saturn rules politics, and also structures any house in which he resides to the extreme, whereby a position of power and respect is offered to the soul. On a positive note, Saturn especially in Sagittarius brings a philosophical approach to life. In Osama Ben Laden's case the extreme fear principle is directed towards foreigners, power (US), and structuring and controlling the Middle East. Although he loves to travel, the Saturn freezing principle causes him to travel only in connection with his evil work or in emergency escapes. Saturn is a karmic planet, and the powerful "tower of power" and recognition built over the years, can only crash due to the negative repercussions. Hitler suffered this downfall and his "empire" was crushed.

Saturn in the Tenth House (career/position)

Osama Ben Laden is independent and self-reliant and with Saturn's restrictive influence in his 10th house of career he will encounter a series of obstacles. Saturn will make him learn to accept and carry out even the most unpleasant responsibilities of leadership in his terrorist activities. There will be serious karma to repay to the universe, due to his total disrespect of the Universal rules. Sadly enough, no religion has ever taught the true power all humans inherit at birth. Instead, Universal rules were replaced with man-made rules, opening doors to disaster through a multitude of religions and icons, separating countries due to their beliefs. The results are millions of deaths due to religious wars. Osama Ben Laden is, like 99% of the people walking this earth; a robot of the stars. He became a religious fanatic overwhelmed by a set of negative stars. Not knowing the divine universal design, his will can not be applied to counteract the outcome... Ignorance is evil. Omitting those laws written in light (the stars) can only bring about serious penalty to mankind.

Uranus in Leo (work) - 1955-1962

Osama Ben Laden is confident and has the help needed for organization and has also excellent leadership abilities. Since he finds it difficult to tolerate restrictions of any kind, he can be defiant and rebellious toward any form of authority. Uranus (the rebel) does not follow established trends, and in fact Osama Ben Laden's religious values are lethally different to what others consider acceptable.

Uranus in the Sixth House (work)

Uranus' desire for freedom and eccentricity supports a position where Laden calls the shots—a deadly job, which is unusual and definitely not routine.

Neptune in Scorpio (religion/deception) - 1955-1970

Osama Ben Laden is driven to uncover and impose his own religious convictions through the deadly sign of Scorpio which rules his 9th house of religion and receives the Dragon's Head. On a positive chart this celestial position brings a keen interest in medicine, Astropsychology, research and the metaphysical sciences.

Neptune in the Ninth House (religion/deception)

Osama Ben Laden is a super idealist, and the blurring Neptunian power in the 9th house of faith shuts down his rationale. The regeneration principle takes place when pursuing religious endeavors. On a more advanced chart, philosophical, spiritual and mystical studies are favored. Keep in mind that the Middle East is ruled by Neptune (religions/deception) and doesn't support metaphysical studies. The controlling governments do not support any mental exploration, especially generated by the West. This mental manipulation (religious poisoning) allows them to keep a firm control over the uneducated masses, as education leads to freedom of thought and action. No one was there to educate his young spirit. Its Neptunian, inborn tendency to become fanatical about the imposed beliefs, impaired his good judgment and turned him (and many others) into a religious extremist. This position favors a tendency to exaggerate religious endeavors and produce also loud and righteous ministers. The soul has lost all sense of rationale and lives by the codes and the book.

Chiron in the Twelfth House (martyr)

Osama Ben Laden is highly spiritual and doesn't really belong to this physical world. The 12th house rules the subconscious life, and Chiron probably induced deceptive psychotic "visions," knowing that souls born in March are especially prone to abusing drugs, chemicals, and alcohol, leading to hallucinations. In this case the reverse puritanical essence to reach perfection, acts as a powerful religious psychological drug and may also induce mystical, spiritual or supernatural experiences (many trance channels have Chiron in the Twelfth House). With the tendency to see things (and people) the way he wants them to be rather than the way they are, Osama Ben Laden is seriously deceiving himself. He may also feel that it is his duty to make sacrifices so that others can be helped, so he created a fanatic movement dedicated to social, religious and political reform.

Pluto in Leo (facing the world) - 1938-1958

This generation saw the birth of greater autonomy and self-rule among the world's nations. You may learn more about Pluto (death/rebirth) in Leo, Cancer, Virgo, Libra, Scorpio, or Baby-Boom, Baby-Wasted, Baby-Buster, and the Death-Wish generations, in "The Power Of The Dragon." Osama Ben Laden was born with Pluto (fanaticism/death) in the 7th house of open enemies, and nurtures an irrationally strong subconscious desire to fanatically solve the world's problems.

Pluto in the Sixth House (work/service to the world)

Pluto, the planet of death and drama, rules Osama Ben Laden's daily work. On the negative side, Pluto rules the mafia, the night, hidden activity, and deadly plots. On the positive side, Pluto rules the FBI, CIA, the police force, secret service, and it induces a strong desire to be of service to others. I am hoping that these Plutonic agencies come to acknowledge the powerful meaning found in Astropsychology, rather than ignore its existence. Pluto's natural ability to get to the root of deep-seated problems also breeds advanced Astropsychologists and healers. A positive Pluto will not tolerate corruption and injustice in society and will work to expose those responsible. In the case of Osama Ben Laden, all these plutonic forces have been misdirected to inflict death for support of both his political and religious agenda.

Osama Ben Laden's North Node in Scorpio in the 9th house - (Read The Power Of The Dragon for information on the dragon's head and tail)

.http://www.drturi.com/dragon3.html

Dragon's Head and Tail location for the whole world by the year:

• November 5, 1956 to May 21, 1958 Dragon's Head in Scorpio, Tail in Taurus

• **Real** - Scorpio / Bin Laden's **Hidden** dragon Sagittarius (9th house)

Key words for a negative Scorpio Dragon

You are often jealous, resentful and dangerous

You are a masochist with a lust for death and drama

You use your metaphysical power the wrong way

You can't let go of people and you are secretive

You enjoy night and attract the wrong crowd

You hate the cops and you have gone to jail

You reject life

Key words for a negative Sagittarius Dragon

Your philosophy, religion or your guru is the only right one

You won't change your mind, your views or your beliefs

You believe that animals are better than humans

You won't challenge what has been written

You are afraid of pursuing real education

You have been religiously poisoned

You think you are above the law

North Node (Dragon's Head) in the Ninth House

In past lifetimes Osama Ben Laden led superficial lives with little reflection or meditation. During this lifetime he will be forced to broaden his awareness and seek knowledge on a higher, more philosophical level. The less he talks, the more he will learn. Travel and exposure to foreign cultures especially the US and Europe would also expand his perspective. As a rule, all souls are trapped on the Tail of the Dragon and in the case of Osama Ben Laden, the lesson of expanding outside one's country and opening up to foreign cultures is totally omitted. The worst of his Dragon's Tail in the sign of Taurus is his stubborn reluctance to let go of the past and grow with the rest of the world. The full power of the deadly Dragon's Head in Scorpio in the house of higher learning, foreigners and religion is misused. This mishap will cost many of lives in the name of religion, and will bring to an end within the next few years, the deceiving age of Pisces. The dragon's tail (Oct. 2001) presently resides in Sagittarius with the planet Pluto. After the painful passage of Pluto (expiration) in Sagittarius (religions), the world will be ready for a more balanced universal religion. The well adjusted, Uranian spiritual teachers will demonstrate a higher expression of the stars, left hidden in all religions of the past. They will introduce a new image of a God, free from fear, full of love and attention. These futuristic "religious" leaders will combine their teachings with a more comprehensive, scientific understanding of the manifestation of the Creator, throughout the Universe and the stars.

What the vast majority of "the faithful" all over the world, including Osama Ben Laden do not know is that,

Astrology is the basis for all religions in the world's history, this includes their own. The old science of Astrology has been and will always be the most diligent work available, for those who are seeking the real truth. Mastering the universal mind and building a cosmic consciousness is not an easy task, but with Uranus (the awakened) now in charge the children of the world will subconsciously reject all established dogmas and aim for a much higher education. The new children of the universe will swim upstream, into the 3rd eye of true wisdom, back to their original birthplace, to the stars.

"Mythology is what grownups believe, folklore is what they tell their children, and religion is both."

~ Cedric Whitman

Lastly, Divine Astrology (Astropsychology) is a much-needed tool to allow spiritual regeneration in its purest form to all. Admitting the Divine Essence of the stars in, to clarify the human experience on this dense physical world, is a serious contribution for future generation's mental welfare and survival. Lastly for the purpose of happiness, peace, and love for all, when Astropsychology is once accepted as a solid discipline in our colleges and Universities, it will provide spiritual awareness, emotional stability, and hope for all mankind.

Important note:

Never forget that the future of mankind depends on the reincarnation of the common thought. For every action you will gain an equal reaction. Mankind was made in the image of God. In the eternal fight between good and evil mankind has always succeeded. It is important that all of you join me in daily prayer, in order to go against evil itself. You do not need a special day or special time for prayer. It is an intrinsic part of the human psyche promoting hope, love, and peace to the world happening at all times with your help. Ignorance is evil. The true evil in any terrorist endeavor is ignorance and the world must grow with the true knowledge written by God in the light through the stars.

"God created the stars in the heavens for more than the sake of beauty. He gave them to us for interpretation so that we may live a more productive life"

Dr. Turi

****

How Does Astrology work?

So how astrology does really work? To really understand this dilemma you must realize that your brain is nothing more than a sophisticated computer reacting to an outside stimuli produced by the stars high above. Like a radio or a television set, your brain (no matter how complex it is) is tuned to see, feel, react, create and so forth, in a certain way. This very sophisticated "spiritual muscle" is simply a physical tool attached to a physical body with a very definite physical function. Simply explained, the Universal mind generates impulses through the celestial bodies in waves which are picked up by the human brain, and all the manifestations are the myriads of our potentials as humans. I will use another example to help you to assimilate this fact.

When you type on your computer, you are the outside intelligence or a God to your PC. The physical manifestations are the keyboard, the screen you look at, the complexity of electronic components in the computer's metal box etc. All is locked inside the box. Your computer is simply obeying and reacting to your physical impulse and touch via your fingers hitting the keyboard. Thus again, your brain is a physical tool reacting to a much higher order or frequency coming from the universal mind or the stars. I will try another example to help you assimilate my theory. To find out what makes a genius, scientists dissected Einstein's brain. Of course they did not, and will not, find the answers to what it means to be human, by doing so. Thus thousands of your tax dollars have been and still are wasted in fruitless research.

Looking for the physical processes of a mind (let's say a computer) will not bring a full understanding of that tool. But once you are done studying this computer, it is already obsolete. A new computer, more powerful and complex, comes along with more functions and new parts. There goes the scientist again, wasting money with their research trying to find out the weak and strong parts of that computer (the brain). Why don't they go straight to the factory (the Universal Mind) and see how it is put together at the source, that is my question to those educated mental snobs. But again, this research has its benefits, for if the computer gets broken; they can use their knowledge to fix some of its physical parts. It really amazes me that those students and professors alike are looking at that small peace of dead meat, hoping to find out the workings and complexity of the human mind. When will they realize that this fleshy computer (the brain) is simply responding to a well hidden motherboard of sophisticated universal functions, called the Universal Mind? They are looking at the screen of the computer not realizing all its ramifications. What a waste of time and money...

There is absolutely no difference between your brain and the brain of Einstein, or the brain of a killer for that matter. Its function, size, weight, wiring, and purpose is exactly the same. The only difference is the initial celestial program inserted at birth. Thus our scientists must stop speculating and making up new scientific and stupid words to look "educated". They MUST look above their heads and not down if they are to uncover the golden key of what it means to be human and to know the workings of its psyche. The majority of us are walking robots, walking batteries, with two sides of the brain, two eyes, two arms; two legs and we all walk on two feet. This is the obvious distribution of both the physical and spiritual manifestation at work. It's much like a light bulb which illuminates once you plug it in. The more power is sent to the bulb, the more brightly it will shine. The power, meaning spiritual knowledge acquired in previous lives, turns into the gift of light to shine on others. Man is not born equal. If a soul has mastered spiritual lessons he will be born with a highly spiritual set of stars, and will perceive more "light" than another person. And if the soul learnt and mastered mathematics in a previous past life, he will not only enjoy math but will excel in it. This person will be a fantastic engineer or a famous architect by birth and will aim in that direction, as predisposed by his stars. Then another who has spent many lives mastering music, might very well become another musical genius like Mozart or Beethoven. The same applies physically; one might be born with long legs and will easily win many races.

To Teach Astropsychology

Do not confuse Astrology and Astronomy. Astronomers will tell you the movement of the stars, their distance, composition, and position in our solar system. That accurate information is very valuable and helps the human experience to further its incredible purpose in colonizing space in the future. Realize the fact that astronomy is a by-product of astrology that deals only with the physical manifestation of the universal mind. Those scientists to predict the time of an eclipse stole and used the Clay tablets of old astrologers. In doing so, they challenged the ultimate celestial purpose of God throughout the symbolic signs of the Zodiac and fueled a general loss of man's cosmic consciousness. The dramatic results are quite depressing, with the chaos experienced on so many levels, and especially with the children literally executing each other in our schools. Infringing on God's celestial rules brings a serious penalty to mankind and its progeny. Astrology is the breath of God, it brings spiritual regeneration, solid direction, physical and spiritual wealth, power, and rebuilds self-esteem. For the sake of our children, Astrology and its therapeutic values must be reintegrated in our colleges and universities. Astrology is desperately needed for all the souls on this earth, and now is the time.

It has long been recognized that there is a need for a new simpler astrology that would meet the requirements of the beginning student of this old science. In this introductory course and this book, I will attempt to meet these needs. Please keep in mind that as was Nostradamus, I too was born and raised in Provence France. I spent the last 30 years of my life re-kindling the work of the great Seer. This eminent Renaissance man did not have a watch or a computer, thus he did not care about the mathematical jargon encountered in today astrology. As did he, I too explored the Universal Mind with my telescopic inborn gifts, and gave special attention to the symbolic values found in each sign of the Zodiac. Looking into the great Universal Mind with a microscope and giving attention to a multitude of details such as risings, aspects, etc. could cause you to lose sight of the big picture. The calendars and the very astrological methods he used were in many ways very different and extremely simple.

By learning Nostradamus' Divine Astrology or Astropsychology, you will finally gain the golden key of what it means to be human and gain a new powerful cosmic consciousness. If you have previously learned astrology, it might assist or work against you. It's like learning the piano; if you have developed bad habits, you will have to work harder to correct them. In any case I am fairly confident that you will still make measurable progress and master this course if you persevere in your research for true knowledge. Please, keep in mind that I am not debunking modern astrology; I have just spent too much time, money, and efforts to no end following that direction. Hard core, old fashioned, mathematically oriented modern astrologers may not be able to enter the intuitive domain of Divine Astrology and should pursue Astronomy. A very strong Mercury location (mental power) might affect your 3rd house (the learning process), or perhaps this planet may reside in an earth sign, such as Capricorn, Virgo or Taurus. Your natal Tail of the Dragon might also reside in an earth sign, making Divine Astrology a little more difficult for you to assimilate. If you are a novice to the stars, this might not mean a lot to you just now, but it will later, once you've completed this book.

I will try to keep the mathematical definitions as simple as possible, and by doing so, will expand on the subtle meanings of the astrological symbols. The study of Astropsychology or Divine Astrology is a based upon a straightforward even simple method and I will guide you through the concepts. If you're reading or listening to this course now you must continue to do so with patience. With time and repetition you will develop a subconscious reflex and automatically absorb the meaning of the terms needed for you to master the secrets of the Universal Mind.

The whole idea of Astropsychology is to learn and master the twelve departments of the human experience. This spiritual language can be used to categorize anyone's states of consciousness and levels of awareness, fate, health and all that it means to be human. As you proceed to listen and learn with this course, you will recognize that the ancient astrologers were not nut cases, but great cosmic and philosophical geniuses. They saw us as the children of the universe, and knew our direct relationship with the cosmos. They also knew of the challenges ahead, and left us with their incredible astrological legacy. In our common search for the truth, we will find our higher selves and recognize our own godly natures. We all have been made in the image of mighty God. Thus by finding our selves, our celestial gifts, and our creative potentials, we will find God. Never forget that, the spark of life is in our soul, and the future of mankind is based upon the reincarnation of our very thoughts. When you have found yourself, you've found God, and when you have found God, you will have found yourself. Incidentally, in time and space you have set this all up... However you do not have the luxury or the potential to realize this fact just yet. You are operating at a low vibration, in a very dense physical world. By learning and mastering the secrets of the universal mind, you are bringing your spirit to a much higher level of awareness, and this book will help you build your own cosmic consciousness and enter the ultimate third eye to true knowledge.

Far from being a dead art, astrology continues to thrive. Because its works so well, it continues to have many followers. Man and King alike use astrology. Examples of some of the famous people who used it are: Lady Diana, both French Presidents Jacques Chirac and Francois Mitterrand, Saddam Hussein, Ronald Reagan and his wife, and the list continues indefinitely... Many psychologists, psychiatrists, surgeons, attorneys, MD's, clergyman, police officers, actors and writers, and members of the government have used my services and have taken my course. Sadly enough we are also aware that astrology has its abusers, those practitioners who seriously diminish the integrity of the real science. They are in it for financial purposes only. You will find those famous names in your local newspaper horoscopes, magazines, and insulting psychic television programs. My teaching is legitimate, practical and rewarding. In any case do not hesitate to comment, and direct your feedback to my website, www.drturi.com. I welcome any remarks, critiques, and suggestions that could improve either my teaching method or future courses.

SYLLABUS

You have the option to take the Astropsychology class either on cassette tapes or live. I have two taped classes you may order by mail. You have the choice to order either the Astropsychology Course #1, or the Advanced Astropsychology Course #2. At the end of the class a test is given to check your reflexes and your knowledge of the information. The first test will focus on your general knowledge of the subject and your spiritual "reflexes". The second test is much more advanced. It elaborates on the hidden forces of the chart and builds more of those reflexes. The second test will consist of not only the subject matter covered in the first tuition but will graduate you to an "Astrophile" or an Astropsychologist, and not an astrologer. This means you don't deal with numbers, trines, sextiles, degrees, solar returns, Saturn returns, and all the usual mathematical jargon. Leave this to modern astrologers or astronomers, as you cannot afford to confuse or scare your client. Make it easy for him and simply deal with your heart, intuition, and symbolism. Without a well built reflex, your only option to "read" someone in any circumstance is by carrying an ephemeris, a big book or a laptop computer. How practical does this sound when you have only a few seconds available to read a person anytime, anywhere? This is what my course is all about. You won't need anything, just a remarkable knowledge and a lightning reflex and you will do just that when you graduate. Remember, before being a science, astrology is an art, and in mastering Divine Astrology you will be dealing with a new canvas of energies. Go to my website for the current details. www.drturi.com

OVERVIEW

What we will do in this tuition is extremely simple. We will examine the twelve specific energies that command mankind's universal psyche. Those energies are laws that command our destiny via the stars. There are twelve signs of the zodiac and these translate into twelve months, twelve hours, twelve apostles, twelve sins, twelve inches, twelve jury members, the twelve tribes of Israel and the twelve musical notes. Twelve is simply an obvious metaphysical number.

The wheel which makes the astrological chart (or houses), is nothing other than a watch. Numbers have replaced symbols to satisfy the rational or scientific mind and to emphasize mathematics in this world of physical structure. I will teach you to identify the astrological chart as an accurate, simple and easy to read art form, as was intended by the ancients.

All signs have equal strengths. As do the stars (rulers), they are all both positive and negative and will manifest themselves either way. Thus, each planet's energy is a like a spiritual current creating a positive or negative influx. To fully understand and translate the entire picture painted by a chart, you must look at the entire chart, including the location of the natal Dragon's Head or Tail (read The Power of the Dragon), not just your sun sign, moon sign, house or planet. All must be taken into consideration.

Behind every one of these "stars," spiritual energies order the planets and signs of the zodiac, and there is a physical reaction and in some cases effective healing power. There is a therapeutic value in the stars, this has been lost in the name of science or ignorance, and that is why this world is in such a chaotic state. Incidentally, five thousand or more children each year commit suicide, because their spirits lack of regeneration. Many have lost hope, no one talks about them, and a sad feeling of despair takes over. Who cares about those children? Who will tell them who they really are, their strengths, and the right direction to take in life? What about their natural gifts and where they do belong in this harsh world? Is there anyone out there who can tell them such comforting and reassuring facts about themselves? With widespread ignorance, constant fear, negative news, what can be done for them? Well the results are there and they are obvious. Without spiritual regeneration, a slow, destructive process is then established, and a need to escape reality and its torments becomes first a necessity, then a way of life. Drug and alcohol abuse, is the sure way to release anyone from reality and their sense of terrible failure. Worst of all, in the name of their deity and specific church, numerous religious groups form formidable barriers against mental exploration. Their method is to poison these souls with the threat of eternal death and burning hell if they dare explore the universe and astrology. Other unlucky children are raised by mental snobs, skeptics, scientists, or atheists, who block them from gaining this vital cosmic consciousness with its desperately needed spiritual regeneration. However it is through lucky breaks, curiosity, hope of a better life, or strong desires to beat all odds, that those children will stumble upon my work, one of my students, and the stars. This is one of the many ways to gather the essence of true knowledge and assure that the healing and regenerative principle will occur. Doing so will enable them to exist and grow, and not perish.

Your job as an Astropsychologist is to promote someone's power the best way you can, in order to bring the relief and faith they so desperately seek in your guidance. Your responsibility as an Astropsychologist is to accurately translate the will of the cosmos and stimulate a more productive life for your client. Keep in mind that whoever comes to you for help, will mostly need your support and understanding. Many cannot talk about their problems to those close to them, because of the mismatched temperaments produced by the stars. Many become introverted, depressed, and feel as if God is punishing them, and guilt will turn them into religious fanatics. They do not realize that to really find God, one must realize he is God. The godly message then becomes available, and they are allowed to "read" the signs (stars) through a higher level of consciousness. The advanced souls can also perceive its obvious manifestation on this dense physical world on a daily basis. Sadly enough, we all have limits, and cosmic consciousness--or the mastering of the Universal mind's secrets--is not for everybody.

An afflicted Mercury (assimilation of information or curiosity) in an earth sign produces skeptics, scientists and atheists. A Mercury (mental power) affliction close to the planet Neptune (deception/dreams) in Pisces (religion/faith) could also cause the soul to miss the golden message of the stars. Those born with Mercury in an earth sign, would rather be digging into the stock market, building gearboxes, or exploring politics, and they rationalize all on a practical level. Meanwhile the Neptunian Mercurial soul would rather sit in church, pray to whatever god, and wish to leave it all to Jesus to work a miracle. You can see the extreme behavioral attitudes all around produced by certain celestial afflictions. The Just middle is called balance and is so rarely found. The advanced souls intuitively "feel" the reality and manifestation of other dimensions of communication. Still, these young souls sooner or later will need to regenerate their spirits, and they are the ones who will come, knock on your door and say, "hey, what is in my future?" Other unlucky lost lambs will fall pray to organized religion and support their local church's manipulations, endeavors, and their doctrines.

You must be ready to help every one of them, regardless of what level of intelligence or spiritual advancement and soul maturity. When doing their chart, if you see something heavy such a strong deceiving Neptune (religion, drugs, Prozac, alcohol), or Saturn (depression, fatalistic, mental snobs), you still have to professionally and carefully pass on your message without hurting their archaic belief systems (faith) or self-esteem.

Metaphysical Rule:

The Future is nothing more than the reincarnation of Your Thoughts

A magnet will NOT attract a piece of wood! Thus, if you are constantly negative and depressed, (working in a mental institution, terminal patients' hospital, working in a mortuary or with negative people etc.), you are simply promoting and working for negative energy. By surrounding yourself with this, you will attract negativity, thereby hurting your own aura and fate. Souls who operate in this type of environment have not upgraded their vibrations, and must see their own emotions in action. Many hospital ER workers take home the drama of a busy night and therefore learn more about human nature. That was a karmic choice they made, and it is very honorable to alleviate someone suffering or save a life. However, I did it myself, and I can tell you that I am so glad I moved away from that dramatic environment. Leave this type of work to karmic souls, as you can make a choice to work for the light, for happiness, and the children of tomorrow, on a spiritual level. One of my best friends worked in the ER department, and the legacy it left on his psyche is just terrible if not destructive, to his whole being. Just ask any Vietnam War veteran, if he had the choice, would he actually choose to see, feel and endure that hell out there in the jungle? This plausible answer will give you more understanding and prove my claim.

My Philosophy: As Astrophiles, we are light workers, the life preservers for the many who come seeking support, comfort and guidance. We are working for knowledge and health, and we have to promote men as God. Incredible as it may sound, we are a part of that great design so we are allowed to learn, understand and use, those incredible tools (the stars). Those secrets are locked in the universal mind, and it is my philosophy (you will have yours, as this is a sensitive topic): Man has written the bible. But God created the stars. God cannot be confined. God cannot be structured in a church, synagogue, temple etc. God is you, God is Me, and God is a butterfly, a tree, a flower, a little cat, the sun, the moon and anything else that is alive and beautiful, on all the infinite and unseen worlds, including our own. All is that and that is all! Life in all its forms and purpose needs respect. Once more, in time and space YOU have set it all up, created it all, but YOU do not have the luxury to appreciate this fact.

Do you think a fish can play the piano or use a computer? Do you think a fish can conceive and realize another world above his roof of water? Maybe the fish has mixed feelings, because he can perceive and hear things above water. His vibrational system (his reality), starts and finishes in a body of water, and his limitations are set. His reality is his only world .

This highly rational and practical vibrational system (our earth), will support neither your awareness nor ability to realize that you're a God and the only master of your destiny. You have asked, so you shall receive, the information for which you have literally been enslaved to search. You are finding answers in my book. It was no accident that in your research into the light, you were geared towards reading my book! But beware, your Minister will tell you that when Jesus (and Elvis!) return (soon they hope), you will be thrown to hell to burn forever, for reading this book! It scares me when I see and hear those religious motor-mouth schizophrenic ministers on national television. Their mental sickness is not even perceived by the poisoned audience. Critical thinking is not an option; they are walking-talking books with no words of their own, and it is the children who are at such risk to this mental encumbrance.

Remember the stars are objective, they don't feel, they don't think, they just do what they were intended to do. In time and in space there is no time and no distance. I do not pretend to have all the answers or own the golden keys of what it means to be human. But I do have some valuable celestial explanations for your investigation. You will have to take your own awareness, and build your own knowledge to higher levels, by examining the provided information. I will teach you all the secrets I know about the Universal Mind, and this will take time. I am going to put you on the runway of perception to a true reality, and from there you will have take off. I can only put some wind under your wings, but in no way will I tell you how high you can fly… This depends on you, your own efforts, your own desires and most of all, your own natal stars. At the end of this book you will jump, think and run at a much higher speed, in a much higher dimension. This will be the result of your observations and understanding of the dynamics of our universe. It might take you a while to really assimilate such knowledge but with time, your spiritual reflexes will be built. You will then understand so much more about yourself and others . The opportunity and ability to do real counseling will be given to you.

Serious shame is on those deceiving psychics on national television and those newspaper horoscope writers. They hurt the integrity of what professional Astropsychologists have to offer. Karma is never far away for those mental manipulators, and if France wants to get rid of them, so be it. But not all New Age light workers are wastes of time money and effort. You will understand your client on a deep and accurate level. You will have the "key" to explain the reason behind the destructive thoughts or feelings. You will be able to explain exactly the course of action to take in anyone's life. You will realize deeply, the desires which manifest, and recognize a vice from a gift. You will perceive it all, but sometimes you will not have the words to explain it to your client. You will be much in advance of your client to really explain, unless he can speak your very refined star language. The worst will be when you see the stars in full action but a reluctance of many young souls to accept or even see the obvious effects. You will speak a much more advanced dialect and many will not be able to identify with you any longer. Inside your soul, you will be the only one to "grasp" and know the answer. You will have to bear this cross until your last day on this earth. However, this insight can only help you to help others in the long run, and that is the true reward.

Building Reflexes Through The Housing System

Divine Astrology as a rule always starts by Aries (House # One)

Sign	House Number: Ruled by:
ARIES	House Number 1 – Ruled by Mars
TAURUS	House Number 2 – Ruled by Venus
GEMINI	House Number 3 – Ruled by Mercury
CANCER	House Number 4 – Ruled by Moon
LEO	House Number 5 – Ruled by Sun
VIRGO	House Number 6 – Ruled by Mercury
LIBRA	House Number 7 – Ruled by Venus
SCORPIO	House Number 8 – Ruled by Pluto
SAGITTARIUS	House Number 9 – Ruled by Jupiter
CAPRICORN	House Number 10 – Ruled by Saturn
AQUARIUS	House Number 11 – Ruled by Uranus
PISCES	House Number 12 – Ruled by Neptune

House Number One: Aries

House Number One	Aries
History: Mars rules the kingdom of animals and regulates how they treat themselves in combat. Survival, instinct of animals and their weaponry falls into this category (sharp teeth, horns, claws, deadly stingers, poison etc.) Hitler was born in April, under the constellation of Aries. Aries/Aryan race. His stronger desire was to create a superior Aryan (Aries) race.	Aries is the baby of the zodiac. Aries is ruled by the planet Mars (a.k.a. the "Red" planet). Mars is also the planet of anger, called in Greek mythology "The Lord of War", it rules man, the color red, iron, steel, knives, guns, bullets, mechanics, and to some extent the desire principle, new enterprises, challenges, and the brain.
Name in Greek Mythology	The Lord of War
Planet	Mars
Animal	The Ram
Country	Germany
Energy Field	Aggressive, competitive, masculine, destructive, impatient, selfish, Speed/action.

House Number One (cont...)	Aries
Energy Field (cont...)	Motivated by an inferiority complex wondering if "I" am good enough. Thus, Aries goes out head-strong to show the world (and himself) often violently to prove his point.
Color	Fiery Red
Body Part	Head, Brain
Mineral	Iron, steel
Personality Trait	"Me" (myself, my world, I am) Cardinal.
Other Associations: In a woman's chart, the location of Mars by sign and house indicates her desire principle and the best man that would fit her. In a man's chart, how he will show or prove his masculinity (and go hunting for his female!) The desire principle of Mars can be applied positively or negatively in the subject's life. It may also indicate serious injuries or how violent death can enter the subject's life.	Aries learns by errors. Like its color red, associated with fire, you can tell an Aries not to touch, he will! Because of his aggressive nature, he is bound to get hurt. Like the child who doesn't know better, what does it do but touches what is forbidden, then realizes that it should have listened and taken heed. Unless born with more advanced stars, this is basically how Aries learns in life.

House Number Two: Taurus

House Number Two	Taurus
History: Disappeared civilizations and their religious groups chose the Bull (Taurus) as a symbol of wealth, solidity, fertility and power. Incidentally, many well established financial institutions have also picked the Bull. As the Christians subconsciously picked the fish (the sign of Pisces) to represent their own religious values, many financial institutions did the same,	Taurus deals with possessions. The second house is ruled by Venus and indicates your financial potential. How much you will make or how you spend your resources, is in this house. The second house also deals with self-esteem, wealth, security, and power. Taurus is steady, strong, reliable and hard working. It rules singing, massage, beauty, money, security, solidity, wealth, aesthetics, and banking.

House Number Two (cont...)	Taurus
choosing the Bull or the sign of Taurus.	
Name in Greek Mythology	Venus, the planet of love, beauty and aesthetics rules Taurus. Venus is the daughter of Jupiter, The Lord of Expansion, Spirituality, Protector and the Great Benefactor.
Planet	Venus
Animal	The Bull
Country	Switzerland
Energy	Feminine, beauty, love, aesthetics, money and art.
Color	Blue
Body Part	Neck, throat, thyroid glands
Mineral	Copper
Personality Trait	Mine (Possessive, "My home", "My husband", "My car") Fixed.
Other Associations	The solid world of wealth and banks.

House Number Three: Gemini

House Number Three	Gemini
History: Mercury is the closest planet revolving around the sun. Tiny Mercury rules the post office, communication, transportation, journalism, writing, reading, talking, the rational critical thought and intellectual exchanges. The position of Mercury at birth depicts the ability to assimilate and pass on information in a very specific way. A strong Mercury will produce a gift of youth and lots of fidgeting or worse, a jack of all trades.	Incidentally, Einstein, Clinton and Dr. Turi are all "suffering" from ADD, Attention Deficit Disorder Contrary to what science want you to believe, those having this condition are born geniuses, and simply tire at being taught traditionally. The universe has provided these unique individuals with gifts to learn at a faster pace, and they assimilate information quickly. They must be challenged outside any current classroom setting that wishes to

House Number Three (cont...)	Gemini
	keep "all" children on the same page of the book, all at the same time. A.D.D. sufferers are gifted children and the valiant spirits who relish in forging new realms of human originality.
Name in Greek Mythology	The Messengers of the Gods. He is the God with wings on the back of his feet or heels, or a representation of speed and information passed to other celestial Gods. Communication and transportation.
Planet	Mercury
Symbol	The Twins
City, State	New York , LA Cities
Energy	Dashing, quicksilver, swift
Color	Electric Blue
Body Part	The nerves, arms, hands, lungs and fingers
Mineral	Mercury (Note: this mercurial agent is extremely sensitive to changes in temperature) and used in many devices.

House Number Three (cont...)	Gemini
Personality Trait	I perceive and I adapt, I talk and love jokes. Mutable.
Other (Learning Habits)	The negative side of Mercury's energy is displayed with lies, cheating, stealing and argues their point to no end. Mercury rules also the radio world where undeveloped souls get to listen and learn things they will not hear in church or other traditional institutions' means.

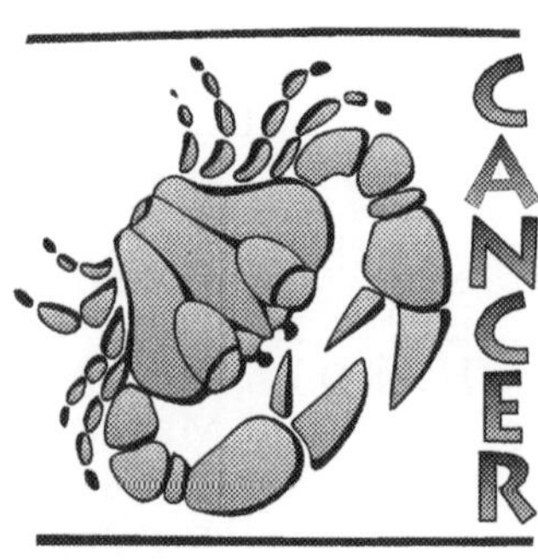

House Number Four: Cancer

House Number Four	Cancer
History: Because of her short distance from the earth, the Moon has a very strong impact on the human psyche. The words lunatic and moody used subconsciously by mankind, are sure physical reactions felt upon the world as she travels through the belt of the Zodiac. The moon cycles are still used by the farmers (almanac) to improve productivity of their crops. This Universal Clock also commands women's menstrual periods, and both the Moon and women share the same twenty-eight-day time period. A masculine or afflicted moon predisposes a woman to "escape" her female duties and will compete within men's	The moon is the closest satellite from the earth. The energy of each star bounces back on the moon. She is far from being a lifeless rock. She is the heart of the earth creating the tides, ruling the psyche, our emotions, family, home, and security. Whatever house the moon resides in, will tell you whether or not a woman can cook, clean, and take care of children. From birth all the way up to puberty, the natal moon position will affect a child. (The emotional response to

House Number Four (cont...)	Cancer
professional worlds such as the Army the Navy or taking boxing.	home life will be induced by the moon passage through each sign and its waxing and waning cycles. Hence, there are twelve different ways for child to perceive and "feel" and relate to its family and home life.)
Name in Greek Mythology	Mother of Fertility
Luminary	Moon
Animal	The Crab
Country	The United States of America
Energy	Intuitive, reflective
Color	White
Body Part	The Breasts, the stomach
Mineral	Silver
Personality Trait	Round face, watery eyes, emotional, protective, white complexion and moody. Cardinal.
Other: The moon's location in a female chart indicates whether a woman is domestic or not. A woman born with an afflicted moon will not cook, clean and will avoid raising children.	She rules our five senses (hearing, taste seeing, smelling, and touch). Your moon's location shows how you react to your environment and how you feel about yourself and your own world.

House Number Five: Leo

House Number Five	Leo
History: Center of the universe, the life force number one. During the day every planet shies away, only the Sun shines. As much as we need the Sun to survive, the life giver can also burn it all, as experienced in the deserts of the world where the scorching Sun destroys all chances for life. This produces an egocentric soul loaded with spiritual pride.	Leo controls creativity; playfulness, children, the opportunity to shine, luck, gambling, love, romance, speculation, the seat of attraction between human beings, fame, stage, life, beauty and music. Wherever the Sun is located in your chart, an opportunity to use the creative forces of the Sun is given to the soul. Fame is often the result for the hard working soul.
Name in Greek Mythology	Sun God
Planet	Sun
Animal	The Lion
Country	France, Italy

House Number Five (cont...)	Leo
Energy	Regal, brave, domineering, noble.
Color	Red-orange
Body Part	Heart, spine (the back)
Mineral	Gold
Personality Trait	"I Will", Honorable, Prideful, Egotistical yet easily hurt. Fixed.
Other (Learning Habits)	Leos always look to the stage. Their love is selfish but dedicated and powerful. Leos are competitive and enjoy children and sports of all kinds.

House Number Six: Virgo

House Number Six	Virgo
History: In opposition to Pisces symbol of Christianity ruled by Neptune (deception). A religious nun choosing to "marry" a deity. Response to a subconscious wish for purity and chastity rejecting earthy "dirty" sexual thoughts and habits.	The sixth house rules work and service to the world, including health, detail, perfection, organization, and office work. Keywords: Purity, criticism, sarcasm, paperwork, office work, dieting, the elimination principle (bowels), nature, the rain forest and the Virgin Mary.
Name in Greek Mythology	The Virgin
Planet	Mercury
Animal	Domesticated pets

House Number Six (cont...)	Virgo
Country	Holland
Energy	Feminine, modest, virginal
Color	Green
Body Part	Nervous system and the intestines
Mineral	Mercury
Personality Trait	I analyze
Other (Learning Habits)	Industrious and hard working. The strong sense of perfection often results in loneliness due to a high critical attitude. This way of thinking seriously diminishes the attraction between human beings and leads the soul towards religious confinement (a nun) or loneliness. Virgo must realize that no one is perfect, not even themselves. Mutable.

House Number Seven: Libra

House Number Seven	Libra
History: Option given to the soul to learn and master both the physical laws generated and printed by man (biblical material, governmental rules) and the spiritual laws written in light (astrology) via the Universal Mind and the stars.	The position of Venus by sign and house indicates the type of love a woman is able to offer to a man. The shopping power of a woman, her artistic taste and what she expects or reacts to in terms of love and affection from a man.
Name in Greek Mythology	Goddess of Love and Beauty
Planet	Venus
Animal	Deer (Bambi)
Country	Austria

House Number Seven (cont...)	Libra
Energy	Feminine, lust, affection, luxury, attraction.
Color	Light Blue
Body Part	Lower back, kidneys
Mineral	Copper
Personality Trait	I balance
Other (Learning Habits)	Libra is much happier with a partner aiming for harmony, seeking love and peace at all costs. If their good nature (diplomacy) is mistreated or challenged, Libra will strike with the sword of justice. Libra's motto is justice and balance. But to live by the sword, you must also die by the sword. Declaration of peace or war! Cardinal.

House Number Eight: Scorpio

House Number Eight	Scorpio
History: Option given to the soul to rise above jealousy, resentment, revenge and destructive thoughts. Through dramatic experiences the soul is forced to change and accept the changes. Area of life where passion and destruction will affect the subject drastically and where serious growth is needed. The option given to the soul to rebuild witchcraft residue for the well being of society. Reaching for true power by house and sign is a possibility.	Scorpio symbolizes Life and Death and the regeneration principle. Pluto is the farthest and smallest planet in our solar system, and in some ways, a magical planet (secretive, deadly and passionate). Pluto, ruler of Scorpio, rules life and death, the police, the mafia, sex, witchcraft, high science, corporate endeavors, (money of other people) taxes, insurance, investigation, sex, legacy, and the potential for learning and teaching metaphysics. Full power is often reached by house and sign.

House Number Eight (cont...)	Scorpio
Nickname	The Planet of Life and Death
Planet	Pluto
Animal	Scorpion
Country	Russia
Energy	Mysterious, powerful black or white magic
Color	Scarlet
Body Part	Sexual organs (Genitals)
Mineral	Plutonium
Personality Trait	I desire.
Other (Learning Habits): Ours (wife and husband's bank account together). Pluto (life and death) affects generations. Kids killing each other in colleges and Universities were born with Pluto (drama) in Scorpio (Death Wish generation). Those children do not regenerate positively from the world and affairs of Scorpio. (See "The Power of the Dragon"). You slowly will die if you don't respond to the eighth house's demands.	Here lies the deep world of the spirit. From where black or white magic emerges, the ultimate power of witchcraft you possess, and what you have earned in a past life that is now due to you. Wherever Scorpio is in your chart you are a "witch" or a "wizard." This is the area where your real regeneration principle takes place. (Pluto can be found in any of the houses). Fixed.

House Number Nine: Sagittarius

House Number Nine	Sagittarius
History: Because of its incredible mass and gravity, Jupiter's purpose (the protector) is to attract debris from outer space, as experienced with the Shoemaker-Levy comet. One of Jupiter's roles is to make the earth a safer place for all of us. Jupiter's location in the chart indicates where your past lives as an Indian came from. It also denotes your degree of philosophy and your love for nature and animals.	This sign rules good fortune, religion, philosophy, the Indians, teaching, codification of thought (the Bible), changing the law, expansion, wide-open spaces, traveling, pets, foreign lands, foreigners, and how you will attract or deal with foreigners. Jupiter predisposes interaction for learning and teaching of (archaic or advanced) spiritual knowledge for the good of mankind.
Name in Greek Mythology	The Archer; The Great Benefactor
Planet	Jupiter

House Number Nine (cont...)	Sagittarius
Animal	The horse (half-man, half-horse). Sagittarius symbolizes your constant desire to go to foreign lands and to push yourself into a philosophy other than your own (to travel far and wide in search of the "truth"). The upper part of the horse is half of a man, which represents clarity, the traveler in foreign lands. The bow and the arrow represent the constant desire to aim for the truth found overhead, or in the stars against the animalistic codification of thoughts or organized religions.
Country	Australia, Spain, Portugal and some parts of the United States (Arizona, California, New Mexico etc.)
Energy	Ambitious
Color	Light brown
Body Part	Thighs, Hips
Mineral	Tin
Personality Trait	I see a direct approach.

House Number Nine (cont...)	Sagittarius
Other: (Negative Learning Habits) The Horse or the crusaders dying for and promoting a specific religion and deity or religious war. (Positive Learning Habits): The traveling man or the intelligent research and ultimate realization of God speaking through the stars and the teachings of cosmic consciousness to the world at large.	They are traditionally educated (professional students of the law, conventional education and religions). When aspected negatively they are literally stifled by their own righteous religious views. They speak only by the book and have not much critical thought of their own. Religious and moral crusaders, pushing religious codes producing loud ministers and organized religions' speakers. Mutable.

House Number Ten: Capricorn

House Number Ten	Capricorn
History: Capricorn is a KARMIC sign. Rules: Your career, public standing, and the elderly. Whatever sign rules your 10th house of career, or wherever Saturn is located by house, you will have a career commanded by that sign. The job of Saturn is to structure and control. It represents your accomplishments or manipulation of others to get to the top of the mountain.	Capricorn's purpose is to climb the mountain of success. Saturn's ultimate use and higher purpose is to be used for the wealth of all, not for self-gratification. Capricorn is the oldest living sign of astrology. This sign was chosen by the ancients (and Christians) to represent the Goat, the head of the devil, to represent your career. Why? Because Capricorn rules structure and manipulation, (to tear down, then rebuild). Evil simply tears down and structures to gain power unto itself. Capricorn is the engineer of the zodiac.

House Number Ten (cont...)	Capricorn
But Saturn is right there and watching you, or KARMA. Example: Hitler was born with his moon and tail of the Dragon in Capricorn. First thing he wanted to do was to tap into the political world of his time. Then he used and he abused the political structure, but Saturn then tore him and his structure down. Saturn will help his children by giving them razor sharp, engineer types of minds, and abilities to see things as they are. Thus the gift of organization and structure. They are great Architects and were born with the power to visualize.	It rules traditionalism, politics, the structure of organized religions and the government mental manipulation behind them. They may shoot and kill each other, step on each other, lie and cheat. Capricorn rules snobbery, wealth, classical music, and the past. Capricorns are the most down to earth and practical of all the signs. Capricorn wants to make money and gain recognition within the population. They are the politicians and the engineers of the zodiac. They will climb and withstand rain, snow, and wind to get to the top of that mountain. The motivation is often greed, money and power. On a more positive note, Capricorn tears the old down to rebuild a stronger and better society.

House Number Ten (cont...)	Capricorn
The extreme is also a possibility when the souls avoid failure by drinking, using drugs or seeking refuge in dogmatic religious endeavors. Capricorn can be as practical or impractical in thoughts and actions.	Capricorn rules all abusive branches of the government and politics including your tax dollars (religious donations) returning to the source.
Nickname	The Devil – Evil, manipulator, gold digger.
Planet	Saturn
Animal	The Goat
Country	England, all buildings and cathedrals
Energy	Restrictive and structural
Color	Grey and deep brown
Body Part	Bones, joints, skeletal system, skin
Mineral	Zinc and fabricated steel used for war
Personality Traits Other: Negative Learning Habits): Combined with a Dragon's Tail in Capricorn, an earthy chart indicates many spiritual and karmic lessons must be learnt during the life of the subject. Unless advanced, Capricorn is a down to earth sign. Like other earth signs (such as Virgo or Taurus), the soul	"I use" (positive) and "I abuse" (negative). Capricorn must learn to be objective and perceive the big scheme of things, not just the little details. Once Capricorn masters its witchcraft residue (head of evil), it can use its fishtail and swim faster than any other sign using the knowledge of the stars. Capricorn, like other earth signs, needs to learn but often fails to understand, that which is

House Number Ten (cont...)	Capricorn
will have difficulty in using intuition and perceiving the stars at work on this dense physical world. Hence, they are rational signs and naturally concerned or interested to use Man's weakness to gain positions of power and respect in this physical manifestation.	unseen or not touched, doesn't mean it doesn't exist. This attitude slows down the progress and success of the soul. An advanced Capricorn will inherit tremendous creativity and incredible artistic talents. Cardinal.

Note: Wherever Capricorn is placed in your chart, you cannot take shortcuts. Saturn is cold and calculating and watches your every move. Saturn or Capricorn is even more critical than Virgo. Saturn is a planner, and rules all codes of structures. A young Capricorn soul manipulates and controls you and seeks to organize your talents and make money from you. Remember a negative Saturn is cold and calculating and a devil at heart. He makes no "bones" (pardon the pun) about tearing you down in order to build you up again, as he relishes in using or abusing you. Capricorn is the power of structure and one of its aims is to control the mass psyche via organized religion. Saturn rules all Governmental offices and all politics. On a positive note the power of Saturn is used constructively for others and society. Where ever your Saturn is located in your chart, the option to use or abuse is given to you. This area is of a karmic nature where errors must be paid in full by the soul.

Note: In early U.S. History, the English (England, ruled by Saturn) helped the forefathers to structure the basic political laws (or government) of what is called today, the great nation of the United States of America.

House Number Eleven: Aquarius

House Number Eleven	Aquarius
History: Uranus is called in Greek Mythology "The God of the Sky" and regulates everything above the earth, and the universe including the future of mankind itself. The symbol of the man and the jar is a representation of translated Supra Knowledge collected from the universal mind into the jar and the flowing water (the translated celestial wisdom) offered to his human fellow beings. I am myself an Aquarius. Those born in February attract also UFO experiences	Rules: Friends, wishes, group activities, the genius quality of man. Universal love, the intellectual, eccentric, independent, futuristic, the New Age, high technology, electricity, the impossible and the incredible. Aquarius also rules the UFO phenomenon, the high science of astrology or the secrets of the Universal mind, the sudden releases of energy, earthquakes, weather, hurricanes, tornadoes, tidal waves and volcanic eruptions to name a few.

House Number Eleven (cont...)	Aquarius
.Name in Greek Mythology	The Water Bearer
Planet	Uranus
Animal	Large and unique birds
Country Energy	Japan and France Electric, shocking
Color	Electric blue
Body Part	Circulatory system, shins, ankles and the high intuitive parts of the mind.
Mineral	Uranium
Personality Trait	I know
Other (Learning Habits): More than any other sign, Aquarius becomes the target of religious fanatics, established institutions and the favorite victim of the ignorant and the worst and badly informed (young souls) elements of our society. Often much too smart or perceptive for its own good. The running water represents the nourishing divine element flowing endlessly to a society thirsting for knowledge .	Portrayed as the man whom has the natural gift of cosmic consciousness given to him through the stars (Aquarius rules astrology). His purpose is to master the impossible, and offer it to humanity. He is the inventor, the enlightener, the spiritual awakener, the original intellectual master, the genius, and the eccentric and independent free thinker. Einstein was born with a Dragon's Head in Aquarius. Fixed.

House Number Twelve: Pisces

House Number Twelve	Pisces
History: It takes 2000 years for one sign to teach its lesson to the world. In 1945 we left the deceiving world of Pisces and entered the incredible age of Aquarius. Uranus' influence will allow man to realize his direct relationship with God and the Universe. Indeed Pisces is the most difficult sign and house of the Zodiac. The soul is enslaved to swim upstream (like a salmon) towards its birthplace, or the stars. Religious poisoning, fear, guilt, the past, uncontrolled imagination is the negative fish swimming	Rules: The undoing, the subconscious, our dreams and all chemicals such as gas, drugs, and alcohol. Neptune rules depression, imagination, asylums, hospitals and jails. He also controls all forms of religions and synagogues, churches, temples, exotic places, gurus, cults, the oceans, mysticism, and the 12th house of the subconscious. Pisces is a KARMIC sign. It was "subconsciously" chosen by the Christians to represent their particular doctrine and religious teachings. Neptune is a deceiving planet and rules the Middle East and the destructive belief powers of pious fanatics and religious

House Number Twelve (cont...)	Pisces
downstream. Pisces is the last sign of the zodiac. It has gained all the strengths and all the weaknesses of all the signs of the zodiac and is a terminal sign. Usually the last life on this level of consciousness.	warfare plaguing the world in the name of deities, religions, doctrines, and belief systems.
Name in Greek Mythology	Poseidon - Lord of Deception
Planet	Neptune - Water
Animal	Fish
Country	Middle East
Energy	Deceptive, illusive, artistic
Color	Deep Dark Blue
Body Part	The feet
Mineral	Producing plastic and oil
Personality Trait	Believer, dreamy
Other (Learning Habits) Constantly challenged in the current of life. Being pulled in opposite directions at the same time. One fish is seeking ultimate knowledge and is swimming up towards the light or the stars. The other one is swimming downstream and follow religious dogmas. David Koresh	Pisces house and sign induces the most difficult lessons of all. This is where you will have to challenge all that you have been taught to believe since childhood. Your strength is to use your critical thinking and swim out of delusion, deception, drugs, bad habits and induced fears. Test of your will and your intuition. The option to build your cosmic consciousness and learn all about the stars,

House Number Twelve (cont..)	Pisces
And Rev. Jim Jones were swimming downstream leading other Neptunian followers to their deaths. Neptune rules drugs and islands. The entire group of over a thousand people died poisoned with drugs and in a secluded island in the name of ignorance under Jim Jones' rule. Deception and religious wars are the legacy of any Neptunian's leaders.	metaphysics, spirituality and creativity. You will find that the intangible will enrich you. Neptune is very deceiving but he can also be very rewarding if you swim upstream. Creativity to the extreme is offered to the soul. Mutable.

Pisces is a Karmic sign and has no fate of its own. His knowledge becomes his fate. The fish must swim upstream in a relentless current with no relief. Night and day the stream will drag the fish down towards deception, drugs, alcohol or religious fanaticism. By using the will (which is stronger than the stars) Pisces can cut the rope of the past physically and psychically. The soul is then allowed to experience the purest and cleanest water of all to realize his oneness with God. The soul has then gained cosmic consciousness, power, freedom, and peace in its own godly nature. Much of this knowledge has been lost or cast aside by abusive governments or in previous past life endeavor such as a nun, a priest or a minister. The ultimate challenge and delusion is imposed upon the soul wherever Pisces and Neptune resides in the chart.

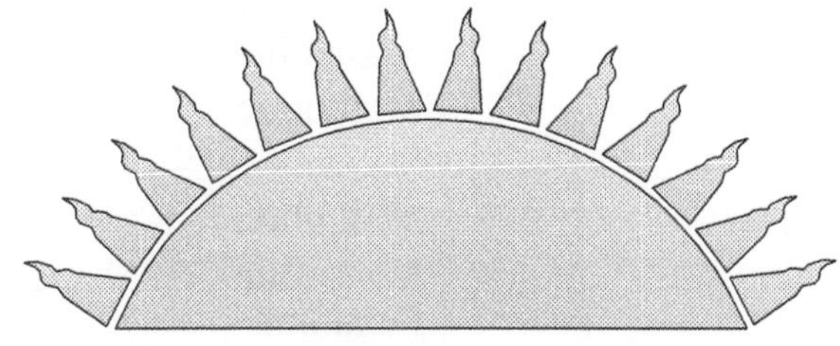

I am now going to teach you the elements and qualities affecting each sign of the Zodiac.

ELEMENTS

FIRE	EARTH	AIR	WATER
Fast	Steady	Intellectual	Emotional
Eager	Practical	Talkative	Intuitive

FIRE	EARTH	AIR	WATER
Aries	Taurus	Gemini	Cancer
Leo	Virgo	Libra	Scorpio
Sagittarius	Capricorn	Aquarius	Pisces

QUALITIES

CARDINAL	FIXED	MUTABLE
Aries	Taurus	Gemini
Cancer	Leo	Virgo
Libra	Scorpio	Sagittarius
Capricorn	Aquarius	Pisces

MASCULINE and FEMININE

Aries	Masculine
Gemini	Masculine
Leo	Masculine
Libra	Masculine
Sagittarius	Masculine
Aquarius	Masculine
Taurus	Feminine
Cancer	Feminine
Virgo	Feminine
Scorpio	Feminine
Capricorn	Feminine
Pisces	Feminine

OPPOSITES

Aries - Libra	Aries (I am)	Libra (we are/I balance)
Taurus – Scorpio	Taurus (I have)	Scorpio (we have/I desire)
Gemini–Sagittarius	Gemini (I think)	Sagittarius (we think/I see)
Cancer – Capricorn	Cancer (I feel)	Capricorn (we feel/I use)
Leo – Aquarius	Leo (I create)	Aquarius (we create/I know)
Virgo – Pisces	Virgo (I analyze)	Pisces (we dream/I believe)

DESCRIPTION OF EACH OF THE TWELVE HOUSES

House One ♈	Aries	The soul's purpose. The soul incarnates into the physical body, the ego. The main purpose of its reincarnation on this specific world. (There are trillions and billions of vibrational physical and spiritual worlds.) No time, no distance only eternity to grow wiser.
House Two ♉	Taurus	The soul's options and opportunity to make money and accumulate possessions. Power and greed. It also affects the self-esteem of the soul. Money and self-esteem are connected. See how you feel going to work riding an old bicycle or driving a new Ferrari.
House Three ♊	Gemini	The soul's thinking and communication power and its ability to assimilate information, to learn, to teach, write etc. Critical thinking and fate with brothers and sisters.

Twelve Houses	Description	(cont....)
House Four ♋	Cancer	The soul's upbringing. Options to establish security, nesting, and feelings. The soul's emotional processes involving home, parents, mother, food, real estate and clothing.
House Five ♌	Leo	The soul's creative process and opportunity for love and romance, fame and fortune and all speculations. The attitude, aptitude, experiences, and type of children he will procreate.
House Six ♍	Virgo	The soul's service to the world and opportunity given to work. Mental and physical health habits. Organization and critical thinking at work. The purity and chastity principles of the Virgin Mary.
House Seven ♎	Libra	Opportunity offered to the soul for partnerships and performance with others. How and whom the soul relies and attracts others. Relationship to the world, open enemies, contracts, justice, marriage, balance, and harmony.

Twelve Houses	Description	(cont...)
House Eight ♏	Scorpio	The soul's option to unite for power and merge physically, sexually and financially with others. Corporate finances, insurances, death and metaphysical matters. The option given to the soul for regeneration, investigation, and the re-building of witchcraft residue.
House Nine ♐	Sagittarius	The options for the soul to travel and seek the truth. Publishing, teaching, learning, traveling, philosophy, education. The codification of thoughts producing religious philosophies. Relationships with foreigners and experiences in foreign lands. Indian cultures and wide open spaces.
House Ten ♑	Capricorn	The soul seeks honor and a higher purpose. Options for career and a degree of accomplishmeats. Opportunity and attraction to reach or learn from those in positions of power. Politics, old age, father, structure, critically observant, the engineer. All-powerful established organizations and the government.

Twelve Houses	Description	(cont...)
House Eleven ♒	Aquarius	The soul's option to seek and serve the world at large with supreme and special physical or spiritual data including astrology. Advanced technological organi- zations such as NASA and other Universal enterprises. Universal thought, changes in the status Quo. The wishes supported by friends or institutions offered to the soul. Your gifts in Astropsychology are learned and shared in this house.
House Twelve ♓	Pisces	The soul dreams about finding himself or God. Confinement, possibility for addictions. Secret enemies, guilt, the past, deception, illusion, religious institutions, sacrifice, hospitals, jail. Sickness or freedom of the spirit through the use of imagination, the arts, music, dance and poetry.

****

MEDICAL ASPECTS OF ASTROPSYCHOLOGY

Aries (Mars); head, hair, the brain

Taurus (Venus); neck, thyroid glands

Gemini (Mercury); arms, hands, respiratory system, lungs

Cancer (Moon); stomach, breasts

Leo (Sun); heart; spine, back

Virgo (Mercury); intestines, digestive tract

Libra (Venus); kidneys; purification principle

Scorpio (Pluto); sexual organs; reproductive area

Sagittarius (Jupiter); thighs; hips

Capricorn (Saturn); joints, knees, bones

Aquarius (Uranus); circulatory system, the shins, calves and ankles

Pisces (Neptune); feet, toes, mucus membranes

Note: Pisces individuals are extremely sensitive to chemicals of all kind including alcohol and all doctors' prescriptions. Clients born with a Pisces Tail are cautioned to find out all they can before ingesting a prescription drug and should thoughtfully check on the possibility of side affects. With Pisces Tail, there is a natural reaction against chemicals no matter what they are!!! Remember, souls born with a Pisces Tail should use every precaution, or avoid ingesting any foreign agents altogether. Many young children in the name of ignorance, have died this way. The ignorant medical scientists refer to this dilemma as "infant death syndrome". Sadly enough, not long ago CNN reported that two parents wanted to help their few months old baby who was crying all night long. They took the child to the Children's hospital and the doctor diagnosed the child with a stomach problem. A drug prescription was established to ease the baby's pain. The baby will never cry again, he died soon after ingesting the drug... So many deaths are suffered this way and so little is known by the disinclined scientific medical community, and an unwillingness to explore Neptune's power and the medical aspects of my work.

* * * *

PLANETS

Moon = emotional response (the domestic scenery)

Venus = love, creative response (the arts)

Mercury = intellectual response (communication)

Mars = desire principle (competitiveness)

Sun = fame, creativity (enlighten the world)

Saturn = fear principle (karmic planet)

Jupiter = the codification of thought (laws)

Neptune = seeks to find God (imagination)

Uranus = Universal Truth (originality)

Pluto = regeneration (life and death)

Note: A good Astrophile will realize and remember that each planet will display both its positive and negative energies on the subject. However, just because the energy is there doesn't mean the person will display this power (positively or negatively). It is up to your education and intuition to detect the energy. If somebody approaches you with various questions, always guide the soul towards the positive aspect of the stars. Make him realize also the negative energy which is present, but emphasize the positive only. You will help that person tremendously. For instance, you cannot say that because somebody has Mercury in Pisces, he will not be a good mathematician. Tell him to concentrate more on numbers and details but insist on making him aware of the natural intuition, creativity, imagination and spiritual values found in Pisces. Subsequently, while less energy is found in one sign, the strength needed may be found somewhere else in the chart. A solid tail in Capricorn or a practical moon in Taurus will help the dreamy Pisces to deal with the physical world and you must detect these facts before asserting or assuming anything to your client.

Unless A Person is an Aries, he will usually have "three chances" for a mix of energies from one sign. Let's use the Pisces energy as an example. For instance, a Sagittarius will have Pisces as his 4th house, making that a Pisces/Cancer (ruler of the 4th house) energy. Next, he may have the planet Neptune (Pisces) in Libra, making that a Pisces/Libra mix. His 12th house is Scorpio but ruled by Pisces, so that makes it a Scorpio/Pisces mix. Therefore a soul is not limited or confined to the use of only one strength of an energy, and this increases his depth of character.

* * * *

THE MOON

Until puberty, a child is guided almost entirely by his natal moon more than the other planet in his chart. The rest of the stars do not yet FULLY activate the child's psyche. For example, a child is much too young to suffer depression because of the burden of his career (Saturn). His attitude and beliefs are also affected by his parent's moons dictating certain conducts. A mother with a moon in Scorpio may have an abrasive attitude that would hurt a child with a soft Pisces moon. If that same child had a father with a moon in Aries, the child would be affected by both moons. When the child matures, his natal moon (stronger or weaker by position sign and house), activates and he begins to rule his own life, or follow what has been established by his first teachers. Thus if a parent is set by the moon to be religious and the child is not, conflicts may occur later on with the less advanced parent. Taken to the extreme, if the child is set to be religious due to a pious natal moon in Pisces or Cancer, and reinforced by the mother during the upbringing, the child could also react violently to a form of what he perceives as anti-religious conduct, (abortion) taken by women. In extreme cases he could become a religious killer (Salvi/Osama Bin Laden).

Now don't forget, the moon also represents the domestic scenery and how a mother or a teacher will react to this child. If the teacher, mom, or anyone else, has an unsupportive aspect to the child's natal moon, chances for conflict, stress and negativity are very strong possibilities. This indicates why the local schoolteacher born with a very practical, detail oriented and perfectionist moon in Virgo, would be a teacher to begin with. However, if the teacher is not educated in Astropsychology, she will not be able to understand that child to the degree of any students of Astropsychology. Thus because a child is perhaps "afflicted" with A.D.D. (remember this is a gift not a disorder!), she will be very concerned about the child's education and mental welfare (Virgo rules also health). Thus innocently enough, she will contact the parents and suggest to have the child "investigated" by the school psychologist. Realize that this person too, educated traditionally as are the majority of law-makers and teachers, is totally ignorant as to the star's impact upon this child. Following the school psychologist's recommendation, another ignorant mental snob then makes the ever so important decision to prescribe the poison Prozac or Ritalin to your child.

Even if you're man, and the moon resides in a feminine sign, you will naturally be concerned with food. This will predispose the masculine soul to cook and clean as a woman would or should do. This indicates whether a woman was born to be domestic or not.

THE FLUCTUATIONS OF THE MOON

The moon's fluctuations play a vital part in our lives. The moon controls our psyche. This is due mainly to the moon's impact or gravity upon the earth. As we know, the magnetic pull of the moon upon the earth is strong enough to continuously roll the tides. Also, our body consists mainly of water. Consequently, the moon moves all bodies of water, including ours. Our response to the fluctuations of the moon is nothing more than our subconscious reacting to the power of the moon upon human psyche, emotions and domesticity.

Never forget that the ancients used the moon's fluctuations in planting and harvesting crops. Thus, seeds were planted upon the waxing moon, which yielded a bountiful harvest.

There are three signs in everyone's chart controlled by the element of water, Cancer, Scorpio and Pisces. These three water signs will undoubtedly feel the moon's pull and energy in a specific house during the waxing and waning periods more so than other zodiac signs. Meanwhile, regardless of your birth sign, you have 3 water signs affecting your housing system. In that respect the moon fluctuations will affect those three houses tremendously. Realize that knowledge is power and by the end of this course, you will know where those three house are located and how to use the moon's fluctuations to your advantage.

THE MOON'S CYCLE

Waning and Waxing Period

The moon cycle is about one month or respectively 28 days. The new moon time is called the waxing period. During the time from the new to the full moon, is the time for you to go out and meet new people, sign contracts, and promote your life. The time of the waxing moon is metaphysically and spiritually filled with subtle forces that you will not necessarily see or touch. These forces are protected during this time of the moon's fluctuations. The Value of the Moon Cycle Law is: Remember, when first entering a house you may buy, when meeting someone new, when signing a contract or traveling to a different country; the first time you touch new ground, you are giving birth to a section of your life. After the Full Moon it is the time of release and cleansing, a time to clear, get rid of the old, and turn inward.

People born during the time of a new moon period (waxing moon) are more inclined to be extroverted, healthier and happier. The opposite is true for those born after the full moon period, when the moon is waning. They tend to be just the reverse, hence more introverted, not as healthy, and tend to have more of a karmic life.

NOTE: There are 12 energies or 12 zodiac signs, affecting you in each House 1-12; and 10 planets (Mars,

Venus, Mercury, Sun, Moon, Pluto, Jupiter, Saturn, Uranus, and Neptune. Thus, within each house and within each sign, energies co-mingle. Additionally, these are the laws of exchange: positive/negative, up/down, black/white, man/woman, front/back, God/devil. Without opposites there would be no chance for life. Opposites are the natural order to life. In understanding physics, we can only acknowledge that the other side of this physical world relates to a spiritual world, which we do not see, but feel. This spiritual manifestation has its own set of rules, which are written in light via the stars.

* * * *

THE POWER OF THE MOON

Universal Law Explained

Remember this sentence? "*There is a tide in the affairs of man, when taken at its crest, leads on to fortune.*"

--Wm. Shakespeare

I personally believe that, at least subconsciously, there is an awareness of the planetary gears or the timing, involving man and our closest satellite, the Moon.

Every day which God has created, sees the procession of stars across the vault of the sky; they have followed the same path through the heavens, tracing the immutability of the cosmos and its constellations, which have spoken to the wise since the beginning of time. This work will explain in detail the subtle energy produced by the Moon's passage through the twelve houses and signs of the Zodiac. These houses govern the twelve facets of our lives, and the rhythms of our cycles, emotions, finances, consciousness, homes, children, careers, friends, wishes, fears, loves, personalities and all that goes to make up our sorrows and joys. Depending on the mystical rhythm of the Moon and her relationship — harmonious or discordant — to the constellations and houses of the sky over which they rule, she will govern our human activity and give birth to our vices and virtues. The infinite and concealed dance of the Moon through the Zodiac affects not only you, but all of us. You are a "microcosm" or a child of the Universe and there is reason for you to be. You are a part of this incredible physical and spiritual structure called a "macrocosm."

Sir Isaac Newton wrote "for every action there is an equal and opposite reaction." We are what we think, having become what we thought. This statement emphasizes that for every thought or action there will be an effect.

This is what I call the "Universal Law," the causes-and-effects of the yin and yang recognized as the law of KARMA. The Moon is by herself responsible for much of our and the world's fate. By the tracking of the Universal Law and using Starguide, you will be allowed to see this lunar impact and reaction every day of your life. Obviously the waxing and waning periods of our closest satellite produces the daily process of tides. Thus, women will have not only a spiritual but a physical manifestation (menstruation), and all of us will be responding subconsciously to the words "lunatic/moody." Without opposite forces at work there would be no reaction nor any life possible on both the spiritual and physical planes. To my knowledge, our so-called "dead" satellite is very much alive, and much more than a rock hanging above our heads. She is a vital part of a Divine celestial design; she is the beating heart of the earth. Vigilantly observing her whereabouts will aid in understanding the real psychology of man.

I always said, "The Moon is a little more than a dead rock hanging above our head just for the sake of beauty." I just hope that in the future, the psychology fields will invest a little more and do some research on the subtle forces generated by the moon, and how her passage through the Zodiac really affects the human psyche.

For instance, a soul born with a feminine moon in a water sign such as Pisces will be extremely susceptible to the moon fluctuations. Especially if the soul inherited a negative moon sitting right on the Dragon's Tail and is not aware of it. Or in some cases the moon is badly aspected by Saturn, the Lord of depression. Now; the unaware psychiatrist or psychologist does not know about the 28 day cycle of the moon and its direct impact on his patient's psyche. Hence, he or she will be classified as a "manic depressive " and come once a month (victimized by the waning moon) in need of more destructive anti-depressants. Chances are Neptune will now hook the soul and he become addicted to the prescription drug. Thus the oblivious doctor will use this "manic depressive," and empower the mighty and expensive insurance and drug industries. In the name of ignorance, slowly but surely the patient loses himself in the quicksands of Neptune while the doctor, the insurance and the pharmaceutical industries all benefit. This is happening now to thousands of children, and yours could be the next victim unless we stop this nightmare soon.

The Changing face of the Moon was revered and understood by the ancients as an aspect of the feminine and idolized as the Lady of the Night who ruled over fertility and magic. Your awareness of the Moon's passage through the Zodiac will enable you to discover a basic structure of energy patterns that underlie the changes and circumstances of your life. This is indeed the purpose of a good astrologer, his main objective being to reveal an order or meaning beneath or within that which often appears to be a random or chaotic situation. The Moon's passage through the housing system is one expression of the archetypal structure we call a cycle. While many of the formally educated scientists have lost their cosmic consciousness, it has still remained hidden within astrological values and basic astrological foundations. By visiting my site www.drturi.com and reading both your free daily or monthly forecast, you will soon find the incredible values of predictive astrology when practiced properly.

All the signs of the Zodiac, the twelve houses, and the numerous astrological aspects are based upon God's higher order in the established, interstellar cycle. Their subtle meanings are derived from a particular place or function to each other, and all operate within the ordered cycle as a whole. Our lives unfold according to our specific cyclic pattern, interacting with the Universal cycle. Discerning the Universal Mind at work is difficult. Those gifted at birth will naturally understand the cosmic mind, using their inborn intuition and objective mental tools. However, when properly educated, anyone can learn to further his cosmic consciousness and realize his close relationship with God and the Universe. It often starts with a willingness to expand the consciousness, and the simple realization that what cannot be seen or touched doesn't mean it is non-existent. That is what makes a real scientist or a truly intelligent person, the ability to respect the essence of the word "investigation"! Sadly enough, the majority of these educated souls fear ridicule, and may also take the risk of abandonment by their peers or churches, simply by investigating that which is disallowed. Those methodical scholars will never be able to penetrate the spiritual domain of the stars in my research. Those scholastically oriented souls are plagued at birth with a limited view and conception of the unknown. Usually a weak planet Mercury (the mind), a phlegmatic Uranus (inquiry) in an unassuming earth sign (rationale) is the logical reason for the soul's inability to reach a higher level of understanding. Their minds resemble closed nutshells which inherited common and limited astrological formations which deprive them of experiencing the highly cosmic realities outside that shell. To them, the moon is nothing other than a dead satellite orbiting the earth with no more purpose than to produce the daily tides.

The obvious structure of the Moon's cycle is derived from the fact that it consists of a beginning, middle and an end. Thus, the monthly lunar cycle suggests by observation that it is divided into two halves. During the first half, the movement is outward as our close satellite travels away from the area of space occupied by the Sun. As this happens, the powerful light of the Sun increases, "waxing" (positive) on the white face of the Moon. The turning point is symbolized by the Full Moon; it reverses motion. The Moon begins to approach the Sun as the reflected light on its surface "wanes" (negative), until they meet again at the New Moon (new start). Halfway between the New Moon and the Full Moon, we notice another important division point where light and darkness are equal on the moon's surface. At the first waxing quarter, the light is increasing, while at the last waning quarter, it is decreasing. These simple astronomical observations can only provide the scientist's mind with knowledge for interpreting the physical lunar cycle's phase. The positive cannot exist without the negative. It takes two forces for anything to be. Therefore the scientist should know that an intuitive domain exists in opposition to the rational domain, and be able to investigate this realm.

There is so much behind this "lunar manifestation," that as a child, I began to feed my own critical observations. I always thought the moon to be something more than a frigid white globe orbiting around the earth. Many times in the darkness of the night, I found myself staring at her, wondering about her hidden power. She is the swiftest of the planets, passing through the 12 signs of the zodiac in about 28 days. I knew that sooner or later, I was to uncover her subtle way and find the answers. To me, all those stars in the night sky, shining above my head, were more than beautiful luminaries lighting the way in the dark of the night. It does, however, take more than one's five regular senses to tap into her subtle manifestation upon our psyches and life in general. Nothing happens randomly in the universe, and the timely return in full each month surely indicates an ultimate order. Month after month, I patiently watched her becoming New and Full, and I learned my first and one of the most important lessons in metaphysics: "The undiluted truth is not to be found inside my limited world, but in others and the Universal mind."

Being so close to the earth, the Moon's magnetic pull (gravitational force) is so great, that she is solely responsible for the daily process of the tides. Therefore, curiosity, observation and comparison became the key elements to promote my cosmic consciousness. As I met her, becoming full and new, month after month, I slowly began to understand her powers. By constantly watching my environment, friends and family members, she began to speak about her clear and visible impact, and astute control over man's psyche. As the years went by, I realized her uncompromising role over the sea, and I became more aware of her powerful impact on our daily affairs. I made notes day after day, week after week and month after month, realizing the consequences of ignoring or adapting to her passage through the twelve signs of the Zodiac. Later on, I learned that the farmers of the past followed her fluctuations for the betterment of their crops.

Then I carefully put my observations to test in my life and the lives of those around me. It did not take long to realize that by respecting the Universal Law, my life became much more productive. Her positive and negative effect on man's emotions, actions and reactions became so obvious to me that I decided to make a full-time job telling others about her. As I watched the news in times of a full Moon, I understood why people became destructive, "lunatic," eccentric, moody and psychopathic. I then named it the Uncompromising Universal Law. Since then, as a professional Divine Astrologer, wherever I am needed, I am teaching the merit of this simple and valuable knowledge.

When you first learned how to drive a car, you were carefully introduced to the rules of the road. You learned that you must stop at a red light or follow a road sign, as your very life depends on your doing so. These are the codes that you have learned, and they must be respected anywhere you happen to go in the world. Following established rules will take you safely wherever you have to go. Sadly enough, too many people do not respect these rules, and innocent people have died accidentally. Awareness, knowledge and respect of these rules are desperately needed. However, the spiritual rules established by God, written in the constellations, have been misplaced. Only a minority is aware of the impact produced by the moon, and the rest, the majority of us are completely ignorant of these Divine rules. The result is seen during a Full Moon and each time the moon is crossing a destructive sign. This lack of awareness turns into a formidable chaos, producing despair, drug addiction, depression, violence, criminal behavior . . . and the list goes on and on. Know that ignoring either the physical or spiritual rules will lead any one of us to pay a heavy penalty.

So-called "holy wars" have plagued man all through the ages. Ignorance and fear cast aside the real Universal message. To my mind, the millions of deaths produced by continuous religious wars all around the world are good examples of the destructive power of fanaticism. I realize that everyone's relationship to God or many gods is deeply personal, and that no two people feel the same way. My great mother taught me that God is love, beauty, education, responsibility and knowledge, a belief I have steadfastly clung to. I have noticed the dualistic nature of life, man/woman, front/back, up/down, black/white, yin/yang, positive/negative, the ultimate law of opposition. I soon began to realize that nothing would exist without its counterpart, and this Law of opposition was much too obvious to be challenged or ignored. I began to wonder if God would be without the Devil. One month is made up of 2 two-week periods, one year of 2 six-month periods. From the New Moon (the black dot on your calendar) to the Full moon (a circle on your calendar), the light is green.

Those two weeks are called "the waxing time." Then when you see her full, white and round, the light is amber. Those two weeks are called "the waning time." As she starts her positive waxing time, you should plant your seeds for life. Go out, meet new people, socialize, become engaged, get married, buy a new car, go shopping, sign important contracts, travel, visit family members and generally promote all you can during this positive trend. My "Moon Power Starguide" has all the New and Full Moons available for entire year. Also, Starguide tells you when and in which sign the New Moon or the Full Moon will mature. You can use this knowledge to master the outcomes of all your endeavors. Initiate ideas or projects as she climbs happily in the heavens. Then when she finally becomes full, be aware of the approaching "yellow light," as these signals show a time to slow down and reflect. Use your will to fight depression, clean your house, prepare your next move, write letters but don't send them just yet.

Observe and listen to all the people around you. Many will suffer the waning Moon's power and will become negative, moody and lunatic. Watch the news and see for yourself the dramatic differences in the two periods. However, good things can happen during a negative period. This means, officially, that somehow you started "that" situation during her waxing, positive time, and you are now being paid off. Bad things can also happen to you when the Moon is supposedly positive. It might only be a tap on your hand, compared to what you could have really experienced. Keep in mind that you have been going through your life not knowing — not using the Universal Law. You did not interact with the Moon's fluctuations (the gearbox of our system) and many gears (your experiences) have broken down. Apply your knowledge right away and take the time to invest your understanding in Astrology (the dynamics of our Universe).

The Universal Clock also commands women's menstruations, and both the Moon and women share the same twenty-eight-day time period. Work non-stop around the Moon's passage throughout every sign of the Zodiac, and then her deepest secrets will by yours. As she travels through the belt of the Zodiac, she resides in one sign from two to three days , and pours the energies (positive or negative) found in that specific astrological sign over your emotions. Never forget that an ultimate higher order has been established, and the essence of our emotional life is within. Learning and adapting to the Moon's power will help you to understand what it really means to be human. This lunar consciousness will lead you towards understanding your own strengths, with the ability to use them to promote your life, while minimizing your weaknesses day by day!

Some people often say, "But Dr. Turi, I cannot live my life this way. New Moon or Full Moon, I have business to take care of!" Well, I understand the dilemma, but to me it sounds like, "Dr. Turi, the light is red, my car is stopped at the light, but I can't stand still any longer and must proceed, because I am going to be late for my appointment." Go ahead! You see, you came and asked for spiritual rules; I gave them to you, and now it is up to you to deal with them. You took the chance and were curious enough to "ask". Now that you have received the "discipline," it's up to you to abide by the rules. The world is not necessarily ready, willing or unenlightened pertaining to this "lunar" code, but you are! The idea is to plot well ahead and synchronize with the universal law when planning your important endeavors. It is as simple as that.

Since the dawn of time, the Creator has shown his truth to the humble, a truth that is hidden from the vain blinded by worldly pleasures, but which is written in the skies, which nightly speaks of the glory of God

--Nostradamus

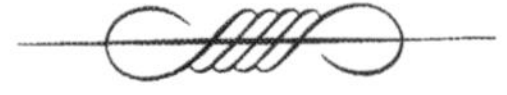

PLACEMENT OF THE MOON IN EACH SIGN

Moon Signs

The position of the Moon regulates your emotional response to life. Her location by house and sign indicates, in a woman's chart, her domestic ability, and her home life. Any planet in relationship to this placement could seriously affect the feminine values of a woman. Thus, a woman born with the Moon in a fire sign will be very competitive but won't spend much time in the kitchen. However, if the Moon is located in the fourth house (ruled by Cancer, the sign of domesticity), or in a water/earth sign, she will be very domestic. Thus a man born with the moon (home) in Cancer (food) or in the fourth house will naturally be a good cook.

Children are strongly affected by their natal Moon locations until puberty. Your awareness of the strengths or weaknesses of that specific sign, or residing planet(s) can make a strong difference when raising your child. The "Moon Power" will directly or indirectly affect all signs of the Zodiac, without any exception. Her passage through the sky's 12 different Astrological signs will have a direct impact on your (and other people's) psyches. Thus, she becomes the mediator of our virtues and vices.

Note: This research is based on a general overview of the Moon throughout the signs. Other assisting planets and the location of the Dragon's Head/Tail will greatly affect the general characteristics and outcome of the following information.

Aries Moon ♈ 	Masculine/Fire sign. Not domestic, the diamond and baby of the zodiac. The soul is able to develop a new level of consciousness. Aries is controlled by Mars, prone to accidents and is apt to learn by mistake. Powerfully emotional, competitive, and impatient. This lunar position could bring friction with family members, especially the mother. In times of trouble, with aggressive Mars (war) living at home, the family could resemble a battle zone. Patience and diplomacy must be practiced at all times. This is a great position to channel the spirit of Mars into constructive endeavors — real estate, construction, administration, writing or any profession demanding strength, initiative and fast thinking. For one more intellectually inclined, the Martian mental power can be used to produce a book or run a business from home. A word of caution, Mars rules danger and fire, thus if you are born with Mars (fire) in Cancer (security), or in the 4th house (home), insuring the house against fire is recommended. Children born with this Moon position must be taught respect and discipline at an early age. Those born with a Moon in Aries may retire in a semi-arid region with all of the comfort needed for a well-deserved rest.

Taurus Moon 	Feminine/Earth sign. Domestic, solid, strong, steady and dignified. This soul attracts beauty into the home. This lunar position demands a strong sense of security and induces patience and domesticity. This moon location is exalted, and will ensure a beautiful home during the course of the subject's life. If Venus (love) resides in Taurus or in the 4th house (home), a need for beauty and the purchase of expensive ornaments will promote a form of security and wealth in the home. Candlelight, soft music, and good food are found in the homes of those born with the Moon in Taurus. Solid and security-oriented Moon in Taurus people must guard against jealousy and stubbornness. The upbringing can either be experienced in a wealthy or destitute environment according to the location of the Dragon's Tail and its accompanying karma. Diligent and hard workers, these souls will sooner or later establish a solid and secure base of operations regardless of their stars. Children born with this Moon position must be taught that money is not all that they need and to share what they own with others. Many people born with the Moon in Taurus will spend the last days of their existence surrounded with comfort and luxury.

Gemini Moon ♊ ☽	Masculine/Air sign. This soul is versatile, extremely talkative, likes to tell jokes, intellectually stimulating; has a gift of youth, double form of personality, and rules communication. He is fast, nervous, will need discipline to listen and to do his work; generally classified as an Attention Deficit Disorder (A.D.D.) child. By nature this placement of a moon is not suppose to follow the codification of thought. Mercurial, witty, and many-sided. This lunar position gives the subject youthfulness, a double personality, and an aptness in communication. This soul may be forced to often change residency during the course of his lifetime. Many individuals with the Moon in Gemini will make their homes a place of teaching and learning. Mercury rules communication, and a large library with interesting books is often found in their homes. This lunar position gives the subject a great need to communicate with all family members. He must be taught at an early age to focus, concentrate, and to finish what he starts. Gifted in communication, those souls learn foreign languages quickly and are adept with cameras. On a negative note, the child must be taught against stealing or lying. The numbers 2, 4, 6, and 8 will mark their lives. This is a great position for producing books or conducting a business from the base of operation. Many born with the Moon in Gemini may spend their last days on the outskirts of a large city or in a foreign land.

Cancer Moon 	Feminine/Water sign. This souls is domestic, introverted, with double lunar impact. Emotional, sensitive, and intuitive. This Moon (security) position gives the native a strong appreciation for food and a gift in cooking. Indeed, the Universal Law (based on the Moon's fluctuations) must be respected. Depression and sorrow may result in times of a waning Moon. This is due to the heavy impact of their ruler the Moon, on their sensitive psyches. However, opportunities will arise and progress made by understanding and practicing the Universal Law. These people have a strong need for security and are very concerned with family matters. Usually, unless there is a strong affliction, the mother and child have a positive rapport. A protective, nurturing attitude is another legacy found in people born with the Moon in Cancer. Childbearing and nourishment are a source of happiness for those born with this Moon's location. Children born with the Moon in Cancer are very sensitive and must be taught to stand for themselves. These souls may spend the last days of their lives close to a body of water or on an island.

Leo Moon 	Masculine/Fire sign. Leo moons are extroverted, seek the limelight, enjoy throwing parties, are domineering, like to organize others, act like a kings or queens, but are not domestic. Magnanimous, child-like, and openhearted. The Sun's energy mixed with this lunar position gives the native a zest for life, organizational skills, and the gift of command. Cheerful and loving, these souls need to shine in the family circle and will go to great lengths to protect their loved ones. Being young at heart themselves and fond of children, they usually produce large families. Artistic pursuits can be induced at an early age by one of the parents, leading the soul toward a premature fame. The strong desire for action may lead the soul toward sports or outdoor activities. Children born with the Moon in Leo are active and artistic by nature and should be encouraged to further their natural gifts. Discipline and respect for others must be induced early to avoid future confrontation with people outside the immediate family. Young Leo Moon souls love animals, particularly horses, and may be touched by fame in growing up with them. Children born with this Moon position must be taught to respect others and to follow the rules. The last resting-place may be in wealthy, famous surroundings. France and Italy may also be in their retirement plans.

Virgo Moon 	Feminine/Earth sign. These souls are domestic, perfectionists, with a cleanliness attitude, a sub-consciousness fear of disease, fussy, organized, and detail oriented. Methodical, precise, critical, and health-oriented. This lunar position gives the native penetrating eyes, a strong desire for perfection, and an ability for working with great detail. Usually the need for a clean and organized environment is strong and obvious. Also present are domestic abilities and a gift with plants. Many who have inherited this position like to knit or do garden work. People born with Mercury (communication) in this Moon's position must guard against criticism and gossiping. In an unbalanced chart, this Moon produces an over-concern with health and may force vegetarianism on others. Incidentally, with a heavy Moon's position in Virgo, the native may completely disregard health rules and become a heavy user of narcotics and alcohol. As a rule, Virgo Moons do not like messiness and may miss the benefits of healing their bodies and minds with pets. Being unnecessarily concerned with detail may also blur those souls' cosmic consciousness. On a more positive note, the advanced Moon in Virgo is aware of the necessity of keeping the body in good health and would do battle to further education for the good of all. Managerial abilities and discipline are also found with this Moon's location. Children born with this Moon position must be taught to guard against an over-concern with health and details. The soul may find its last resting-place close to a big, natural garden.

Libra Moon  	Masculine/Air sign. Here there is a strong desire for partnership, avoids being alone, seeks peace, balance, harmony, and diplomacy. They excel in both psychology and artistic abilities which require sensitivity to harmony and balance. This lunar position gives the native a soft attitude and a gentle approach to life in general. The impact of Venus (harmony) on the domestic scenery will bring love, romance, candlelight, and good wine. These souls need to surround themselves with luxury and valuable objects. Many of them will be born to use their gifts of interior design. However, when confronted, a Libra could become warrior to take seriously. Partnership is a necessity for this soul, and he is a real shot of luck to any man or woman who deserves his diplomatic, loving manners. As air signs, Libra moons like to get involved with advanced intellectual or artistic types. These souls need mental stimulation and expect the same loving and fair treatment in return. A natural flair for psychology, the arts, and the legal system is found in this position. Children born with this Moon position must be raised in a well-balanced environment and taught to make up their own minds as soon as possible. The soul may choose its last resting-place where everything needed for happiness is found in perfect harmony.

Scorpio Moon ♏ ☽	Feminine/Water sign. This placement manifests a dramatic upbringing, a piercing and stinging tongue, anger, magnetic eyes, ultimate power, metaphysics, sexual power, and terrific intuition. Also present is power, magnetism, sensuality and mysticism. This lunar position gives the native penetrating eyes and a will to survive dramatic experiences. Usually the mother becomes either a great friend or a great enemy. Abuses and dramatic happenings are thrown to the soul in his upbringing to prepare him or her for some serious karma to process. With Pluto (death), this position needs constant control, and a strong desire to restructure the domestic scenery is always present. Elizabeth Taylor was born with a powerful Moon in Scorpio, which indicates the reason behind her numerous marriages. Dramatic loss will be experienced by the soul, as seen with Nostradamus who was born with the Moon in Scorpio. He lost his two children and first wife to the plague. Many times, the child is born out of wedlock, rejected or in some cases, the mother dies when the child is at an early age. Sometimes sex, drugs, and alcohol are involved before the birth of the child. The child is then placed in institutional care, as an orphan would be. In young souls, resentment and jealousy are also found with this Moon's position. Many killers and sex offenders are born with a Moon in Scorpio. As always, when the Moon crosses this sign, death is all over, secrets are uncovered and serious dramatic happenings occur.

Scorpio Moon (Cont...)	See my Starguide for full guidance and predictions. From "hell to heaven," is a good way to express a Moon in Scorpio when it comes to the soul's last resting-place. Princess Grace of Monaco (France) was born with the Moon in Scorpio and her last resting-place in the South of France was a fantastic dream come true. However, her dramatic, accidental death, driving the French Riviera, is also a sure sign of the power of the stars upon her fate. Children born with this Moon position must be allowed to be left alone and to understand at an early age the depth of their mystical nature. On a negative note, a dramatic end follows a long, painful imprisonment, liberating the soul from its small and dark cell. Scorpios usually reach all their dreams and end their lives happily on an exotic island.
Sagittarius Moon 	Masculine/Fire sign. This person loves wild and open spaces, foreign lands, he is the freedom lover, risk taker, adventurer, and truth-seeker. He is by nature philosophical, cheerful, and communicative. This lunar position favors learning and teaching, forcing the native to travel far, and eventually residing for some period of time in a foreign land. The upbringing is usually strongly affected by one of the parents imposing certain religious beliefs and conduct. If exaggerated, this "attitude" may, in turn, be imposed on others, thus creating problems in close relationships.

Sagittarius Moon (cont...)	The strong desire to "philosophize," to travel and communicate may also bring instability on the domestic scene. The smart ones will work it out and live in a mobile home (or a boat) in constant closeness to Mother Nature. Pets (especially horses) are usually found with this Moon location and a strong desire for freedom will always be present. This Moon's location predisposes the bearer with a cheerful attitude, faith, and a form of luck. Children born with this Moon position must be allowed to recognize and understand God in all forms and should stay clear of religious dogma. Born with great talent in communication, they are driven, both mentally and physically, to faraway places where the opportunity to philosophize with all cultures and diverse opinions will be offered. Wide-open spaces, deserts, and rough nature will appeal to them as a last resting-place in this world.
Moon in Capricorn 	Feminine/Earth sign. A Capricorn moon is domestic, the engineer of the zodiac, observant, precise, builder, and a manipulator. They are practical, organized, and methodical. This is an ideal Moon position for those interested in politics, mathematics, and architecture. Hitler was born with the Moon in Capricorn and it is said that if he had not got involved in politics, he would

Capricorn Moon (cont...)	have been the greatest architect in Germany. Natural gifts of attention to details and great observation skills are usually present. As in the infamous case of Hitler, who misused this Moon's position, it produces political fanatics and manipulators, leading to destruction as represented by the head of the goat (devil). Karmic Saturn sees it all, and brings his children to despair and depression when the laws of cause and effect are ignored. On a more positive note, many successful souls from all walks of life were born with this Moon position. Perfectionism, snootiness, criticism and an over-concern with health may also be present if the Moon is badly afflicted. A strong appreciation of classical art is also found for these self-made souls. Stimulated by power, wealth, and position, many Moon in Capricorn souls will marry older partners. However, the old ones may be able to "afford" a much younger and prettier partner! Strongly committed to their families, they strive for security their whole lives. Many of them are gifted with cooking abilities and others will join the real estate industry. Children born with this Moon position must be allowed to understand and respect the status and values of others. The last resting-place may be in the highest building and wealthiest part of

Capricorn Moon (cont...)	town, a representation of their successful sign, a goat reaching the icy top of a high mountain.
Aquarius Moon ≈ ☽	Masculine/Air sign. The Aquarius moon soul is independent, open-minded, sociable, a person with a wide ranges of interests. He does well generally with mathematics, science, art, music and literature. Ingenious, independent, and original. This Moon position has produced many inventors and great Astrologers. The natural, freethinking process and strong desire for emancipation may interfere with the family's traditional values. Many have to leave the security of their homes at early ages, due to their eccentric attitudes and unwavering desires to travel the world. Friends and group organizations appeal to them and many hold psychic or Astrology séances in their homes. Uranus (hi-tech), ruler of Aquarius will channel incredible information through them, providing they understand the importance of crystallizing their thoughts with the help of a computer.

Aquarius Moon (cont.)....	Strong-willed and fixed, they will not tolerate dogma, ultimately rejecting it. They provide friends with love and support in times of trouble, but insist on the same returned favors. Aquarius rules the future and the UFO phenomenon. Many of them consciously or not, have a direct relationship with extraterrestrials. Poisoning the mind with fears and failures of the past may produce depression and panic attacks in the long run. Children born with this Moon position must be allowed freedom of thought and critical thinking. Souls born with a Moon in Aquarius may choose to live the last part of their lives in a specific high social group, which provides friendships and the original mental activity for which they strive.

Pisces Moon 	Feminine/Water sign. The soul is attracted to the intangibles such as gas, drugs, alcohol, jails, religions, hospitals, and asylums. It's susceptible to drugs and chemicals and should be made aware of this. Positively, it has the ability to offer the purity of light, the real light (ultimate knowledge, wisdom and power). On a negative aspect, the soul should stay away from alcohol and drugs. This moon attracts religious values, and in extreme cases may produce fanatic religious killers and suicides. It can be seen in serial killers such as Dahmer, or high profile murderers like O.J. Simpson and the religious terrorist (a Pisces) Osama Bin Laden. The last resting-place may be a jail or an island which itself is ruled by Neptune. It's prone to create self-imposed guilt and an inability to let go of the past. The soul has no grounding with the Moon in Pisces (dreams, deception, and imagination). Intuitive, psychic, and artistic. This Moon position is a karmic one and could indicate a constant spiritual search for identity.

Pisces Moon (cont.)....	Indeed, it is a beneficial position for those providing for the sick and needy. Thus, many Moon in Pisces are attracted to hospitals, jails, caves, temples, churches or similar confining establishments. Loving and caring, the Moon in Pisces native will be attracted to dreams, the subconscious, the arts or medical fields. The advanced ones will promote their natural psychic abilities and become towers of strength to others. However, it is important for them to recharge their own batteries and learn to detach from other people's troubles. The upbringing is usually deceptive and difficult. One of the parents may have dependency problems, or fanatic religious views, imposing the beliefs at a tender age. Paul Jennings Hills (killer/abortion activist) and Dahmer were both born with a strong negative Pisces in their charts, indicating rigid moral-religious code and sexual repression, which led them to devious acts of killing. Pisces rules hospitals, mental institutions, asylums, churches and prisons, clearly indicating how, where and why the soul might have to endure such horrible penitence. The ideal fish swims upstream like a salmon, and leads many of us to the real light of spiritual freedom. Children born with this Moon position must be emancipated from all forms

Pisces Moon (cont...)	of fear and religious dogma. The negative Pisces Moon soul may end its life by suicide (usually in jail, ingesting drugs or by water accidents), or mental institutions. The positive Pisces will retire close to the ocean where they can provide their well-needed spiritual support and appreciate the colors of the sunset. The true Pisces recognizes the Universe as his church, and the stars the commandments written in light. The progressive fish ultimately reaches cosmic consciousness and self-realization where he finds himself in God as a God himself. Pisces or Neptune's location is indeed the most difficult area of the chart for all human beings.

Since the dawn of time, the Creator has shown his truth to the humble — a truth that is hidden from the vain blinded by worldly pleasures, but which is written in the skies, which nightly speaks of the glory of God.

— *Nostradamus*

VENUS

Venus is the daughter of Jupiter in Greek Mythology. She regulates love and artistic ability. Venus represents what a woman has to offer a man as far as love is concerned. Venus legalizes your money especially if found close to Jupiter or Pluto. Venus also regulates your creativity and your artistic sensitivity. Most of all, Venus is seen as the planet of love and beauty.

Note: The position of Venus in a man's chart indicates what type of love a man will be demanding from a woman. The position of Venus in a woman's chart indicates what type of love she is able to offer a man.

PLACEMENT OF VENUS IN EACH SIGN

Venus in Aries ♀ ♈	In the first house, it shows how pretty and romantic a person can be. Magnetic, competitive, a bit insecure. Where there is action, danger, and noise, will be where there is a chance to find love. Remember that Aries is a fire sign and rules rock-n-roll, sports, and action. The masculine energy (Aries) is now mixed with the feminine energy of Venus. These people are very creative (Venus) in molding red-hot rods in steel (Aries), and can create beautiful artwork. A Harley Davidson is a complete and solid example of a Venus in Aries at work, or a mixture of noise, power, fire and beauty. Those girls love long dirty hair flying in the wind and are born free and very competitive by birth. Many of them will have to learn the hard way, that love is not just a mix of physical beauty and sexual animal instincts.
Venus in Taurus ♀ ♉	Venus rules the sophisticated sign of Taurus. So here we have a magnetic, beautiful, pretty, handsome male or female individual with high tests for beauty and pleasure. Venus in Taurus can be very possessive and jealous due to the depth of emotion and passion for a lover. Taurus must learn to love with their heads, not just with their hearts. They are usually very selective in giving their feelings away.

Venus in Taurus (cont...)	Not just anyone will do, as they are quite critical by birth. Venus also rules the second house of possessions. Thus, money is in the mind of Taurus and will flow easily to them. Many great artists are Bulls and make money by creating beautiful songs, or with singing (Taurus rules the throat). What Taurus needs most is good food, good massage, candlelight, soft music, and romantic, expensive settings. This is a very beautiful position for the planet Venus to be in. The downfalls are jealously and possessiveness, and problems with letting go of a lover.
Venus in Gemini 	The opportunity is given the soul to experience love on a mental level. Venus is art, while Gemini is communication (writing and reading). Venus in Gemini also produces fine photographers and the ability to generate beautiful poetry. Because Gemini has a double personality, this pairing often indicates a dual nature or someone able to love two people at the same time. Souls born with Venus in Gemini have an intellectual need for mental stimulation, and sexual expression is important to them. Anything less produces boredom and an urgent desire for a new experience. For some, communicating love is extremely important, while others love to exchange funny jokes. A

Venus in Gemini	gift of youth is often present. True or long lasting love is also experienced with a foreigner or in foreign lands.
Venus in Cancer ♀ ♋	This position predisposes the soul to experience the Oedipus Complex. The planet of love and beauty is in the sign of Cancer which rules home, family dad and mom. Souls born in July offer the best care to others. This represents the type of love that only a mother would give to her child, a lover or a husband. Venus in Cancer is very clinging. This placement for Venus is very sympathetic, and the soul is able to give an abundant amount of love. Additionally, in times of trouble or need of emotional support or solid food, that person will show what true care and giving is. A very, very beautiful position for Venus. This is also a very sensitive position for Venus because Cancer has a problem of letting go and is tenacious by nature. If that person suffers emotional wounds they will take a long time to heal. There is a very strong love and respect with their relationship to the family. Remember the planet of arts and money is now in the sign of Cancer. With Venus in Cancer, money can be made with real estate, hotels, or feeding the world emotionally or physically. Venus in Cancer must be cautious not to give their beautiful love to selfish and abusing souls.

Venus in Leo  ♌	This is an extremely magnetic position for Venus. Remember that Leo, "I am King" (egotistical) is also domineering and may put stress on his "subject." They expect to rule you, and in some abusive cases, for you to obey them. Leo will show true love by treating you as the most important person on earth and give you all the gold you deserve. Leo traditionally rules love, gold, children and the arts. Many souls born with this Venus position are gorgeous, and loyal to their lovers. Leo also rules the fifth house and the seat of attraction between human beings and creativity. Madonna and Michael Jackson are Leos, and there is always a tremendous creativity and magnetism surrounding these two great performers. Leo also rules love, romance, speculation, and acting. This shining sign rules France and Italy and that's why people say, "French are romantic."The French language reflects Leo's warmth, and its intonation is pleasant to the ear. Venus in Leo are great actors. They are the individuals who will watch soap operas all day, mostly because they are in love with beauty, drama and love. A mother born with Venus in Leo is certainly able to give much to her children. Venus in Leo will always attract either famous people or extremely gorgeous

Venus in Leo (cont...)	or artistic people. The partner will be in love with love, and in love with the best of what life has to offer. They will want to treat and be treated like a Kings and Queens, and expect a palace for dating or love making.
Venus in Virgo ♀ ♍	Virgo is a highly critical earthy sign. Working on their (and your) health and habits is very important to them. So if you are in love with an advanced Virgo, do not smoke, and be sure to exercise every day. They are also careful of what they and you are eating. Many fall for the extreme power of the "Virgin Mary" and become health lunatics and vegetarians. The reason Virgo should give you her love is because you respond to her high standards for work and health. Virgo always works very hard. A younger Virgo soul will be totally the opposite and will refuse to work, drink themselves silly, and chain-smoke cigarettes. In many ways, Venus in Virgo is simply concerned with offering you the purest form of love. Date a Virgo (or any earth sign!), and you will find very it stimulating indeed, to discuss work and office matters on your date.

Venus in Libra ♀ ♎	Libra rules Venus. Here you have a wonderful position indeed. Venus in Libra is mostly concerned with maintaining harmony in matters of love. Libra traditionally represents the seventh house of marriage, contracts and commitments. Venus in Libra demand perfect habits, beauty, and intelligence in their lovers. Young Libra souls often fall short of offering what they are looking for in their partners and drink too much. An advanced Venus in Libra will be very supportive and choose their words carefully. Their gentle words and beautiful phrases will be fluid, attractive, romantic and harmonious to everyone . Libra rules Astropsychology, and Venus in this sign is at its best position for expression and helping patients. Venus in Libra also produces fantastic interior designers and fine artists. Venus in Libra demands love, respect, beauty, refinement and a balanced behavior in public
Venus in Scorpio ♀ ♏	High drama. Young Scorpio souls will suffer this position of Venus. The depth and intensity of Scorpio's passionate nature could either bring drama, or sting to death the object of love. This attitude is produced by Pluto's (ruler of Scorpio) ultimate desire to control the partner. A woman born with Venus in Scorpio is extremely

Venus in Scorpio (cont...)	magnetic. She is a walking sexual magnet loaded with sensuality. In her powers, she's like a black widow. Always be careful when dealing with a man or a woman who was born with Venus in Scorpio. If you are sincere and forthright, she will make you a happy man. But don't expect any compromising, you had better mean business or else. If she loves you, no one has a chance to take her away from you. Venus in Scorpio is ultimate power and ultimate devotion, til death do us part. Behind her gentle magnetic nature, she's subtle and deadly. Those souls need total commitment from their partners. Like the black widow spider, she eats her prey ALIVE! Not an individual to play with! Venus in Scorpio cannot see life without their partner (life and death), and many will experience their best growth with the affairs of love. The intensity and passion generated by this Venus' position also makes for great artists.
Venus in Sagittarius  	An extremely philosophically oriented soul. Sagittarius rules foreigners, and this position often leads to marrying a foreigner or living in a foreign land. This soul will strive to travel to far away places. The opportunity is offered to the soul to experience a unique type of love. The desire to travel to far away places is strong. The soul will be attracted to people having

Venus in Sagittarius (cont...)	similar values, either religious, or philosophical. There is also a strong respect and love for animals (horses, etc.). Venus rules art, so there is a strong appreciation of philosophical art with this position. Venus in Sagittarius is also intellectually inclined. They are all attracted to knowledge, education, and people who are involved in teaching or traveling positions. They usually get richer physically and spiritually when making a commitment to a special and very spiritual person. The young Venus in Sagittarius soul will only marry a person who has and shares his specific religious doctrine. The advanced soul is highly spiritual and non religious.
Venus in Capricorn  ♑	Venus in Capricorn is a practical and intellectual soul. They are all attracted to people in position of power (the doctor, attorney, mayor, and up-town persona). Venus in Capricorn will subconsciously hang around this "up-town" part of the city. She or he will love having a drink at the Hyatt or the Hilton or some famous upscale location. Loving somebody who has worked hard and established a solid position of power or a position in society

Venus in Capricorn (cont...)	is what motivates him. The young Venus in Capricorn soul is cold and calculating and interested only in your wallet, your accomplishments, and the financial security this brings to a relationship. On a positive aspect, Venus in Capricorn indicates a person who appreciates classical music, fine art and beautiful architectural designs. The soul is willing to work hard and build success with the chosen partner. Venus in Capricorn bestows a beautiful complexion throughout the entire body. This celestial signature promotes the soul to a profession involving the arts and the public eye. This includes work with magazines, communications, photography, and for some advanced souls, the study of Astropsychology.
Venus in Aquarius 	Universal love, freedom, super magnetism and originality are bestowed in this position. Venus in Aquarius brings interest and the study of astrology, music, electronics, etc. The planet of love or Venus is now in the astonishing and sometimes weird world of Aquarius. Thus the planet regulating the sudden release of energy brings unexpected people and experiences into the subject's life (one night stands, original partners and fast in and out relationships).

Venus in Aquarius (Cont...)	Because Aquarius is a fixed sign, once they have found a true mate they can be faithful to one love. This position brings lovers to be friends and friends to become lovers. Souls born with this Venus position will often associate with new age groups, participate in UFO conferences and any and all New Age endeavors. Thus the option to find that special Universal love (i.e., a unique person, that eccentric person). Venus in Aquarius is a non-judging and free loving soul, generating universal love. On a negative aspect the soul seeks all forms of group love or weird sexual experiences (i.e., Mormonism, cults, Satanist leaders etc.).
Venus in Pisces  	Unconditional love is the key with this position of Venus in Pisces. In times of trouble, individuals with this Venus placement will not let you down, as sacrifice is their middle name. Their love is not necessarily grounded and sometimes deceiving. In extreme cases, a very beautiful woman gives her body to a physically repulsive or ugly person, her reasoning being that he also has the right to love and be loved. The Venus in Pisces individual instinctively feels sorry for the other person's suffering. They feel this way without rationally thinking about the

Venus in Pisces (cont...)	situation or the person in question. The behavior is motivated by a strong feeling of guilt, easily manipulated by less honorable souls. In extreme cases, there is also a strong possibility for hidden or deceiving love affairs during the life of the subject. Deception and illusion bring the soul to either total exile or sacrifice, producing extreme behaviors such as prostitution or nuns. (The fish swimming in opposite directions). Guilt is a big problem and they are deluded easily (Pisces' deceptive, illusive nature). Venus in Pisces has compensated reality for fear via sacrificing their own wants and needs for the sake others (Jesus Christ dying on the cross for the sins of others; martyrdom). Pisces rules hidden subconscious motivations, fears, illusions and deceptions. On a positive note, the best to be found in terms of love and sacrifice once the soul realizes its own weaknesses. An incredible position for the performing arts if the chart is supported by more practical stars.

SUN

The Sun Sign represents the area in which you can reach fame, master the light, or enlighten the world. It is your private, unique lesson in life, and one of the major reasons you are here on this earth. The sun is located in either the first house of your soul's purpose, or your second house of money and self esteem. Your Sun location by itself will not depict the way you will get on with other people. Your chart is like a parachute and every planet must be taken into consideration as all planets interact positively and negatively. Simply acknowledge that all stars carry both positive and negative energy. The idea is to keep them in balance, and most of all to be aware of each one of them in a chart. Each Sun Sign has a distinct purpose, and seeks to find the following:

PLACEMENT OF THE SUN IN EACH SIGN

Sun in Aries ☉ ♈	To establish oneself, develop one's personality and to lead.
Sun in Taurus ☉ ♉	To establish financial security and build one's self-esteem.
Sun in Gemini ☉ ♊	To establish, understand, and use duality constructively.
Sun in Cancer ☉ ♋	To establish and learn all about emotion and feed the world.
Sun in Leo ☉ ♌	To establish fame and learn all about ego and power.
Sun in Virgo ☉ ♍	To establish health, service, and maintain a sense of purity.
Sun in Libra ☉ ♎	To establish balance and harmony and justice in all areas of life.
Sun in Scorpio ☉ ♏	To establish power control and regeneration in all areas of life.
Sun in Sagittarius ☉ ♐	To establish education and teach the truth found in the light.
Sun in Capricorn ☉ ♑	To establish a position of power and honors and serve the masses.
Sun in Aquarius ☉ ♒	To establish and lead the world to enlightenment and the future.
Sun in Pisces ☉ ♓	To establish cosmic consciousness and find himself in God.

MERCURY

The planet Mercury is called in Greek Mythology "The Messenger of the Gods." He has wings on the back of his feet, and he delivers messages to all the Gods in the universe. Gemini (ruled by Mercury) is fast and is the sign and planet of swiftness, agility and speed. The ancients represented Mercury as both a male and a female energy, or the yin and yang. Negative Mercury can also produce liars and thieves. Mercury rules communication via radio, television, writing, and reading. Gemini (Mercury) also rules critical thinking and common sense. Gemini is the sign directly against the codification of thoughts, or religion. Gemini is curious, thus may challenge the established rules. Gemini is the attorney fighting, twisting, and using the legal system trying to convince the all powerful judge (Jupiter/Sagittarius) of his case. Gemini is a representation of all the attorneys used by O.J. Simpson (a Gemini Dragon's Head by birth), to get himself out of trouble by using the system to get away with murder. Mercury is indeed the planet of communication. Like a lawyer, Gemini's power is his ability to explore every angle of a situation and convince (sell) others (the jury) with his uncanny wit and use of words.

The highest power for Mercury is in Aquarius. This is where the combined energies of the two previous air signs (Gemini and Libra) mix to make the third and final energy where it is concentrated and at its best position. The same applies for fire, earth and water signs. Thus Pisces is the concentration of the power of Cancer and Scorpio combined together. The progression and dynamics of this energy ultimately adds to and does not take away from anything else in the chart.

MERCURY IN RETROGRADE

Mercury travels in a retrograde motion three times a year for sometimes a month or so. It usually starts a week and one-half before modern astrology dictates in the ephemeris, and also continues for up to two weeks after the ephemeris indicates regular motion. I noticed that well after Mercury had gone in its direct motion, I experienced stress related to this celestial manifestation. Thus I decided, and for good reason, to elongate the timing in my Moon power yearly publications. When in its retrograde motion, Mercury forces every one of us to slow down and stop. Mercury wants you to look back at your life and what you might have missed, thus the past often becomes alive. It is not a good time to embark on anything new such as buying a car, signing contracts, or promoting the future. It is rather a time to "review" what you have or have not done, or reexamine what you have missed. Mercury in Retrograde is a reminder that you have been going too fast in some parts of your life, consequently missing important details along the way. (Refer to my book Moon Power and explore the "Supernova Windows" for the exact dates of Mercury in retrograde).

Note: Mercury in retrograde allows you to look and use the power of Mercury for introspection, inward research. Consequently, during this time, any form of spirituality or philosophical study will always pay off, as your spirituality is promoted to a much higher level. This retrograde period will affect computers, transportation, cars, weather, and appointments (people from the past will re-enter your life etc.). This is a period when events in ones' life must slow down or even stop in order for specific realizations to occur inwardly. Mercury also rules the navigational system of all animals on land and water. Thus a pet can easily become lost, or a whale beach himself as its brain or "computer" receives erroneous information. The "mental snobs" and scientists alike have so much to learn about this phenomenon and should invest in my course. They would certainly save all the tax dollars normally wasted with their stupid and expensive scientific research.

CHARACTERISTICS OF CHILDREN BORN DURING A MERCURY IN RETROGRADE PERIOD

A child born during this Mercury in Retrograde period will be inclined to speak more slowly and will need time to assimilate or grasp information because his mind is working inwardly and at a different pace. For example, if the topic is spiritual or about music, dancing, metaphysics or the arts, the slow and mysterious world of Neptune will support the child's natural ability to assimilate and comprehend this "vibration". This is mostly because Neptune vibrates deeper in its own creative energy. But change the task to mathematics, anything speedy or rational, or normally paced for other children, and he will find the learning process even harder. If a teacher is aware of this Mercury in Retrograde phase they can enhance a child's study habits by: 1) changing the pace in the classroom setting; 2) gearing lessons towards a creative and artistic modes; and 3) focusing not so much on deadlines, and giving the child plenty time to use his natural retrospective. They should enjoy both learning processes, and be patient with his own abilities as a teacher. In this way the children as well as the teacher will cooperate naturally in the needed setting. Again, the "mental snobs" and traditionally educated psychologists have so much to learn about this phenomenon and should invest in my Astropsychology course.

IMPORTANT: Also, keep in mind that a planet with Mercury in Retrograde motion does not reverse the male and female polarity in someone's chart, nor does it make a traditionally negative planet positive. Hence, a planet in Mercury in Retrograde indicates a slow, deep and intuitive mental process. Again, this does not make it negative per say in any way but just different. The opposite effect is to be found with a very powerful Mercury at birth and usually (such as Einstein, Clinton and myself) produces A.D.D., as the child needs to get rid of the mental and physical surplus of energy. This "disorder" is in fact a gift not an indisposition or illness.

* * * *

PLACEMENT OF MERCURY IN EACH SIGN

Mercury in Aries ☿ ♈	Mars (Aries) and Gemini (Mercury) together. The turbo-charged individual. The speaker, the racing driver. You now have the intensity of Aries (Mars) the red planet of danger, action, machinery, and mechanics, receiving speedy Mercury (Gemini). You will see them on the racetrack, they like fast cars. These individuals are most likely to be stopped by a police officer for speeding. Apparently, they don't understand what it means to slow down. Aries rules the body, Gemini the mind. When the energies are understood and

Mercury in Aries (cont...)	controlled properly, the soul has the potential to use the turbo-charged energy very constructively either in the world of communication or in the world of action and danger.
Mercury in Taurus ☿ ♉	Venus (Taurus) and Gemini (Mercury) together. Taurus rules the banking industry, the second house of money, possessions, security and self-esteem. Chances are this individual will be attracted to the world of security and finance. Remember that Taurus does not only deal with money for money's sake. With Venus, it also rules the arts, massage, beauty, and cosmetics. With Mercury ruling communication, there will also be an interest in sales. The fastest, most intellectual planet of all, Mercury in Taurus stimulates anything related to money, sales, beauty and the arts.
Mercury in Gemini ☿ ♊	These individuals are talking machines at the worst. They run their mouths constantly and don't know when to stop talking. Telephone bills will be extremely high. In young children this Gemini/Gemini

Mercury in Gemini (cont...)	location will have parents wishing their child would stop talking for just a minute. Teachers too will find them an annoyance in the classroom setting. To counteract this excitable energy, one should be patient with them, instill discipline, and take the time to explain to them the importance of education. Remember, these children were born to talk and are born writers, translators, and photographers. They are gifted in communication and can harness that positive energy with proper guidance. Hence, the possibilities for these individuals are limitless, as the power for expression is magnified to such a degree.
Mercury in Cancer  	Moon (Cancer) and Gemini (Mercury). These individuals mix anything directly related to the 4th house of Cancer, with sales, communication, and telephones. Remember that Cancer rules clothing, real estate, security and food. The mind is very concerned with home, family, and security in general. These individuals have sharp minds that will not be blurred by imagination or fear when the moon is waxing. After the full moon, when the moon is waning, the individual could become

Mercury in Cancer (cont...)	"lunatic and moody." Don't forget that the moon is in charge of all the water signs (Cancer, Scorpio and Pisces). Intuition plays an important part with those born with Mercury in Cancer. It would do well for them to listen to their intuition in times of trouble. They should avoid signing important commitments after the full moon and proceed during the new (waxing) moon, as Mercury rules writing, reading, contracts, and paperwork.
Mercury in Virgo 	Mercury (Virgo) and Gemini (Mercury): The mind is concerned with affairs related to general health, homeopathic medicine, clothing, plants, criticism, and detail. These individuals are the perfectionists of the zodiac. They do well with computers, typewriters, with every little detail of moving parts, speech (such as computer programmers). The mind (Mercury/Gemini) is concerned with perfection (Mercury/Virgo). Virgo is also know as "The Virgin Mary" (purity, perfection). For example, individuals with this placement in their charts will do well communicating via writing and or

Mercury in Virgo (cont...)	speaking about diets. Thus, Mercury will manifest itself into the perfectionist world of Virgo.
Mercury in Libra ☿ ♎	Venus (Libra) and Gemini (Mercury): In the fair sign of Libra, the mind is concerned with equality, and able to look at both sides of the question and come up with a well balanced answer. (Note: As its symbol suggests, she carries a sword and the scales of justice. Libra -- war and/or peace). Libra is the sign of psychology, and chances are the person will also be interested in the more advanced practice of Astropsychology. Libra rules the legal system; the mind is naturally tuned to legality and justice. Libra is ruled and controlled by Venus and with it an interaction or attraction to the arts. Advanced souls born with Mercury in Libra will pursue the metaphysical fields, philosophy, Astropsychology and the legal system. Many are also born interior designers, due to their aptitudes for balanced arrangements with colors and design. With Mercury in Libra, the written word will be beautifully balanced and could translate into beautiful poetry.

Mercury in Libra (cont...)	Additionally in this placement, it will lead individuals towards jurisdictions legalities, and contracts etc.
Mercury in Scorpio ☿ ♏	Pluto (Scorpio) and Gemini (Mercury): Probably one the best positions for investigators. Scorpio rules science, research, medicine, metaphysics, corporate endeavors, investments, insurance, sex and the police force. Scorpio rules ultimate power. The mind is much like a radar device in this placement. Mercury in Scorpio constantly investigates. Not only what you say, but also what is said in reply to you. These individuals are able to listen intently to a conversation, and are always on the "look-out" for something you try to hide from them. The regeneration principle takes place on the intellectual level through their acute investigative nature and powerful mental abilities. They will be able to recognize the value of your feelings through your speech and can read words you think. Be careful when you deal with Mercury in Scorpio as sarcasm is often present. These individuals are born cops, profilers, and will penetrate your deepest secret through their powerful intuition. When you ask them for your opinion you will get the undiluted truth. You may not like their bluntness, but you asked them and you got the plain truth. It is not exactly in

Mercury in Scorpio (Cont...)	their nature to be diplomatic. Mercury rules speech and Scorpio has a stinger (sarcasm). NOTE: If you have a moon in Libra (or a strong Venus in your chart) it will tone down the strong sarcasm found with Mercury in Scorpio; this would add more diplomacy. They love science and research (forensic medicine). They are the ones who are not afraid to open a dead body to find out how or why the subject died. Pluto (Scorpio) rules life and death. Therefore, when Mercury is in Scorpio, the option to uncover anything and everything is given to the soul. Life and death matters, legacy and insurance also attract those born with Mercury in the sign of Scorpio. To illustrate the point, here is a fable for those with Mercury in Scorpio or the Scorpio in general: A Scorpio came to a toad and said, "I need to cross the river." The toad said, "Hey, I'm not going to carry you on my back, you're going to sting me in the middle of the river, and I'm going to die." Scorpio said, "I would not do that, and have both of us die." "Are you sure?" asked the toad. Scorpio replied, "I am sure." So they both got in the river to cross with Scorpio on the toad's back. As Scorpio sat on the toad's back he stung him. The toad yelled, "Why did you do that? Now we are both going to die and drown." Scorpio commented, "No you are going to die, I just did what I was born to do!" Moral of the story: Always be on guard when dealing with a Scorpio, no matter where Pluto or Scorpio is placed in the chart.

Mercury in Sagittarius 	Sagittarius rules the codification of thought and higher education. Mercury is the ruler of Gemini, and in Sagittarius it's in opposition. Gemini regulates the curious and critical thinking process, against Sagittarius' acceptance. The critical and curious educational process will somehow conflict with the world of established knowledge of Sagittarius. This means the individual will be tremendously educated and all education will be given through books. Mercury in Sagittarius believes in the printed word, or the written word of the Bible, as truth. Mercury's critical intellect and natural curiosity will challenge the world of Sagittarius. The soul will explore all books (a professional student) and will gather the facts from reality and challenge what is accepted as truth by society. The mind will search for the facts by traveling the world. An attraction to foreign lands, philosophy, the Indians and all matters related to the world of Sagittarius becomes a vivid interest. These individuals possess traditional knowledge and become great teachers of philosophy, religion or common laws. However there is a big difference between education and intelligence.

Mercury in Capricorn  ♑	Of all the earth signs, Capricorn is the most rational and practical. The soul will be down to earth, organized, and is seen as the engineer of the zodiac. Capricorn rules politics, structure, organization, power, snobs, wealth, England, the Queen, classical music, and high society. Mercury in Capricorn is very productive and comprehends the ramifications of any situation or business. Mercury in Scorpio uses intuitive power whereas Mercury in Capricorn uses rational thought. Mercury in Capricorn can make their own lives miserable because they are overly rational in their thinking. They see everything and behave like detectors, that is -- the way you talk, the shoes you wear, the car you drive, the watch you wear, the ring you have, the way you keep your hair, etc. Note: Capricorns realize everything by watching and asking questions. Capricorns are the masters of practical detection. Mercury in Capricorn has the potential to structure absolutely anything to which he puts his mind to accomplish. As a rule, Capricorn tends to stick to what has been accepted and will stick to tradition. The advanced Capricorn soul will take a chance to expand its mind and make use of its fishtail to grasp astrology in a detailed and clear manner. Astropsychologists born

Mercury in Capricorn (cont...)	with Mercury in Capricorn will do well once the mathematical aspect of the old science of astrology is put aside. Mercury in Capricorn is very precise with detail. However the intuition derived from the symbolic power found in the signs must be allowed to flow freely. He is at the heart of any situation, a scientist! Mercury in Capricorn, negatively aspected, produces manipulators of situations and scientists and mental snobs. This is one of the best positions in astrology to master and structure any form of education. The longer in academics the better! The more practical the studies, the better! Again, with Mercury in Capricorn, these souls are very concerned with power, and a studious upbringing in academics will provide the platform for them to launch their careers. This position of Mercury brings about thoughts of old age, retirement and general security. The soul wants to move quickly in a position of power with all the honors, title and big paychecks. Mercury in Capricorn must not let irrational thoughts plague his mind. He must use his thinking wisely, study hard in school, and get into an area of interest and

Mercury in Capricorn (cont . . .)	work his way up. Capricorn rules politics and many Mercury in Capricorns are geared towards governmental positions. A child born with Mercury in Capricorn will be very sharp and a steady studying machine. If given a successful area of study the soul will reach a position of respect through his academic accomplishments.
Mercury in Aquarius  ≈	Aquarius (Uranus) rules anything to do with the future and originality. This includes astrology, New Age endeavors, the unknown and the UFO phenomenon: He is the inventor and the genius of the zodiac. His mind is able to tap on the occipital realm of consciousness and use a mixture of intuition, high intelligence and objectivity to reach the incredible. No other Mercury position is able to use the mind to such dexterity. Intellectual signs are air elements found in air signs leading to intellectual power. The extreme

Mercury in Aquarius (cont...)	originality of Mercury in Aquarius will need much more than what traditional education can offer an advanced soul. Aquarius rules also electronics, aeronautics, radio and television. Universal matters (understanding in a broad way) and objectivity, are foremost with Mercury in Aquarius. This favors any matter related to the Universal Mind or Astrology. The sign of Aquarius rules universal love and is in opposition to Leo. The sign of Leo rules the 5th house of love and romance (selfish love), while Aquarius rules the 11th house of Universal love of friends and wishes. With Mercury in Aquarius, there is an abundance of concern for the world at large. Thus, mindful and intellectual, Aquarius bestows the gift of universal love as the highest form of respect and understanding to us all.
Mercury in Pisces ☿ ♓	Intuitive and artistic, Mercury in Pisces has a natural rejection to mathematics and details. If the fish swims upstream, the mind will be concerned with the arts and the spirit. If swimming downstream, the mind will be preoccupied with religion, drugs, alcohol, and suffer all forms of guilt. These individuals have the potential

Mercury in Pisces (cont...)	to become great teachers and writers because of their powerful imaginations. Their downfall is the dismissal of rational thought and letting destructive imagination take over. Imaginative fears and phobias come naturally with Mercury in Pisces. As seen with Michelangelo's gift, the powerful imagination leads to an incredible artistic talent. On the negative side, Mercury in Pisces will dream all day long of a course of action instead of taking practical decision and acting upon it. This position attracts religious endeavors, where the icon or deity takes all time and efforts from the soul. An unusually fatalistic trend of thoughts could lead the young soul to the use of drugs and alcohol, leading to madness or homelessness. On a positive side this mercurial position allows the soul to dwell with highly artistic or spiritual matters such as hypnotherapy and astrology.

MARS

Mars rules the color red. It rules steel, machinery, and the country of Germany. Mars principle is to lead and discover any potential by its placement in the chart. In Greek Mythology Mars is called "The Lord of War." It demonstrates the raw nature of man, and rules the animal kingdom. It shows how man could treat man when at war and how animal treats animal in nature. Mars' location by sign indicates the ability to face and deal with danger and the will to survive. Here we see the rough energy of man and its animalistic desire principle. In a man or a woman's chart, Mars always indicates the desire principle. Mars in the female chart indicates subconsciously the type of man she is looking for and his masculinity. Mars in the man's chart indicates how he will show his masculinity, (hunting) or the way he will seduce a woman. His virility and his masculinity will be shown to you through the location of his natal Mars.

PLACEMENT OF MARS IN EACH SIGN

Mars in Aries  	The planet of war into its own sign produces turbo-charged individuals. Remember that Mars is the ruler of Aries or the baby of the zodiac. The soul is on a new level of reincarnation and individuals born with Mars in Aries will learn by mistake. Aries rules the head, brain and face, thus the soul is accident prone to these areas. There is not much time for planning for those born with Mars in Aries. In a woman's chart Mars denotes an assertive, competitive and impatient woman especially if she was born under a fire sign. Those people nurture an inferiority complex and need to affirm themselves immediately with action. You must diligently explain to this soul its impatient and competitive Martian nature and to control impatience. Those souls can accomplish miracles if the energy of Mars is applied constructively to any project. Mars in Aries is an asset but because of the aggressive nature of Mars in its own sign physical and spiritual damage to the soul is a high probability. Mars' location in your chart will give you the strength you need to become a leader in the affairs ruled by the house.

Mars in Taurus  	Taurus is ruled by patient Venus and the bull will bring practicality and patience to the soul. Mars in Taurus brings the solid power to reach balance and harmony needed in the subject's life. All the fiery intensity and tremendous energy of Mars is under the supervision of the steady bull bringing practicality and steadiness to the soul. Subsequently, Mars in this sign is less prone to make or suffer mistakes. An idea of how Mars in Taurus can affects someone's life: Taurus rules the Second House of possessions and Mars rules anything to do with war. Chances are the Mars in Taurus soul will invest in guns, dangerous tools or anything that cuts or is hot. The world of finance is into the world of Mars and could produce an artist cutting diamonds or designing jewelry as Taurus rules also products of the earth. Therefore making or spending money with these dangerous or beautiful items is possible. Mars in Taurus also produces prominent leaders in the financial world. Remember too that Taurus rules the arts, music and singing-- thus Mars' energy could also propel the soul towards those endeavors.

Mars in Gemini ♂ ♊	Here is the planet of war and action receives the intellectual power of Gemini ruled by Mercury. The soul could be verbally aggressive when under attack because Mars is war and action. Hence, Mars in Gemini communicates constantly and will not listen well to others. Mars rules the desire principle, so it stimulates a strong appetite for the world of communication-writing and reading, talking, and selling. The entire world of Gemini is now stimulated by the red energy of Mars. Realize also that Gemini rules brothers and sisters, thus Mars in Gemini could steer war with brothers and sisters. Gemini also rules photography and brings about an interest in this field. Remember also, as Mars is the planet of danger and war, wherever Mars is located in your chart indicates where danger may enter your life. A woman born with Mars in Gemini will tend to get bored quickly if the partner is not mentally stimulating. This will induce infidelity in both genders if the energy of Mars does not find a productive way to express itself. Shooting matches are also common with this position.
Mars in Cancer ♂ ♋	The red the planet of war in the family sign of Cancer. This sign rules food home and security. A strong desire to make and own a house will affect those born with Mars in Cancer.

Mars in Cancer (cont...)	Many have in their hearts and minds, the perfect house planned and designed. They will strive to improve the value of their home and with it the danger to hurt oneself with sharp instruments or dangerous tools. Those born with this Mars placement must learn about the Moon fluctuations (see my yearly Moon Power). Doing so will be very valuable for home improvement or real estate projects. Cancer rules the stomach, and in the medical aspect of this work, always tell your clients not to eat when they are upset because of the possibility of developing ulcers caused by stress. These would come from either the use of hot sauce, red pepper or most of all being depressed and changing the food into poison, burning the walls of their stomach. Again they should not eat when they are upset. This placement of Mars in the sign of Cancer will induce interest or professions involving home, restaurants, hotels, real estate, clothing and general security.

Mars in Leo 	When two fire signs connect, sparks are anticipated in all the affairs regulating the Fifth House. Leo/Sun, the house of love and romance, receives the Martian turbo-charged energy reaching for the stage. The individual has a strong desire to succeed and will work excessively. Mars' desire principle will aim at the world of Leo (love, romance, children, creativity, music, etc.). The soul is prone to accidents or violence in the affairs of the heart. In the medical aspect of Astropsychology, Leo rules the heart while Mars rules sharp instruments (suggesting surgery). They may be prone to heart attacks inducing surgery if they abuse their bodies or the good life. Mars in Leo will also be very demanding to his children. With Mars the soul is very concerned with success, while Leo rules fame and children. Traditionally the Fifth House rules the affairs of love, romance, and children. It is important to care and guide the children diligently and not destroy their creative nature by making too many demands. Mars rules danger, violence, action and fast sports. Leo loves any form of sport and will breed anything from a football player to a race car driver. Those souls are totally stimulated by dangerous or violent sports. On a negative side an unhealthy desire for fire could be generated and in the worst case, an arsonist. If Mars' destructive energy goes undetected and is allowed to express itself, the creative principle becomes violent and destructive. On a more positive note the desire is there to create a large family.

Mars in Virgo  	Virgo rules health, paperwork, details and general organization. Mars in Virgo produces a strong desire towards perfection in all areas of the subject's life. Mars in the sign of Virgo breeds the "workaholic," due to the service principle found in this sign. The strong desire for perfection and accuracy can also bring about stress and disagreement with co-workers. On the positive side, Mars in Virgo will gear the soul towards organizational and health endeavors. Remember Mars is the desire principle. On the medical aspect of Astropsychology, Virgo rules the cleansing process and the digestive tract. Virgo rules anything to do with elimination and cleansing. Mars also rules sharp instruments used in surgical procedures. This position produces detail-oriented, precise surgeons. On a negative note, Mars in Virgo generates problems with the lower abdomen or intestines which could require surgery. The digestive tract might be sensitive to changes in diet especially when certain foods are omitted (omitting red meat and becoming a vegetarian). In some extreme cases Mars accentuates a strong desire for virginity (Virgo is the Virgin Mary). The desire for sexual abstinence brings about chastity and translates into a nun marrying a deity such as Jesus. In doing so, the subconscious Martian desire for purity is then established.

Mars in Libra ♂ ♎	Libra is ruled by Venus and this is the sign of partnership and marriage with Mars, the planet of war. The desire principle is for partnership, justice and commitment. If there is any planet in astrology that needs refinement, it is the planet Mars. Mars' aggressiveness and war-like attitude is smoothed over with the influence of peace-oriented Libra. Souls born with Mars in Libra nurture a strong desire to reach balance and harmony in all areas of the human experience. Thus many explore the world of interior design, Astropsychology, the law, or the arts. Mars in Libra nurtures a deep desire to fight for the weak and oppressed (someone like a " Zorro"). Those born with Mars in Libra must recognize their limits and avoid entering friend's conflicts. The aspiration to build a solid partnership can conflict with Mars' aggressive nature. This often destroys the established harmony of a marriage. Recognizing and using both the Venus (love) and Mars (desire) principles accordingly, a chance to maintain harmony in matrimony is a strong possibility.
Mars in Scorpio ♂ ♏	Scorpio souls are classified as either the Lizard or the Eagle of the zodiac. Scorpio rules the medical field, life and death, sex, investigation, drama and passion. Mars in Scorpio is in its most positive or negative position. The Martian energy can be applied

Mars in Scorpio (cont....)	to any creative or destructive actions for or against others. The young soul (Scorpio/Lizard) will be the one that rapes others and stabs them to death. The desire principle of Mars (for good or evil) is operating in a most passionate way and depicts its very sensitive and drastic position. Police profilers and psychologists alike are missing an incredible amount of real information pertaining to the born killer. Hopefully many will acquire true knowledge and educate themselves with Astropsychology. The energies of both Pluto (power) and Mars (desire) can also be granted to an advanced Scorpio/Eagle and have very different and productive outcomes. Pluto rules both the police force (investigations) and the mafia. The advanced soul would not misuse the Scorpionic/Martian energy by destructively repeatedly stabbing an individual to death for sexual purposes. The Eagle would rather be the homicide detective or forensic scientist and gather all the facts. His efforts would in time put the killer or sexual offender behind bars away from society. Remember that Scorpio rules the medical field, life and death, investigation, and Mars is the planet that rules sharp instruments. The Martian/Plutonic desire principle is applied into the world of life and death and investigation. This position breeds people who work for the CIA, FBI

Mars in Scorpio (cont...)	and the police force. Souls born with Mars in Scorpio are totally fearless in front of death. They are in fact stimulated and regenerate in situations of supreme danger and death. They also observe their own reaction and their own behavior in front of death. On a negative note this position induces the destructive emotions of an abusive husband who ends up dead or in jail after confronting the police force. Mars in Scorpio in the 7th House of marriage could attract abusive partners where ego and will would battle to death. On a more positive note there is no limit to what an Eagle soul can accomplish with the deadly mixture of Pluto and Mars in the chart. Astrophiles are advised to counsel a Mars in Scorpio client to exercise control of their powerful emotions and to let go of any suffered offense. Mars in Scorpio individuals make bad enemies. They are the resentful individuals who have strong vengeance streaks towards wrongdoers. A black or white attitude is often present and translates into "either you kill me or I kill you". This is not an enemy to have in any way shape or form.

Mars in Scorpio (cont . . .)	So think twice when you deal with somebody who has Mars in Scorpio. Scorpio rules the genital areas in both men and women. Surgery or inflicted danger in these areas is a possibility. A negative young Scorpio soul will lead a nightlife where drugs, alcohol, and sex will play an important part. Thus a strong Venus in Scorpio, Mars in Scorpio, Mercury in Scorpio, or Dragon's Head or Tail in Scorpio is prominent in the chart. Here, the true Scorpionic regeneration principle is meeting the desire principle of Mars. The house where this incredible duo is located is an area of extreme danger or extreme accomplish-meats. Find out where Scorpio and Mars are in your chart and work positively so regeneration and rebirth will take place safely.
Mars in Sagittarius 	In the medical aspect of Astro-psychology, Sagittarius rules the lower back or the connection between man and the horse. Mars in Sagittarius could induce back problems or injury. A chronic back problem could also be present and you may want to suggest investing in a good, firm mattress, as this will help their backs immensely. One of the best ways to ease the pain is to take a hot shower and run the hot water on the back and to do a series of light stretches.

Mars in Sagittarius (cont...)	Mars in Sagittarius produces a strong desire for travel, education and bringing knowledge to others. Often, the acquired knowledge is codified and based on what was learned earlier in the subject's life, and could easily produce righteous preachers and religious fanatics. Mars is war and desire, and many are willing to fight and in some extreme cases, die for their convictions. The desire to teach and educate others is produced by both Mars and Sagittarius. Their lack of critical thinking will accept archaic religious material written thousands of years ago (such as the Bible). Mars in Sagittarius produces strong subconscious desires to promote peace and truth through printed material and rules. On a more progressive note Mars in Sagittarius' energy is used to aim for higher knowledge, symbolized by shooting the arrows into the sky towards the stars. This soul is blessed with true enlightenment, a solid cosmic consciousness, and will travel far and fast to teach the new found truth. Mars in Sagittarius stimulates an interest in working

Mars in Sagittarius (cont...)	with animals. You will often find a strong Mars in Sagittarius working with pets, dogs and horses (greyhound or horse racing). Mars in Sagittarius enjoys the desert and wide-open spaces where speed danger and fire stimulate the soul.
Mars in Capricorn  ♑	This is a good position for the unruly planet of Mars to be because of the down to earth and practical attitude of Capricorn. Capricorn is a natural engineer (structure) and combined with Mars (explosions & fire), it could produce a scientist. The energy of Mars in Capricorn often produces a strong desire to fight for the system and lead the soul in a position of power within the government (Army/Navy). The soul strives for a position of structured power. Mars can also be used destructively, and produces weaponry designers. Many souls born with Mars in Capricorn are operating as great officers in the military. The desire for war (Mars) meets Capricorn's desire for status and power. A strong desire and involvement with politics is often present.

Mars in Capricorn (cont...)	The chosen career will involve fire and danger such as police officers and navy generals to concerned fireman. For better or for worse, Mars in Capricorn will support the system hoping for the government to support them in the last part of their lives. On the medical aspect of Astropsychology, Capricorn rules the knees, the joints and the skin. With dangerous Mars in this sign, accidents and surgery are a strong possibility. Work could be done on the knees by replacing a joint, or fixing a bone, or surgery on the skin (face-lifts). Capricorn rules old-age, and is the oldest living sign of the zodiac. Mars in Capricorn may brings about a business where the elderly are taken care of. Mars in Capricorn supports a strong desire for mechanical endeavors and engineering, leading to careers with Uncle Sam. Misuse of power and snobbery characterizes this position of Mars in Capricorn and can be used for better or for worse.

Mars in Aquarius  ♒	The desire principle is within the world of Aquarius (the New Age). Mars in Aquarius will gear the soul towards anything futuristic and universal. Involvement in high tech computers, Universal Love, enlightenment, including astrology and UFOs, is often present. The Aquarian energy of the future receives the desire principle of Mars. Mars is the planet of war while Aquarius rules groups. Here you could have one assembly fighting another group such as New Agers versus religious fanatics. Aquarius rules the Eleventh House of wishes and friends. Mars in this sign indicates the type of friends a soul will attract within its group. The common force of Mars is applied for the specific purpose of the group. Mars in Aquarius could indicate where danger can enter your life because of the aggressive friends' endeavors. It could indicate the use of Mars' energy for sports endeavors with teammates. Aquarius likes sports and has an attraction to group organizations. Aquarius rules electricity and any form of radiation. So when born with Mars is in Aquarius a chance for electrocution or lightening accidents is a possibility. On the medical aspect, Aquarius rules the area below the knees and part of the inventive brain. The soul is constantly geared to explore avenues involving the future of mankind through invention and originality. There are strong desires to promote freedom, universal love, mental exploration and the New Age.

Mars in Pisces  	Mars' desire principle can be applied for the fish to swim upstream or downstream. On the negative side, harmful emotions and self destruction by abuse of chemicals, drugs and alcohol is stirred by the power of Mars. Positively, Mars will support all artistic and spiritual endeavors, pushing the creative values of Pisces upstream. The desire principle of Mars within the undoing, extraordinarily ethereal world of Pisces could conflict the soul. Mars in Pisces supports a strong desire to enter the world of religion or philosophy. On the medical aspect, Pisces rules the feet. Water is where danger can enter the life of the subject. Tell your client to be careful around water and not to put stress on the feet, especially when running, so as to avoid injury. Mars in Pisces mixes fire and water, attracting danger in jobs such as commercial divers or underwater welders and boat racing. The desire principle is to compete and deal with both fire and water. Neptune (Lord of the Seas) rules Pisces and hospitals, churches, synagogues, institutions, asylums, and deception, where the strong desire to alleviate mankind's suffering can be exercised. Pisces regenerate from their feet. Pisces needs water and regenerates from the magnetic fields of the earth. Subsequently, it is not a good idea for Pisces to spend too much time barefoot on carpeted, concrete, or wood floors. Pisces should walk barefoot on the grass or on the beach to help the regeneration principle.

SATURN

Saturn rules structure and rebuilding. He tears down in order to rebuild stronger and better, and is the principle of hard work and dedication. Saturn is a gloomy planet producing the fear principle. Saturn also rules the freezing code, as in frozen foods. Souls born with a strong Capricorn, the Moon or Dragon including Mercury in this sign, possess strong rational minds to solve any problems. A young Capricorn soul will have problems dealing with spirituality or metaphysics because of the strong rationale and sense of practicality. Capricorn's symbol has a fishtail which symbolizes metaphysics. Like other earth signs such as Virgo or Taurus, Capricorn should use his fishtail and realize that though something cannot be touched, cut in pieces or explored physically, does not mean it does not exist. You will want to use a rational approach when explaining mysticism to them such as: although they cannot see or touch the rays emitted from a microwave oven, a television set, a computer or radio, the rays are still there manifesting into images, sounds etc. It is sometimes quite a challenge for a young soul to understand the value of the intuitive domain and the impact of those stars upon us. However, Capricorn has good eyes and is very observant. Thus once educated, he will acknowledge the obvious working of the Universal Mind upon mankind's psyche.

Saturn represents the career area, public standing, popularity and general structure. These stimulate positions or careers with large corporations, governments, or cities. Saturn is a Karmic Sign and he is called in Greek Mythology the "Great Malefic." Wherever this planet or sign resides in a chart, it denotes much of your karma and in some ways your past life. You may have collapsed and suffered losses but Saturn wants you to do it again and do it right this time around.

SATURN AND THE MEDICAL ASPECT

The freezing-fear principle

On the medical aspect of Astropsychology, Saturn rules the skin, bones and the knees. Because of the Fish Tail in the Goat symbol, it is beneficial to teach the person to use the Universal Law, to follow the waxing and waning of the Moon. Illness and disease come faster within the location of Saturn by house or sign. The "Great Malefic" induces depression, negativity, lack of survival instincts, and refusals or inabilities to regenerate with spirituality. Slowly but surely the decay principle takes place spiritually then physically. The door is now open for disease and death. Your mission is to re-establish a regeneration principle through creativity, education, hope and faith and love to the subject.

PLACEMENT OF SATURN IN EACH SIGN

Saturn in Aries ♄ ♈	Because of the freezing power of Saturn, the competitive qualities of Aries and its anger are tempered and sometimes even stopped. Aries wants to go forward but Saturn makes him cautious, generating a fear of expressing the power of Mars. This insecurity will translate into excuses not to advance such as; I'm not good, I cannot do it or I will fail, etc. The Martian soul must learn to structure and build confidence in himself. In some cases the opposite is experienced and the Aries' power takes over pushing aside Saturn's cautious nature. The young soul jumps without thinking about the consequences of the harsh lessons which follow. Learning by mistake is often the case. With Saturn in Aries, the soul must learn to rebuild his or her entire self esteem, and the entire personality. These are the people staring at themselves in front of the mirror for hours, looking for every possible reason not to act in the game of life. The young soul will anticipate all possible failures and see only a world of failure. The Saturnian detective and cautious power is in full action slowing down the Aries enterprising spirit.

Saturn in Aries (cont . . .)	Saturn is on "the self" when in the first house in Aries. Saturn in Aries on the medical aspect of Astropsychology produces chronic depressions, headaches, sinus problems and dizziness when bending down too quickly. Aries rules the head but Saturn restricts the amount of blood and oxygen going to the veins complicating functions of the brain to work freely. Saturn's freezing principle affects any area of the chart he is found in. Counteract the chilly power of Saturn by positive thinking, exercise, and ingesting red meat, hot sauces, red wine, herbs and vitamins. All that Martian food will provide aid to neutralize Saturn. Again Saturn rules the freezing principle. The very fear principle will act as a motor force, propelling the soul towards a position of leadership where quick action and right judgment to avoid danger is concerned.
Saturn in Taurus  	Saturn's fear principle will be felt with security and possessions. The reaction produces a tendency to overwork the mind and body. Saturn in Taurus breeds financial wizards and bank builders. The soul can also be geared to work in banks, beauty parlors, or with the arts, etc. Usually money was

Saturn in Taurus (cont...)	easily gained with the soul in previous lives and in some occasions, wasted or used to control others. If you have inherited Saturn in the sign of Taurus you must realize the real value of people and not their possessions. The fear principle produces a constant apprehension of not having enough money or establishing security. On the medical aspect of Astropsychology, Taurus rules the neck. Counteract neck tension with hot water bottles, acupuncture, gentle massage, etc. (Tea Recipe for soothing the throat: Boil two cups of water. Place a ½ teaspoon of fresh hyssop and a dash of fresh cinnamon into a tea strainer and put into a cup. Pour in one cup of boiling water and let the tea steep till warm. Add organic honey to desired sweetness.) Also, it wouldn't hurt to elevate the feet and place a hot water bottle on or around the pelvic area. Capricorn is a winter sign while Taurus rules the neck and throat. Whenever the weather gets cool the stress will be felt in your neck, so make sure you protect that area. Keep a sweater handy, and your neck fully protected against the cold air. Even if you have to get the mail or throw away the garbage keep this area protected. If air conditioning or a fan is blowing on your neck, have the vents redirected to blow away from you. Remember to stay away from drafts on your neck and shoulder areas.

Saturn in Gemini ♄ ♊	Saturn's freezing power will be felt in communication and in some cases produces speech problems. There is also an inner apprehension of not speaking well, due to a lack of education. Gemini being an intellectual air sign needs to express ideas but Saturn's restrictive power has to be dealt with and produces fears of this nature; "am I going to say the right thing, am I going to look stupid, do you think I am educated enough?" Saturn in Gemini forces the soul to be scared and insecure about what he knows and what he says. Saturn in this sign will send the person to the library and turn the soul into a professional student to counteract that fear. On the medical aspect of Astropsychology, Gemini rules the lungs, arms, fingers, legs and the nervous system. Counteract nervous tension with yoga and neutralize the acids in the mouth by gargling with warm water. Relax a bit. Elevate your feet to take the strain off the lower lumbar region. Try not to strain your voice by taking short breaks after each sentence if you must speak. Fight allergies by vaporizing the room and making sure windows are closed to avoid drafts (plug in the vaporizer and pour menthol and eucalyptus oil in the well to vaporize the room). On a positive note this position produces great speakers, writers and prominent salespeople.

Saturn in Cancer ♄ ♋	Saturn's fear principle will be felt within the home and the family. Stress will be experienced in all affairs related to general security. Often pressure and restriction is imposed upon the soul at an early age and during the upbringing. Sometimes it forces an elder person (Saturn rules old people) to take care of a child due to the mother's or father's sickness or inability to take on responsibility. Saturn in Cancer is making the soul constantly worry about close family member's security. Saturn in Cancer indicates a serious fear of not being able to establish and gain security, food or a home. To counteract this inner fear, Saturn guides the soul towards hotels, restaurants or careers in real estate. On a positive note, many souls will reach a high position of management and will work for the welfare of children, as Cancer rules the family and security principle. Others, more spiritually inclined, will flourish and work as Astropsychologists, to free and feed the soul spiritually. Saturn in Cancer works in restaurants to fill the stomach, but when Saturn in Cancer works on the spirit, it fills the mind. Spirit is the way of freeing and bringing security. Cancer rules the stomach and the breasts. Saturn in this sign tends to retain water. Moderate your salt intake and to counteract Saturn, do not eat when under stress or when you are upset.

Saturn in Cancer (cont...)	Take a stroll along the beach, go to the park and walk on the grass, rejuvenate by relaxing on the beach or on the grass, feel the warmth of the sun. Don't drink cold beverages or add ice to water because the cold freezes the digestive juices and enzymes. As a general rule do not consume beverages that are too spicy, too hot or too cold. Learn to relax your mind and your tummy will thank you for it! Also, sip rather than drink your beverages. For medicinal purposes feel free to add a mint leaf, a piece of fresh ginger, or some fennel seeds to help the stomach discomfort, or add all of them if you like, you decide. Tea Recipe to make the tummy feel better: Add to boiling water, fresh mint, a slice of fresh ginger and fennel seeds. If you want it sweet, add a licorice tea bag and let it steep 'til "just right." curl up in a warm cuddly blanket, turn on some soothing music, recline back and relax. If you live near a beach, (Cancers love the water) grab your cd, headphones and say hello to the sun and sand!

Saturn in Leo ♄ ♌	The soul experiences Saturn's fear principle in love and creativity. Often a fear of fame and fortune or bringing children into this world is present. Leo rules the fifth house of love, romance, children, the arts and creativity, and with it the option for a woman to create a child. Saturn in Leo freezes the reproductive organs of a woman making pregnancy difficult or impossible. The same applies for a man with Saturn freezing the subject's procreation principle. In some cases the restrictive power of Saturn is so strong the child may be born premature, deformed and dies. Saturn's rules karma and all parties involved have specific reasons to suffer the losses. Usually this position indicates a mother who is extremely concerned with her kid's education and welfare and constantly worries about them. In some extreme cases the parent becomes much too concerned and overbearing. One of the parent's own failure to reach fame is a subconscious motivating fear and they become much too concerned with the accomplishments and success of their own child. Saturn (the parents) in Leo (the child) forces the child to be on stage at a very early age and work harder to reach for (their) best through the child. The parents make the child compromise childhood for fame and success. The parental thrust

Saturn in Leo (cont...)	denies the child his childhood by pushing him into adulthood, responsibility and accomplishment much too early. Saturn in Leo also indicates a practical reason to be in love attracting a much younger or older person. This could produce a con artist or a gold-digger. Medical Aspect: Leo rules the heart, thus the possibility of a heart attack due to stress. A fear of death and decay is often present forcing an over concern with health matters and exercise.
Saturn in Virgo ♄ ♍	Souls born with Saturn in Virgo have a fear of not establishing a good service to the world. Virgo rules also health, perfection and organization. Two earth signs coming together with Capricorn (career) and Virgo (service to the world) they get along quite well. Virgo is an intellectual sign and relies on its critical mind to deal with details and organization. Saturn helps Virgo along constructively to bring about completion and structure in all endeavors. Virgo is fussy and picky while Saturn is motivated for a position of power in a structural world (the astronomers, the scientists).

Saturn in Virgo (cont...)	Thus perfectionism is brought to its highest level. With this combination, there is not much left for intuition or imagination. Only the "fear" of what can be done properly or whether it is done well enough is plaguing these concerned individuals. Saturn rules wealth, career, public standing and honor, while Virgo rules service or a less glamorous position. This brings about the fear of not being able to perform good service, and becomes the motivating factor to reach a high position in the corporate world. Medical Aspect: Virgo rules the intestines and the nervous system. Saturn in Virgo tends to freeze the already slow digestive tract, and is prone to problems with gas, indigestion, bowel irregularity, hemorrhoids and colitis. Skin eruptions may also surface due to nervousness being internalized. Nature is telling them to not worry so much, to relax a bit more, get some fresh air and sunshine. They should eat better, incorporate perhaps lighter, fresher fruit, lean meats and lamb, and to include steamed leafy green vegetables into their diets. For instance, bananas, apples, and papaya have wonderful properties of adding bulk and fiber internally. These are easily digested and assimilated in times of stress,

Saturn in Virgo (cont...)	and it helps nourish their souls once again. If at all possible they should omit caffeine from their diet, and stay away from coffee and regular tea. It is beneficial for them to take strolls along the beach, go to the park and walk on the grass, rejuvenate by relaxing on the beach or on the grass, and feel the warmth of the sun. Like Cancer who rules the stomach, those born with Saturn in Virgo should not drink cold beverages or add ice to water, for it freezes the digestive juices and enzymes. As a general rule, do not consume beverages either too hot or too cold. Herbal teas for Saturn in Virgo are as follows: For constipation — chickweed, ginger, and rhubarb root (alone or in very small quantities together). For stomach, indigestion and gas – thyme, bay leaves, fennel, ginseng, chamomile, and wild cherry (each alone or small quantity mixed together). For nervousness — chamomile, celery, dill, peach leaves, rosemary, and spearmint, wild cherry (each alone or mixed in very small quantities together). For diarrhea – peppermint, ginger, plantain, wintergreen, fenugreek, hyssop (alone or mix with very small quantities together). Sweeten with organic honey or with a licorice tea bag.

Saturn in Libra ♄ ♎	Here the soul has a fear to make a commitment or sign a contract. They constantly wonder whether a partner is able to give them what they really need. Saturn in Libra produces a high level of divorces or legal activity. The soul is expecting to receive as much as he gives (I do this; you do that, and vice a versa). Libra is the sign of psychology and rules also the legal system. So many great psychologists, legal workers, and attorneys are born with Saturn in Libra. A Saturn in Libra person must realize that he can only receive what he can give. Balance, harmony, justice and fairness is what this position has to offer. There is a very strong sense of justice with Saturn in Libra. In extreme cases, these people nurture a great fear of not being able to make or keep their commitment or get married. Medical Aspect: Libra, which rules the kidneys and Saturn, may build stones there. The kidneys may be lazy and may not perform correctly and with it the probability of surgery.
Saturn in Scorpio ♄ ♏	Here the souls nurture an inner fear of sex or transmitted diseases wondering about sexually adequacy. This position of Saturn is one of the major reasons for many divorces. Someone born with the moon, a Venus or Mars in Scorpio produces individuals with strong sexual urges.

Saturn in Scorpio (cont...)	Saturn freezes the Scorpionic sex principle or may affect negatively the sexual organs. This position of Saturn can also concern the subject mentally (you don't feel good about sex), or physically (small penis, etc). The birthing for woman born with Saturn in Scorpio could be intense and painful.
Saturn in Sagittarius ♄ ♐	Here the soul nurtures a fear of foreigners and foreign lands and may avoid traveling. An avid consumption of religious material is seen as the only truth and produces a fear of expanding the mind. The positive aspect of Saturn in Sagittarius is to expand outside of conventional religious teachings and teach others about their new findings. The soul needs to realize the limits of the codification of thought and the damage religious poisoning can do to others or oneself. What is written and accepted as truth by the majority does not mean it is the truth. Saturn in Sagittarius struggles with this fear to expand and seeks to free itself from spiritual limitations. In extreme cases the soul is totally reluctant to expand outside of the scriptures and becomes a righteous promoter of religious archaic materials. On a positive note Saturn in Sagittarius produces great teachers and makes good veterinarians.

Saturn in Sagittarius (cont . . .)	Negatively, it produces a compulsive gambler which firmly, blindly, believes he will hit the jackpot and go home with millions of dollars. It is the same blind and deceptive faith put on a deity. In the worst scenario, Saturn in Sagittarius produces professional students, mental snobs and religious fanatics, spreading their own mental limitations or fears. Saturn in Sagittarius paralyzes the mind from exploring and could induce trouble or danger in traveling foreign lands. There is a deep concern to learn philosophy in general or about Indian cultures. These individuals will have to expand their horizons and learn different ethnic values (religion, philosophy, and metaphysics). Medical Aspect: Sagittarius rules the back and with it problems or surgery on the back.
Saturn in Capricorn ♄ ♑	Saturn the planet of fear in his own sign produces individuals extremely concerned with position, career and honors. The fear of failure is quite strong and concerns of people misjudging them is a high probability.

Saturn in Capricorn (cont...)	On a positive note the soul will build self esteem and courage through setbacks, and the experiences will bring about success later in life. Capricorn is a karmic sign, very patient and honorable. Hard work and determination will bring them to the top of their chosen careers. Medical Aspect: The bones, skin and joints are prone to stress and problems (arthritis).
Saturn in Aquarius ♄ ♒	This is one of the best positions for Saturn. Mostly because the structuring power of Saturn is in the sign of Aquarius or the 11th house of wishes and friends and opportunity. Saturn in Aquarius may bring older friends or difficult friends but in some way will structure wishes. On a negative note there are little or no friends available or a fear of new friends and a fear of groups (militias or guru leaders). To them, building a group brings a sense of security against other groups. Their lesson is to join a progressive group not a dangerous militia or deceiving religious group. The advanced soul will bring about a healing New Age energy group, working towards unity and universal brotherhood. Remember that Aquarius rules mental power and psychic energy.

Saturn in Aquarius (cont...)	The refined energy of Uranus rules the future, and Saturn (Capricorn) rules structure and engineering. Geniuses, astronauts, pilots and inventors were born with Saturn in Aquarius. These individuals are masters in high-tech and make for great astrologers and Astropsychologists. Saturn in Aquarius is in the world of the incredible UFO phenomenon and produces great writers and precise researchers.
Saturn in Pisces ♄ ♓	Pisces is a karmic sign and Saturn is a karmic planet. It is the enlightened Pisces swimming into the light who can perceive the difference between imagination and divine information. This position breeds people who work in hospitals, for the red cross, or for anyone experiencing trouble with addiction to drugs and alcohol. Saturn in Pisces is in a very, very delicate and dedicated position and produces hypnotherapists and natural psychics. Because of guilt and depression the soul can swim downstream and sink into Neptune's deceiving waters. On a positive note the soul is allowed to swim upstream towards oneself or god. Those advanced souls possess true light and can lead anyone into the cosmic realm of consciousness.

Saturn in Pisces (cont...)	On a negative note religion, imagination and depression take over the rational side of Pisces, sapping away the potential for spiritual freedom. Medical Aspect: Pisces rules the feet and toes. Walking bare foot on the grass and or on the sand at the beach allows connection with the magnetic fields of the earth. This position of Saturn breeds true artists once the imagination is used in a productive way. In extreme cases, a fear of madness or hell could lead the poisoned soul to a mental institution or to jail. A fear or love of water is often present and may lead the soul towards oceanic work, oil prospecting or chemicals and medical research.

JUPITER

Jupiter is the largest planet in our solar system. It is called in Greek Mythology, "The Lord of Lords" or "The Protector." Jupiter is the largest planet in our solar system and its enormous gravitational force acts as a guardian to the earth. Thus, as experienced with the Shoemaker-Levy comets, any celestial detritus was absorbed by Jupiter before getting to us and destroying our planet. Extraterrestrial intelligence set up our solar system this way and for good reasons I might add. Jupiter rules the sign of Sagittarius and Jupiter will always rescue and protect his own children by bringing them luck. As represented by its symbol (the horse, the man, the bow and the arrow), Jupiter's energy induces philosophy, traveling, teaching, and breeds truth-seekers. Souls born in December will be dealing with foreigners and traveling to foreign lands. Doing so will bring about knowledge to be shared to the rest of us.

Jupiter's location in a person's chart predisposes the individual with opportunities to learn and search widely through mental exploration and traveling. Jupiter's location by house and sign indicates how luck and growth will be experienced by the individual. Jupiter will bless you with endless good fortune in certain pursuits related to your message. It shows where good karma is due to you. The downfall of Jupiter's impact in your chart is an over concern with the codification of thought, or traditional, academic education. Combined with the righteous-faith code, Jupiter's exaggerated principles produces obvious opposites. You will find this crowd operating under Jupiter's rigid jurisdictions in various departments of the human experience such as judges, atheists, scientists (mental snobs) or priests, ministers, and gurus (religious fanatics).

PLACEMENT OF JUPITER IN EACH SIGN

Jupiter in Aries 	You may have inherited a stocky physique with a very competitive mind. In women Jupiter in Aries tends to display itself on their upper thighs and buttocks. You may be born under any sign of the Zodiac and still have these physical characteristics. This is certainly due to a strong but hidden moon or dragon in Sagittarius in your chart. With Jupiter (expansive principle) in the first house, exercise is paramount, as you are prone to obesity. Mental and physical activity or sports are a must if you have this celestial position. Aries rules the head (eyes, nose, teeth, head and brain). The opportunity will be given to the soul to learn and teach others about different cultures and philosophies. On the negative side the Mars desire principle (Aries is ruled by Mars) can ally with the worst of Jupiter

Jupiter in Aries (cont....)	(codification of thoughts), and breed extremists of all sorts. The soul is given the opportunity to educate itself within the world of Aries. He may end up working as an optician, a psychologist, a dentist or in an advanced case, an Astropsychologist. The soul is very concerned in learning everything about himself so as to reach his best potential and lead in the chosen field. As Jupiter also rules teaching, chances are that these people will invest in education. With it comes the option to be leaders in teaching whatever they have learned. Jupiter in Aries induces a strong interest in knowing everything about oneself. Speed, mechanical engineering or anything that has to do with fire, danger and competition will benefit with Jupiter's protection.
Jupiter in Taurus ♃ ♉	The opportunity is given the soul to educate and establish himself and prosper within the financial world of Taurus (banking, finance, gems, massage and aesthetics). Venus rules Taurus, and Jupiter's daughter brings even more artistic value to this lucky position. Jupiter also rules Sagittarius and gambling and the faith in feeling lucky.

Jupiter in Taurus (cont...)	This could bring disaster to the person by producing compulsive gamblers. Jupiter in Taurus will always support endeavors related to products of the earth, aesthetics, the arts, and foreign financial endeavors.
Jupiter in Gemini ♃ ♊	The opportunity is given the soul to prosper within the world of Gemini (communication, transportation, writing, etc.) Jupiter rules also the publishing world and in this sign, promotes speaking and writing endeavors. Many souls born with this position are masters in communication. They fly planes, drive taxis or big rigs, or are international teachers. Many will be radio hosts and promote the sales of books all around the world. As always with Jupiter's sense of faith and rigid codes, the mercurial principle can also produce loud and obnoxious ministers and bible promoters. Jupiter rules luck, protection, expansion, education, and the publication all of the above on a very large scale. A gift of learning and teaching languages is often present and could produce motivational speakers.

Jupiter in Cancer ♃ ♋	Here the opportunity is given to the soul to feed and protect the world at large and prosper within the world of Cancer (family, real estate, food, clothing etc.) McDonalds and other leading food industries are a good example of Jupiter in this sign. Other advanced souls may decide to feed the world in a more spiritual way and you will find this crowd working on programs to alleviate pain and suffering in foreign grounds. Jupiter rules the Indians and wide-open spaces, deserts and foreigners. The soul may operate in any of those areas bringing relief and hope to others. Jupiter's expansive and religious principles could also produce estate planners and the desire to teach others in remote areas. Chances are that the soul will find the resources to build a house or a church in a remote area or in a foreign land. Often the subjects marry foreigners and operate in a foreign country. Cancer is very traditional while Jupiter is morals and codes. On a negative note Jupiter in Cancer induces a deep concern to teach or harass all the family members into the followed or established religious path and respective deity. In a more advanced case, Jupiter's benevolent nature is used constructively by teaching high metaphysics and the respect of nature and animals. Jupiter will always answer your questions if you dare to ask in a big way!

Jupiter in Leo ♃ ♌	Here the opportunity is given the soul to benefit and grow within the world of Leo (fame and fortune, children, love and romance, singing, dancing, speculation and gambling). Chances are the person will spend many years educating himself with foreigners in foreign lands. All the while the lucky planet Jupiter will bring about serious growth and protection in all aspects of the subject's life. Jupiter's principles will bring a strong desire to learn and teach artistic endeavors and with it the option to raise large sums for the children. Leo rules France and Italy and if you were born with this celestial intonation, the options are there for fame and fortune from or in those countries. A French, Italian, or an art teacher from any country is a practical way to represent Jupiter's potential in the sign of Leo. On a negative note, Jupiter's sense of faith and rigid codes combine with Leo's desire for fame, and can produce loud and obnoxious ministers. This lunatic crowd is easily detected by seeing their spiritual religious pride, over- acting, their sense of drama, and wearing enormous jewelry on national stages.

Jupiter in Virgo ♃ ♍	Jupiter's blessings are given the soul within the world of Virgo (health, service, editing, plants, clothing and work). The protective and lucky planet of Jupiter will help these individuals with any endeavors regulating communication (Mercury). On a negative note, the strongly exaggerated religious inclinations of Jupiter, combined with puritanical Virgo (Virgin Mary), can produce interesting characters ranging from health fanatics to religious extremists totally concerned with purity. Michael Jackson walking around with a dust mask to avoid breathing impurities, or a nun's high desire for chastity are good examples of the amplification principle involving Jupiter in this sign. On a more positive note, Jupiter in Virgo produces people responsible for nature, the environment, and they are great organizers. The strong Virgo sense of detail, health and structure is applied constructively for the benefit of society. Hence producing great health and environmental teachers and in some cases the disposal of the physical human envelope or mortician workers. A gift with plants and gardening is often present.

Jupiter in Libra ♃ ♎	Jupiter will bring many opportunities to the soul to learn and teach the best of Libra's world (the law, the arts, (Astropsychology, psychology, interior designing). On a negative note, the strong religious and exaggeration principle of Jupiter, combined with Libra's sense of law, can produce professional students who are reluctant to challenge printed material. A lack of critical thinking can also produce religious fanatics, especially if the subject was born with a weak mercury (the mind). On a more advanced plane, the soul will be given the option to study matters related to all of Jupiter's affairs (the Indian's world, philosophy, foreign affairs, languages and higher laws). Personal involve-meats with business partners and foreigners are stimulated, protected and favored. A strong positive Jupiter in Libra produces world traveling lawyers, judges and proficient diplomats.

Jupiter in Scorpio ♃ ♏	Jupiter will give serious options for education involving Scorpio matters (science, medicine, sex, witchcraft, corporate endeavors, research, metaphysics). Scorpio's secretive, investigative nature and desire for power combined with Jupiter's ethics and rules produces FBI and CIA agents, and all police endeavors. Scorpio is a metaphysical sign but in a young soul's case (the Lizard) or with religious poisoning, the strong passionate nature of Scorpio can and will become deadly. A Jupiter and Pluto mixture is a time bomb waiting to go off, where the soul is willing to die for its deep principles (fanaticism and terrorism). Regeneration always takes place when the old is replaced with the new, and when the soul is forced to learn about different cultures traveling the world. In some cases, a tremendous amount of wealth is exchanged on a daily basis via the stock market. The soul will be put in a position where he will participate in handling others' people resources, and produces insurance agents, state and financial planners and the IRS working force.

Jupiter in Sagittarius ♃ ♐	This is a dignified position where the ruler is located in its own sign, reinforcing both the positive or negative effects of the sign itself. Here the opportunity is given the soul to make a karmic contribution to society for good or for bad. (philosophy, religion, the codification of thought, publishing and teaching). The option to aim and throw the centaur's arrows up (to the stars) towards the Universal Mind, or down into books (religious materials) is given to the soul. With it, there is the danger of missing God's celestial design and manifestation, for the preacher's religiously codified words. These people are great scholars. On the positive side, the soul is given the option to reach for true light and then teach the newly found light to the world via speaking, traveling and publishing. The ultimate goal can only be reached through traveling, mental exploration, critical thinking and mental challenges from foreigners. In some cases these individuals are totally incapable of passing the rigid teachings of their particular religions and appear to the more advanced souls as extremely righteous, nurturing a fear of evil or Satan. The extreme exaggeration of Jupiter meets the extreme codification of thoughts.

Jupiter in Capricorn ♃ ♑	The opportunity is given the soul to learn and teach all the affairs of Capricorn (public standing and career). Jupiter is higher education while Saturn is structure. These individuals tend to stay within accepted norms of education and will reject anything untraditionally proven. The real danger for mental snobbery is produced by the strong desire for a position of power via traditional education. Capricorn rules engineering, architecture and all governmental and political endeavors, while Jupiter rules exploration. Hence it induces traveling in their chosen careers. The soul will excel in foreign lands and with foreigners on many governmental projects. Much of the education is traditional but with traveling and foreign cultures, it will force the soul to open up to a less rigid view of life. Honor and respect is deeply needed with this position and produces physicians, attorneys, city board of directors, political figures etc. In some extreme cases, the soul is incapable of entering the spiritual or intuitive domain, and appears to be extremely limited and judgmental to the more advanced soul. In reality, they are as stupid as they think they are educated, and this is not to be confused with intelligence. The reluctance to expand the mind in spiritual matters is simply a reflection of

Jupiter in Capricorn (cont...)	the deep seated fear of ridicule to the eyes of society. With a more advanced soul, the ultimate structural power of Jupiter in Capricorn is applied to teach unconditionally all areas of the human experience.
Jupiter in Aquarius ♃ ♒	Jupiter's expansive principle is given the soul to master and teach all the values found in the world of Aquarius. These souls undergo tremendous even extraordinary experiences making more rational souls wonder about the reality or possibility of such things. Jupiter's desire to travel, learn and teach, meet the incredible and shocking world of Aquarius. Uranus (God of the sky) rules Aquarius and reigns over space matters, electronics, computers, aeronautics, satellites, discoveries, invention, New Age matters and the future of mankind in general. I was born with Jupiter in Aquarius, and this is why I love to fly helicopters and had four solid UFO experiences and connections with ET's. Much of the world (99%) is totally unaware of the power of the Universal Mind upon its psyche, and is robotic and often victim to the stars. This same crowd laughs and rejects my claims or is totally incapable of understanding people like me, let alone

Jupiter in Aquarius (cont...)	accepting this incredible and real phenomenon. The soul is given the opportunity to explore the incredible and teach it to the world via Aquarius' tools. These tools are such things as radio, television, the internet, etc. The inventor, pilot, genius, New Age Leader, Astropsychologist, and Astrogeologists are Uranus' children and all have very specific missions to bring knowledge from the future against all odds. Bill Gates, the hi-tech wizard is a perfect example of Jupiter (expansion/luck) in Aquarius (electronics/internet). This crowd is usually misunderstood and in the name of stupidity they are constantly harassed. In the name of jealousy and ignorance they often become the chosen victims of young souls from many sources. However Jupiter protects them and promotes their unique mission world-wide where respect, fame, fortune and positions of leadership await them.
Jupiter in Pisces ♃ ♓	Jupiter's strong code is meeting with Neptune's illusive or artistic nature. On a productive note Neptune's artistic talents are promoted and taught in a big way. Neptune is the ruler of Pisces and Pisces deals with many benevolent institutions where financial support is easily gained for promotional and service purposes.

Jupiter in Pisces (cont...)	If the soul is advanced and swims upstream, the option to master and teach all about the subconscious, metaphysics or the arts is offered to the soul. On a negative note the young soul swims downstream and follows anything from a deity to a guru or a foreign cult leader. Valuable time and many resources are wasted reading archaic material and traveling to foreign lands looking for the truth or a guru (Peru, India, Tibet etc.). The advanced soul instinctively knows to look above and like a salmon, begin its long ascent towards its birth place, the light and the stars. Through difficult and sometimes dramatic experiences the young soul is forced to look somewhere else and with it the option to "ask and receive" the truth. The worst of Jupiter's rigid codes and Neptune's deceiving powers have taken the lives of many souls. Some fell victim to David Koresh or Rev. Jim Jones' deceiving leadership. Through mental exploration Jupiter will provide the soul with the highest form of expression through the spirit, the arts and publishing. The hardest lesson of all is to understand and establish "self realization" and the oneness with and as God.

NEPTUNE

Neptune in Greek Mythology is called, "The Lord of the Sea, Poseidon," and rules all oceans and the Intangible. This planet's negative principle supports and promotes the correct use or misuse of all agents found in all chemicals. Neptune's energy is lethargic and dreamy and totally the opposite of Saturn which is much more practical in nature. This is one of the main reasons why Christians subconsciously picked the symbol of the fish, ruled by Neptune (dreams/water element), against Capricorn (practicality/earth element/Saturn) as a symbol to represent evil (or progress/science).

The vibrational forces generated by Neptune affect all physical and spiritual conditions. It's like swimming in thick oil and avoiding all forms of practicality. The soul refuses to work and avoids responsibility by making excuses or worse, abusing drugs, alcohol or medications. This often the results in extreme sensitivity, and month's, even years, of negative auto suggestion brought about by dramatic memories experienced throughout the life of the subject.

Wherever Neptune is located in your chart you are prone to deceive yourself or be impractical. You may also attract deceiving and negative elements or chemicals into your life. Many of my clients born in September (Virgos) fell victim to poisoning, drugs, or alcohol abuse (through the 7th house of partnerships which regulates facing the public), in Neptunian areas, bars, discotheques, after hour locations etc. Neptune is both the most difficult planet to understand and rationalize with and also the most deceiving area of your life by house and sign location. Wherever Neptune sits in your chart, you are bound to be used, abused, drugged, manipulated, deceived and about as practical as a fish trying to live outside the water. You are just as realistic as the minister trying to convince himself by convincing you that he has the right way of life, the right deity and the right church for you. The illusory power of Neptune is phenomenal, and everyday has led millions of people all around the world in an insane dance of deception. This is the reaction expressed by the masses from centuries of religious poisoning. Neptune rules the world of dreams and your personal way to escape reality through your powerful imagination. This is where you can apply your creativity and the arts or religions to see your very beautiful world where all is beautiful and peaceful (paradise?). Neptune allows you to use his powers your way, where you as God allow yourself avoidance of the harsh reality of this dense physical world and its heavy responsibilities. Incidentally, Neptune controls the Middle East (where all the most destructive religions were born). Once more Bin Laden (a Pisces) is a full representation and product of the worst of Neptune's deceiving energy (religion/deception) at work.

IMPORTANT: Remember that Neptune rules the intangible, imagination and deals with the spirit and the subconscious. Neptune has no basis in the world of reality and will manifest himself in this world in various ways. Neptune rules Pisces and being a water sign, relief and insight can come from following the moon's fluctuations. Hence, Astropsychologists must remind their clients to follow the moon's fluctuations and the waxing and waning moon periods. Refer to the book, Moon Power Starguide for daily accurate locations and impact of the moon.

PLACEMENT OF NEPTUNE IN EACH SIGN

Neptune in Aries ♆ ♈	Aries rules the first house, thus Neptune in this fire sign may slow the turbulent personality of Aries. The fire and turbo-charged legacy found in the sign of Aries is sapped by Neptune (water), hence a more spiritual or artistic Aries. Problems of concentration or sleepiness are common but creativity and sensitivity are enhanced. On a positive note, Neptune in the first house produces oceanic explorations (Jacques Cousteau) and movie producers or actors. Aries is a daredevil and an explorer. In this case the Martian desire principle mixed with Neptune's artistic or spiritual talent will go a long way. As always with Neptune, trouble may come from an abuse of drugs, chemicals, or alcohol. Water sport figures and danger in water is also part of a Neptune in Aries celestial configuration.

Neptune in Taurus  	Taurus is an earth sign and brings stability to the dreamy Neptunian house. Taurus is ruled by artistic Venus and induces more love of money and a strong need for security. With Neptune's creativity and Taurus' practicality, the soul will be gifted in the arts. As always Neptune is also deceiving in nature and may alter the Taurus rationale. If Neptune (like any other planets in the chart) is well aspected, the option for creativity is offered to the soul. Realize also that Neptune can also attract deceiving elements in the house he resides. Thus be aware of contracts signed after the full moon and deceiving partners or endeavors, especially those religiously oriented. In extreme cases illegal money is generated by selling drugs or alcohol. Remember that Neptune rules also religions, drugs, gas, oil, the Middle East and alcohol, while Taurus rules money (Al Capone, drug lords and many Arab oil kings). Use only the positive aspect of Neptune, for if you don't, Neptune rules jail, hospitals and mental institutions. This position breeds incredibly creative people and fine singers. Taurus rules the throat and next to Neptune many young souls will be found singing in church, deceptively leading others to invest large amount of money into organized and deceiving institutions

Neptune in Gemini  ♊	The principle of communication found in Gemini meets with Neptune's trickery and breeds deceiving salesman. Neptune rules the oceans therefore leading some souls towards selling or working with boats or fishing equipment. As always with Neptune any deals and sales pertaining to all the affairs (positive or negative) ruled by this planet will plague the subject. On the more productive side, the entire world of Neptune's artistic talents and creativity is also offered to the soul. The opportunity to write beautiful scripts and attractive movies using Neptune's imaginative powers is also a possibility. Neptune in this sign can also produce psychics and refined painters. A mixture of Neptune (imagination) and Mercury (photography) can also produce great photographers. In extreme cases, Neptune's deceiving power is an addition to Mercury's communication skills and could breed compulsive liars and thieves. Dealing with brothers and sisters could also be a source of confusion or deception.

Neptune in Cancer  	Cancer is home and family and traditionally rules the base of operations and the business of real estate. The deceptive impact of Neptune would be felt at home where alcohol and drugs could induce upheaval and harm to the family (child abuse). In a more productive way, Neptune may gear the soul to own a home close to the water, do a lot of fishing, and enjoy the ocean. On a negative note, Cancer rules the womb, so an addicted mother could abuse drugs, alcohol or medications, inviting birth defects or abortion (drug babies). Neptune rules religion and its impact at home could be manifested through one of the parents enforcing religious principles to the family. This attitude usually creates conflicts with some of the more advanced children. On a positive note Neptune in Cancer produces real psychics and spiritually compassionate people. They are concerned with family matters, security and the well being of others (mentally abused etc.) The full creativity and artistic talent of Neptune is allowed to express itself for good or for worse at home.

Neptune in Leo  ♌	Leo rules love, romance, France, the arts, and children in general. On a negative note, the deceiving power of Neptune could bring about drugs and alcohol abuse and unwanted pregnancy. Neptune also rules movie making and in some cases incites child pornography. Neptune's negative elements can also bring about abuse to children from religious institutions. This position invites also secret and deceiving love affairs and could attract low elements into your life (drunks, alcoholics and deceptive people). On a more positive note, Neptune's incredible talent meets with Leo's desire for fame and produces fine actors and dancers such as ice skaters creating beautiful artistic movements with their feet. A good mixture of Neptune and the Sun produces the best anyone can offer to all the children of the world. On the medical aspect, Leo rules the heart, and Neptune medical prescriptions. Abuse of chemicals could alter the good workings of the heart. Any abuse of drugs or chemicals will cause problem in the long run. In some negative aspects, Neptune rules water, and Leo the children, or association with pool related deaths by drowning. You have to keep an eye on these children around water as deceptive Neptune is luring them to the water. This position breeds incredible and caring people committed to working and teaching children.

Neptune in Virgo ♆ ♍	Virgo is health and perfection while Neptune is drugs and alcohol. The structuring power of Virgo can be applied to the handling and mixing of water or chemicals for pharmaceutical and health purposes. Neptune is one of the best placements in health oriented Virgo. On a negative note, Neptune's imagination can override Virgo's critical senses and turn the soul into a hypochondriac, a bulimic or a vegetarian. Neptune rules the subconscious, metaphysics, healing, meditation, while Virgo rules health and cleansing matters. This position breeds homeopathic medicinal workers and the use of the regenerative elements found in all plants. This celestial position produces also highly precise spiritual healers. The strong sense of detail of Virgo is often associated with painting or drawing.
Neptune in Libra ♆ ♎	The positive or negative power of Neptune can find an outlet in the intellectual oriented sign of Libra. On a negative note Neptune's deceiving influence will affect contracts and marriages by attracting misleading associations with Neptunians. Libra rules the law, and the blurring power of Neptune can bring the wrongly accused or unlucky framed subject to jail. On a positive note the intuitive power of Neptune can be used in any affairs ruled by Libra.

Neptune in Libra (cont...)	This celestial manifestation breeds attorneys and judges engaged in maintaining or promoting religious legal endeavors. A mixture of Libra (balance and harmony) and Neptune's creativity can also generate fantastic interior designers. On a negative note this position increases the chances of deception in all matters related to Libra (marriages, partners, legal matters etc.) On a positive note Neptune's healing and creative powers can be used for the well being of society.
Neptune in Scorpio  ♏	A mixture of Neptune and Scorpio can be quite dramatic in many ways. Scorpio rules investigation, death, drama sex etc. On a positive note this celestial manifestation breeds precise Astropsychologists, profilers, and psychics engaged in detective police work. These individuals are more productive during the night and are attracted to the macabre. This breeds coroners and mortuary workers. Neptune rules madness, drugs, jail, religion, hospitals and asylums. A strong probability exists with Neptune in Scorpio for the subject to be involved either physically or spiritually with the positive or negative element of Neptune. The intensity of Pluto, ruler of Scorpio along with Neptune's illusive power, can produce serial killers, rapists and seriously mentally disturbed drug addicts favoring

Neptune in Scorpio (cont...)	schizophrenic endeavors. Simply stated the best or the worst of man's subconscious powers can be used for or against society. The regeneration principle is usually achieved through mental work, metaphysical investigations, science, and research on the working of the human psyche. This is the heart and soul of the police, FBI, CIA, and sadly enough, all the executives of this very special branch in our society are totally unaware of the validity and values of my work. Time will work for me.
Neptune in Sagittarius 	A mixture of Jupiter's codes and Neptune's illusive power can only further the intensity of teaching and enforcing the rules including biblical terms as ultimate laws. This position produces a very sensitive reaction to the country's induced accepted religion. A mix of Jupiter's codes and Neptune's illusive power can only further the intensity of teaching and enforcing the rules including biblical terms as ultimate laws. This position produces a very sensitive reaction to the country's induced and accepted religion. On a negative note the young soul is simply incapable of challenging the written word and cannot use its own critical thinking outside of what has been written. The deceptive and illusive power of Neptune is enforced

Neptune in Sagittarius (cont...)	and codified by Jupiter's high moral codes, making it impossible to challenge. On a more productive note the advanced soul is forced to travel and realizes its own limitations by exploring others people's cultures and philosophies. The very same reluctance to expand outside of his culture, forces the subject himself to realize his own mental limitations and stipulations. One of the challenges is to realize the diversity of governments mental control imposed through religions upon many different cultures and countries predisposing the soul to mental exploration and ultimately cosmic consciousness.
Neptune in Capricorn  ♑	Capricorn rules structure, command, organization and all matters related to the government at large. Like Virgo and Taurus, this earth element will bring practicality to the affairs ruled by Neptune. On a negative note the key word for Capricorn (evil head/devil) is "I abuse." Thus, the use of Neptune's most deceiving powers (religion) is used to enforce a form of mental discipline (ten command-meats) to the masses. In doing so, this brings the option to establish more control for the powerful ruling law-makers' government executives. This brings a form of harmony to the servant, the god-fearing, law obedient and uneducated working society.

Neptune in Capricorn (cont...)	Capricorn rules politics and strives for a position of power and control and will make good use of any and all rigid laws (Hitler had the Moon on the Tail of the Dragon also in Capricorn). The structuring power of Capricorn (the mountain) can also be used through the Neptunian's artistic values to produce highly structured classical art (dancing and opera singers). The high command of Saturn (ruler of Capricorn), mixed with Neptune's creativity, will produce a movie director or a church architect designer. A full manifestation of Neptune in Capricorn has been in place since the building of both the religious icon and its specific religion. Simply another deceiving way for the government to control your psyche using Neptune's pious and illusive powers.
Neptune in Aquarius ♆ ♒	Aquarius rules the future, high-tech and all New Age endeavors. On a negative note the deceptive power of Neptune breeds lunatics like UFO cult leader Marshall Applewhite, who lead his group to mass suicide.

Neptune in Aquarius (cont...)	Extraterrestrial phenomenon is very real but was taken to the extreme by this lost Neptunian soul. As with other religions, the New Age is also a form of religion and has its deceptive Neptunian Captains. They are the gurus, cult leaders and all the various victims of this illusive planet. They are the Jesus of modern times, the crafty prophets attracting and wasting many lost souls resources. Uranus, the ruler of Aquarius, rules television and discovery while Neptune rules the oceans. Here you have the Learning or Discovery channels or the oceanographer. This celestial manifestation can also produce well advanced Astropsychologists due to the placement of Aquarius (universal Mind) and Neptune, ruler of the 12th house ruling the subconscious. The option to uncover the secrets of the workings of the Universal Mind and its direct relationship to the subconscious is a strong possibility. On a negative note a conflict between the past and guilt (Neptune) and the future and freedom (Uranus) can lead the subject to some serious mental problems as seen with cult leader Applewhite's mass suicide.

Neptune in Pisces 	Pisces meets its own ruler reinforcing the potential to reach the greatest highs or lowest lows imaginable in the human experience. Neptune's deceptive or constructive powers are given full expression. The soul may reject all forms of practicality and may escape in a world of dreams, drugs, alcohol or religion (Osama Bin Laden, David Koresh and Rev. Jones). One of the most difficult positions, as the soul is enslaved to swim upstream like a salmon, towards its birthplace or the stars, against an incredible deceitful current. In the worst case scenario, dramatic experiences such as wars destroy the subject's psyche and the will to survive. Prone to serious mental disorders, he then gives up fighting and become homeless. Any form of escape using chemicals is often the means of establishing a form of suicide to exit the harsh reality of a very tangible world. On a positive note the compassion or artistic values of Neptune are expressed to the highest level of creativity for the well being of society.

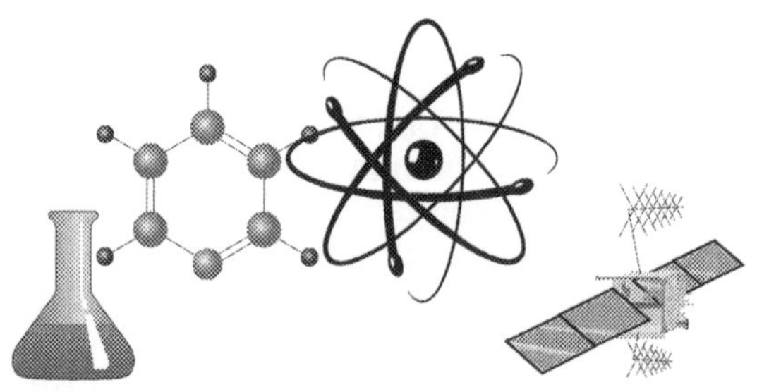

URANUS

Uranus is the planet that rules the future and that which has not yet been realized by mankind's ingenious spirit. Uranus has been in charge of the world since the first explosion of the atomic bomb around the year 1945. Uranium and plutonium have been used to emphasize the worst of the planets' destructive forces. Uranus rules the sudden release of energy and Pluto the process of decay and death. Uranus rules nature's most devastating forces at work (earthquakes, tornadoes, typhoons, and hurricanes). This planet rules Japan where there are more earthquakes and volcanoes per square mile than any other country in the world. Uranus and Pluto rule the liberation of tremendous destructive forces. Uranus rules the New Age, electronics and this planet's shocking power is in charge of mankind for the next 2000 years. The planet Uranus regulates the discovery principle, curiosity, and its element is air (Aquarius). Uranus is inquisitive and extremely intellectual. Keep in mind that Uranus rules the genius qualities of man, including invention, aeronautics, computers, high-tech, UFOs etc. Note also that Japan is the only country in the world that has experienced the worst of Uranus' sudden release of energy, with two nuclear explosions.

Uranus (astrology, UFO's) rules the New Age

Wherever Uranus is located in your chart the opportunity to become a genius or express your originality belongs to you. Whatever sign receives the planet Uranus dictates where one must become special and become an inventor offering futuristic views to the world of science and research. Uranus is not "normal" within the criterion of acceptance in society's standards. Uranus is original and a rebel at heart; he also promotes unconventionality thus allowing the new to take over the old.

PLACEMENT OF URANUS IN EACH SIGN

Uranus in Aries ♅ ♈	Uranus in the first house imposes originality on appearance of the physical body (Aries). Aries is competitive and turbo-charged, and with Uranus' electronic inventive powers, new ideas of weaponry could be generated and applied for war (building bombs, building up high-tech weapons for the purposes of destruction). Uranus in Aries can induce erratic even shocking behavior and impatience. Combining Aries or Mars, the planet of war along with Uranus' electronic energy can also produce scientists researching human cloning intended for war purposes. Investigating other areas of the chart will give a better view as to whether or not that energy will be used properly and constructively. Uranus and Mars together can be pretty devastating to

Uranus in Aries (cont...)	the human race but when both powers are used diligently there are no limits to what can be done with the creation. In certain cases Uranus induces weird appearances, tattooing and piercing.
Uranus in Taurus ♅ ♉	Taurus rules wealth, love, the arts, creativity, banking, financial possessions, solidity, trust, and strengths. Uranus rules high-tech, television and radio. Uranus in Taurus predisposes the soul to spend money (or make money) in all elements controlled by Aquarius (astrology, high-tech, computers, television etc.) Taurus rules also massage products of the earth (diamond/gold) and avant-garde fashions.
Uranus in Gemini ♅ ♊	The critical thinking of Gemini is combined with the intellectual genius quality of Uranus, breeding individuals constantly asking "why and how." Research and science involving any advanced subjects motivate Uranus in Gemini individuals. They are also fascinated with anything that promotes the new age, communications via hi-tech, television, or radio. Many of them are inventors of high-tech communication gadgets. This position also produces pilots, as Gemini rules transportation.

Uranus in Cancer  	Cancer rules the home and Uranus in Cancer brings the electronic gadgets and the use of high-tech and computers (Uranus) into the home (Cancer). Uranus in Cancer indicates also the option to learn or teach astrology from the base of operation and use computers in real estate endeavors. Uranus is very independent and induces stress or a desire for freedom from authority. However, combined with the tenacity of Cancer, there is always a strong desire to go back home where things are stable and solid. This position demonstrates also why a famous chefs (Cancer) are involved and performing "cooking programs" on national television (Uranus).
Uranus in Leo ♅ ♌	Leo rules the 5th house of creativity and the area where a woman will produce a child and give life, because Leo rules love and the sun gives life. Uranus in Leo means also the potential of surprise in the affairs ruling Leo, or a woman's surprising pregnancy. However, the child will be born with some unsuspected gifts and in some cases genius qualities. Uranus in Leo produces extremely magnetic or original people. Leo rules the selfish love principle while Aquarius rules universal love. Uranus in Leo can indicate lovers

Uranus in Leo (cont...)	who have a different view and are attracted to groups where love and sex are expressed freely. Unplanned pregnancy is always a risk with this position.
Uranus in Virgo ♅ ♍	The Virgin Mary's health energy (Virgo) is mixed with new age healing techniques (Aquarius/ Uranus). Combining the Virgo detail oriented, picky, fussy, health oriented spirit of Virgo with computers and high-tech can produce an original way of servicing the world. Uranus' inventiveness in Virgo (work) can also produce interesting inventions, web designers and great gifts with film, computers, and television editing. A great position, producing a pilot or an astronaut.
Uranus in Libra ♅ ♎	Uranus rules computers (internet) while Libra rules partnership and marriage. This often produces a linkage with computers or the use of the internet to find a suitable partner. Libra is balance and Uranus is the sudden outburst of action. Libra is the law, legalities and Astropsychology. Uranus is originality, humanity, uniqueness, astrology, and the New Age. Uranus carries his unique energy in Libra (ruler of the 7th house of partnerships). Thus searching for the original partner (Libra) and an

Uranus in Libra (cont...)	Original, open-minded, unique (Uranian) person. If both individuals have Uranus in Libra a partnership with the chance for growth and unique experiences is offered to the souls. If the partner is too conventional the research becomes the means for regeneration to fight boredom or routine.
Uranus in Scorpio ♅ ♏	Traditionally Pluto rules the eight house of witchcraft, life and death, corporate endeavors and magic. The Uranus in Scorpio subject regenerates by investigating information related to life and death, mystery, medicine and corporate money, and they use computers (stock market). Opportunity is given to the soul to make money with large groups as Scorpio rules corporate finance, with Uranus (hi-tech). Uranus in Scorpio induces a deep interest in metaphysics and can produce precise tarot readers or astrologers. With Uranus in Scorpio they can read you like an "open book." Educated in Astropsychology methods, the power will become extremely accurate in depicting any character. Large sums of money can be made or lost almost immediately. There is also a strong involvement with sex and video endeavors or interests with this position. Security hi-tech equipment is often used in the job.

Uranus in Sagittarius ♅ ♐	Uranus rules freedom while Sagittarius rules wide open spaces. Sagittarius rules also the Indians, the deserts and Las Vegas. Uranus controls the electronic gaming machines used in Las Vegas. Uranus in Sagittarius can produce an electronic gambler. Uranus in Sagittarius is also depicted with an extremely spiritual person mixing the very old and very new Philosophies. Sagittarius and Aquarius are naturally open minded and happy souls and can be very good friends helping you to reach your wishes. The downfall of this position is that Sagittarius (as a priest) tends to follow the codification of thought (religion) and the printed knowledge found in books. Meanwhile, Uranus' universal spirit breathes true star-knowledge, and is reluctant to explore or support the religious Sagittarius and his limited belief system, or the Vatican. Uranus' Spiritual awakener in Sagittarius (dogmas) makes the life of the subject a constant process of traveling and educating, to finally reach cosmic consciousness.
Uranus in Capricorn ♅ ♑	We combine practical Capricorn with Uranus' knowledge of high-tech and computers. Uranus in Capricorn is the builder of success, career, wealth, and public standing

Uranus in Capricorn (cont...)	(Capricorn) in the high-tech world of radio, television, originality, and genius (Uranus). Rush Limbaugh is a good example of Uranus (television) in Capricorn (politics) building a pyramid of success challenging the government
Uranus in Aquarius ♅ ♒	This is the best of the strengths of Aquarius into its own sign. There, the potential to become a genius and to be totally irrational will be expressed in many ways. Uranus in Aquarius is the inventor of the time machine and produces visions of the future. Great futuristic works of art belong to Uranus in Aquarius. The subject is definitely unique in his own creativity and surpasses common imagination. The soul is prone to attract incredible positive extraterrestrial experiences or shocking negative encounters if Uranus is badly aspected.

Uranus in Pisces 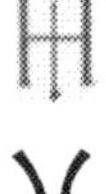 ♓	Pisces (Neptune) rules creativity, imagination, and the world of dreams, drugs, alcohol, illusion, and deception. Hi-tech, electronics, and laser technology is a Uranus manifestation. The two combined will produce an interest in such things as cinematography, movie theaters (Pisces), high-tech, electronics, the future of mankind, new age, UFO's, and movies such as Star Trek (Uranus) or Titanic (Neptune). With Uranus in Pisces the positive fish swims upstream against dogma, fear, hell and the devil and will make good use of Uranus' power in understanding and learning the stars (Uranus). The Uranus in Pisces subject is prone to expand intellectually in spite of any early religious poisoning or conditioning.

PLUTO

Pluto is one of the most powerful planets in astrology and also the farthest planet from the sun in our solar system. Pluto is the planet of life and death, sex, reincarnation, and will transform a worm in the water into a butterfly in the air. Pluto is the planet that controls the productive or destructive masses' reaction. On a negative note Pluto's extraordinary passionate nature breeds fanaticism for life and death. Pluto triggers terrorists and religious fanatics and new forms of life in death. Ancient astrologers carved the scorpion and its poisonous stinger to represent death. Pluto allows the soul to regenerate by house and sign in the chart where the fear of death is absent. Under Pluto's command you will surprise everyone with the inner strengths you possess in the affairs regulating the house.

PLUTO'S IMPACT ON GENERATIONS

Pluto in Gemini: "The hypnotized generation (see The Power of the Dragon)

Adolph Hitler was born in April (Aries) with Pluto's hypnotic power located in the Sign of Gemini in his 3rd house of communication. Pluto was in Gemini from 1883 until 1913. Hitler was talking and hypnotizing this generation that would suffer his political position in command and bring about death to millions.

Pluto in Cancer: "The Wasted Baby Generation" (between 1913 and 1937). The generation following Hitler's birth and fate was born with Pluto (death) in the sign of Cancer (home and family). These are the 10 million Jews and millions of other war victims that died (Pluto) and lost their homes (Cancer). The US, born July 4th 1776 and France July 14 1789, are Cancer/Leo countries and thousands upon thousands of country men died when Pluto crossed Cancer, the sign of family, home, security, and food.

Pluto in Leo: "The Baby Boom Generation" (from 1938 to 1957). Leo is love, romance and children and produced the baby boom generation. After the passage of Pluto in Cancer and the raging wars, the stars had to replenish the world. Leo rules love and romance and Pluto the rebirthing and reincarnation principle opening a new door to the generation of love, freedom, music, sex, and Woodstock (Pluto in Leo)

Pluto in Virgo: "The Baby Buster Generation" (from 1957 to 1971). Virgo rules health and this perfectionist generation needs you to read labels and understand the ramifications of any food or chemicals you ingest. Some are truly health fanatics and turn into vegetarians, hypochondriacs and bulimics. The Virgin Mary (Virgo) wants you to only eat vegetables and grains and exclude meat products. Here, Pluto's fanaticism resides in Virgo, the sign of health, detail and precision. This generation works hard to ban cigarettes altogether. They are the environmentalists and are very concerned with the rain forest, saving the whales, clean air, recycling, fitness, and they build computers and health exercise machines. Often Pluto in Virgo's subjects are too concerned with bureaucracy, health matters and miss the big picture.

Pluto in Libra: "The Gang Generation" (from October 5, 1971 until November 6, 1983). This is the sign of the law (police) and group partnerships sealed by contracts and commitments (Libra) into the house of death (Pluto). Libra rules the 7th house (open enemies), and produces deadly battles of one group against another, or drive-by shootings. This generation needs to be part of a group to regenerate and will not want to stay at home. The gang attitude pervades, "It's me for you and you for me 'til death do us part". They love dramatic, plutonic, deadly situations where they can risk their lives for their partners. They regenerate in the intensity of giving the best of themselves to the group with which they identify and contract themselves. Here the gang is completely stimulated and regenerated with a constant element of death. The lesson of Pluto in Libra is to use the group strengths to build life and master the art of diplomacy. Libra is the sign of peace, beauty, love and commitment but with deadly Pluto, war and death is the only acceptable outcome for the young soul. Libra reminds us to seek balance and harmony in partnerships, contracts, legalities and respect in all our relationships. However, Libra also reminds us that the flip side of peace is war and death. Pluto in Libra is motivated by the justice principle such as; someone has done something wrong to the group and disturbed the sensitive scale, so let's unite and go kill the responsible parties. Pluto rules the police (forces of good) and Libra the gangs (forces of evil).

Pluto in Scorpio: "The Death Wish Generation" (from 1983 until 1995). This young generation born with Pluto in Scorpio is completely fearless in front of death and extremely active sexually. The deadly junk of movies and television programs creates the stimulation needed to stir their need for drama or the sex for which they strive. This generation can only regenerate with the plain reality and facts of life, and many carry a deep subconscious awareness of witchcraft. They do know that there is no death really but reincarnation works based upon karmic residue. They are not religious and actively seek the true knowledge of the stars and metaphysics. At the age of fourteen some youngsters of this generation have made drastic news.

Before this generation's elites get into power, many of them will be killed. The survivors will have a few scars and nurture tremendous physical and emotional stress that will be used to save society from its own collapse and interior destruction. The survivors have something unique to share with the world and a tremendous fate to fulfill. Left unchecked, the Pluto in Scorpio generation has the full power to destroy or bring about miracles to this world. Subsequently, the advanced souls will make it to the top as doctors of the physical or spiritual world.

Pluto in Sagittarius: "The Reforming Generation" (November 1995 until January 2008). Religions as we know them today and the old dogmas, will have to go with this generation. Those new spiritual leaders won't promote dogma, fear, hell and the devil. Pluto in Sagittarius will bestow a form of teaching of enlightenment in understanding the transcendental forces of God through the stars. Life and death will be accepted and not feared supporting a much higher purpose and realization of man's immortality as a God placed on earth.

Pluto in Capricorn: "The Future Builders" Politics and abusive governmental structures as we know them today will be eliminated by this generation. Pluto (death and rebirth) in Capricorn (government) will bring about the best of the universal brotherhood. Understanding and association within a one governmental structure based upon true physical and spiritual guidance will come about. The complete political structure will undergo a total death and the imposed change will benefit mankind.

Pluto in Aquarius: "The Star Child generation" Our relationship with the Universe and extra terrestrials will come to the fore. Extraordinary Hi-Tech tools will be used or offered to mankind by ET's to progress with other life forms in the endless cosmos. The option to exit this fast dying world will be offered to man, so as to fulfill the human race's highest purpose, or be destroyed in the process. The ultimate power of life and death (Pluto) will touch the world of Aquarius (sudden release of energy). Pluto in Aquarius will unleash serious earthquakes, volcanoes, and remind us that the earth is still alive and breathing. She will need to restructure her entire physical self as she did many times before. Pluto in Aquarius will produce a generation of geniuses ready to take on the challenges they will have to deal with. Pluto in Aquarius will bring a full New World with UFO's and extra terrestrials (Uranus). The future, the impossible is becoming possible.

Pluto in Pisces: "The Next Dimension Generation" A total death and rebirth of the psyche of mankind and the ending of a spiritual conception. This generation of psychics and artists will forge ahead, helping the rest of us to discover man's greatest potential of using the super Conscious in time and space. Our knowledge today will be increased thousand fold as far as the subconscious; metaphysics and the intangible are concerned. Pluto in Pisces is the world of the spirit receiving the life and death energy allowing the passage into a higher vibrational system and another dimension. Pluto in Pisces is life and death mixed with a rebirth of the spirit.

* * * *

PLACEMENT OF PLUTO IN EACH SIGN

Pluto in Aries ♇ ♈	Man discovers fire and starts to make his first weapons such as knives and arrows. Aries is the warrior while Pluto is self discovery. Negative-obsession with oneself or the creation of a new race or the Aries (Aryan) race. Positive outcome - dying and rebirthing one self through dramatic experiences. Regeneration with oneself.
Pluto in Taurus ♇ ♉	Negatively aspected it could lead to an obsession with security and wealth resulting in death or jail, as earthy Taurus rules money and possessions. A positive outcome could be Pluto in Taurus calling forth cultivation of the earth (Taurus) which brings life and sustenance (Pluto). Regeneration is reached with the arts and the earth.
Pluto in Gemini ♇ ♊	The negative results could see mental obsession to control and manipulate others, and a nefarious use of metaphysics for personal gain (Hitler). A positive outcome-- the full restructure of the intellectual capacity and common sense through education and traveling. Regeneration is reached with communication, learning, and writing.

Pluto in Cancer ♇ ♋	The negative is an obsession with family matters and food. The positive, a full restructure of the base of operation and rebirthing from a dramatic upbringing. Regeneration is reached with emotion, food and real estate.
Pluto in Leo ♇ ♌	Here you see a negative obsession with love, romance and children producing a Susan Smith-like drama of killing one's children. A positive outcome would be a full positive restructure of love and romance, creativity and children. Regeneration takes place with children, the arts and creativity.
Pluto in Virgo ♇ ♍	Here there is a negative obsession with work and health. The positive outcome is seen in restructures of mental and physical health. Regeneration is reached with nature, plants and clothing.
Pluto in Libra ♇ ♎	You see here a negative obsession with the legal system, partnerships, psychology, marriage, and contracts. Regeneration is reached with the learning of Astropsychology and the law.
Pluto in Scorpio ♇ ♏	Here, a negative obsession centered with jealousy, resentment, revenge, death, legacy and sex. Regeneration is reached with research, psychic powers, corporate endeavors and spiritual exploration.

Pluto in Sagittarius ♇ ♐	Negative obsessions concern religion, education, foreigners and the law. A full death and life restructure into the religious and philosophical worlds of ideology is stimulated. Regeneration is reached with philosophy, traveling, foreigners, and publishing.
Pluto in Capricorn ♇ ♑	Here, the negative obsession centers around career, politics, wealth, building and accepted sciences. Regeneration is reached with all unusual and unconventional material.
Pluto in Aquarius ♇ ♒	Negative obsession with cults, astrology, UFO's, electronics and flying. Regeneration is reached with accepted norms, inventions and practical spiritual science (Astropsychology).
Pluto in Pisces ♇ ♓	Negative obsession with guilt, madness, the past, religion, imagination, hospitals, jails, drugs, and alcohol. Regeneration reached with creativity, exotic places, painting and music.

SUBCONSCIOUS MOTIVATION

SUBCONSCIOUS FEARS:

Aries has a subconscious fear based in the sign of Pisces	Loneliness / not being loved / appreciated / madness
Taurus has a subconscious fear based in the sign of Aries	Inadequacy / being number two / challenged / criticized
Gemini has a subconscious fear based in the sign of Taurus	Financial insecurity / letting go of the past / money / power
Cancer has a subconscious fear based in the sign of Gemini	Death of a brother / sister / limitation of knowledge / traveling
Leo has a subconscious fear based in the sign of Cancer	Not having a home / food and shelter / family protection
Virgo has a subconscious fear based in the sign of Leo	Not accomplishing / reaching fame / health / losing power

Libra has a subconscious fear based in the sign of Virgo	Perfection / losing a job / health matter / doing a god service
Scorpio has a subconscious fear based in the sign of Libra	Husband / wife / Partnerships / finding right laws / contracts
Sagittarius has a subconscious fear based in the sign of Scorpio	Not being able to learn it all / enough power / metaphysics / enough sex
Capricorn has a subconscious fear based in the sign of Sagittarius	Not being close enough to God / the truth / knowledge
Aquarius has a subconscious fear based in the sign of Capricorn	Providing structure for the spirit/ gain honors / high standing position in society.
Pisces has a subconscious fear based in the sign of Aquarius	Not being able to serve the world fully / promoting universal love for the betterment of humankind.

DRAGON'S HEAD and TAIL

Explanation of the Dragon

Sir Isaac Newton wrote "for every action, there is an equal and opposite reaction." We are what we think, having become what we thought. This statement emphasizes that for every thought or action, there will be an effect. This is what I call the "Universal Law", the cause and effect of the yin and yang recognized and accepted as the LAW OF KARMA. Modern Astrology classifies the Dragon's Head and Tail as the North and South Nodes of the Moon. The Moon is quite responsible for the daily fate of the world and directly affects mankind's psyche and nature's forces at work.

Obviously, the waxing and waning periods of our closest satellite will produce the daily process of the tides. The lunar cycle is 28 and half days, which is the same as a woman's menstrual cycle. Thus, women especially have a physical and spiritual response to the moon's fluctuations and will be subconsciously responding to the words, "MOODY and LUNATIC". The scientific community is not yet aware of tremendous impact produced by a Full Moon upon mankind's psyche, and still has no real clue as to the tremendous information available to them. In the name of ignorance or "ridicule" these educated mental snobs are missing out on incredible information. The police force and hospital emergency rooms are also unusually busy at these times. The Moon's subtle power is not yet understood by the scientific community but is wisely used by both the intelligent Astropsychologist and the local farmer. However, many years of tedious observation has shown me that the moon (as our closest satellite) undeniably affects the human psyche and its response to life in general. Without opposing forces at work (positive / negative), there would be no reaction, thus, no life possible on both the spiritual and physical planes. Our so-called "dead" satellite is very much alive, and vigilantly observing her whereabouts will make man grow steadily to cosmic consciousness.

The Dragon's Head

Dragon's Head in Modern Astrology is referred to as the North Node of the Moon.

Divine Astrology and Chinese Astrology refer to it as "Dragon's Head."

This signifies new experiences for the soul (growth, a new opportunity to expand is given to the soul).

The Dragon's Head is the area you must reach in this present incarnation. A form of protection, luck and development is offered to the soul. It is where the universe will reward you if you tap into that sign or that specific house.

The North Node of the Moon is a positive energy, a form of "wheel of fortune", pushing the soul towards new self-realization and sure happiness. Chinese astrologers refer to the Moon's Nodes as the Dragon's Head and Tail, and give it tremendous attention as to the placement in the natal chart. Sadly, practical modern astrologers tend to ignore its very existence and in the process will lose a wealth of valuable information. To my knowledge, the Dragon, itself holds as much if not more, facts and power than the entire complexity of the whole astrological chart! I found the essence of the Dragon's secrets to be a major contribution for success or failure in one's life. Many famous people and the ones that have made history, for good or for worse, have an obvious relationship with it. (See "The Power Of The Dragon").

The Dragon's Tail

The Dragon's Tail in Modern Astrology is referred to as the South Node of the Moon.

Divine Astrology and Chinese Astrology refer to it as the "Dragon's Tail."

The Dragon's Tail is the area of your past lives residue, where your soul feels somewhat more comfortable because it doesn't want to progress and do better for itself. You are somehow stuck here, and the affairs related to this sign and house could lead the subject into drama, difficulties, and sometimes death.

The South Node of the Moon is a negative energy that is a form of "karmic residue", dragging the soul toward his past accomplishments, inner fears, and weaknesses. This build-up of previous incarnations and bad habits must be eliminated, and a chance is given to you by the "Great Designer" to experience something new and grow into a better person. As a rule, we are all naturally riveted by the Dragon's Tail, like a child wanting to stay home instead of going to his new school and facing the cold weather, others, and refusing to progress with the rest of his class. There, at home, (Tail), the soul feels secure and confident with what he knows best. In my research, I have noticed that following the Tail's commands can only lead its owner towards failure, pain, drama, and indeed, may lead to death. In some extreme cases, the Dragon's Tail causes the souls to lead other people into their own dark past life residues, thereby hurting the innocent, trusting souls who follow them. This is evident with such leaders as David Koresh, Rev. Jim Jones, and Osama Bin Laden. Sometimes, for specific karmic reasons, the Dragon's Tail can be used positively and has produced gifted musicians such as Bach and Schubert, born with the Dragon's Tail in Libra.

Here, the souls past life musical talents came to fruition so others could enjoy or learn from them. God allowed these "geniuses" to use their previous live's work to the benefit of mankind, and they were able to accomplish wonders at early ages. The location of the Dragon's Tail is where all of your weaknesses come from. You have been there and you have done that and you have learned those lessons. God will not help you there, and if not aware of the Dragon's Head which promises opportunity, you will hopelessly strive for either financial or emotional security. Sometimes, unexpected experiences such as accidents or the use of chemicals, drugs, alcohol, or medications, will cause the soul to be drawn back into his past life residue. The occurrence is somehow shocking, vivid and very believable. Thus, the soul mistakenly receives spiritual messages from higher levels, based on past life residues (Joan Of Arc), and firmly believes the communication. The purification and progress of the soul can only be found on the "next" experience promised by the location of his Dragon's Head by house and sign of the zodiac. Armed with such powerful knowledge, one is able to detect fiction from reality and make a difference between divine information and pure imagination.

The awareness of someone's Dragon's Head and Tail is a real contribution to detecting the plain truth about the dynamics involving the fate of the subject and the true workings of his psyche. This work was not done to diminish anyone's integrity but to clarify their astral relationship with God and the Universe. We all are children of this magnificent galaxy, and there is a reason for every one of us to be.

Famous Examples:

Libra Head/Aries Tail:

They are lucky in marriage and in attracting very powerful partners (wealth/notoriety). Extremely unlucky with life in general, they may suffer a violent death via the head (Nicole Simpson, John Lennon).

Taurus Head/Scorpio Tail:

Taurus is money. This head/tail produces magnetic, beautiful individuals. Taurus head is a form of attraction into the world of Venus. Scorpio's Tail past life residue is witchcraft, sexual energy, and a strong desire to go back to the world of the unknown, sex and death (Houdini, Heidi Fleiss "The Hollywood Madame."

Dragon's Head location by the year:

To find the tail, go to the opposite side of the zodiac. (See also the zodiac on page141, or "opposites" chart on page 182) For instance, if the Dragon's Head is in Sagittarius; the Dragon's Tail will be in the opposite sign of Gemini.

Head		Tail
Aries	------	Libra
Taurus	------	Scorpio
Gemini	------	Sagittarius
Cancer	------	Capricorn
Leo	------	Aquarius
Virgo	------	Pisces
Libra	------	Aries
Scorpio	------	Taurus
Sagittarius	------	Gemini
Capricorn	------	Cancer
Aquarius	------	Leo
Pisces	------	Virgo

1900 to 1949

	Head
January 1, 1900 to December 28, 1900	Sagittarius
December 29, 1900 to July 17, 1902	Scorpio
July 18, 1902 to February 4, 1904	Libra
February 5, 1904 to August 23, 1905	Virgo
August 24, 1905 to March 13, 1907	Leo
March 14, 1907 to September 29, 1908	Cancer
September 30, 1908 to April 18, 1910	Gemini
April 19, 1910 to November 7, 1911	Taurus
November 8, 1911 to May 26, 1913	Aries
May 27, 1913 to December 13, 1914	Pisces
December 14, 1914 to July 2, 1916	Aquarius
July 3, 1916 to January 19, 1918	Capricorn
January 20, 1918 to August 9, 1919	Sagittarius
August 10, 1919 to February 26, 1921	Scorpio
February 27, 1921 to September 15, 1922	Libra
September 16, 1922 to April 4, 1924	Virgo
April 5, 1924 to October 22, 1925	Leo
October 23, 1925 to May 12, 1927	Cancer
May 13, 1927 to November 28, 1928	Gemini
November 29, 1928 to June 18, 1930	Taurus
June 19, 1930 to January 6, 1932	Aries
January 7, 1932 to July 25, 1933	Pisces
July 26, 1933 to February 12, 1935	Aquarius
February 13, 1935 to September 1, 1936	Capricorn
September 2, 1936 to March 21, 1938	Sagittarius
March 22, 1938 to October 9, 1939	Scorpio
October 10, 1939 to April 27, 1941	Libra
April 28, 1941 to November 15, 1942	Virgo
November 16, 1942 to June 3, 1944	Leo
June 4, 1944 to December 23, 1945	Cancer

December 24, 1945 to July 11, 1947	Gemini
July 12, 1947 to January 28, 1949	Taurus
January 29, 1949 to December 31, 1949	Aries

1950 to 2011

January 1, 1950 to August 17, 1950	Aries
August 18, 1950 to March 7, 1952	Pisces
March 8, 1952 to October 2, 1953	Aquarius
October 3, 1953 to April 12, 1955	Capricorn
April 13, 1955 to November 4, 1956	Sagittarius
November 5, 1956 to May 21, 1958	Scorpio
May 22, 1958 to December 8, 1959	Libra
December 9, 1959 to July 3, 1961	Virgo
July 4, 1961 to January 13, 1963	Leo
January 14, 1963 to August 5, 1964	Cancer
August 6, 1964 to February 21, 1966	Gemini
February 22, 1966 to September 10, 1967	Taurus
September 11, 1967 to April 3, 1969	Aries
April 4, 1969 to October 15, 1970	Pisces
October 16, 1970 to May 5, 1972	Aquarius
May 6, 1972 to November 22, 1973	Capricorn
November 23, 1973 to June 12, 1975	Sagittarius
June 13, 1975 to December 29, 1976	Scorpio
December 30, 1976 to July 19, 1978	Libra
July 20, 1978 to February 5, 1980	Virgo
February 6, 1980 to August 25, 1981	Leo
August 26, 1981 to March 14, 1983	Cancer
March 15, 1983 to October 1, 1984	Gemini
October 2, 1984 to April 20, 1986	Taurus
April 21, 1986 to November 8, 1987	Aries
November 9, 1987 to May 28, 1989	Pisces

May 29, 1989 to December 15, 1990	Aquarius
December 16, 1990 to July 4, 1992	Capricorn
July 5, 1992 to January 21, 1994	Sagittarius
January 22, 1994 to August 11, 1995	Scorpio
August 12, 1995 to February 27, 1997	Libra
February 28, 1997 to September 17, 1998	Virgo
September 18, 1998 to April 9, 2000	Leo
April 10, 2000 to October 13, 2001	Cancer
October 14, 2001 to April 14, 2003	Gemini
April 15, 2003 to December 26 2004	Taurus
December 27, 2004 to June 22, 2006	Aries
June 23, 2006 to December 18, 2007	Pisces
December 19, 2007 to August 21, 2009	Aquarius
August 22, 2009 to March 3, 2011	Capricorn

Key words for a positive Aries Dragon's Head

- You are a genius, an inventor, a leader of the mind or the military
  You have plenty of desire and you were born with an adventurous spirit
  You have a lots of vitality; good self esteem, and you are lucky
  You are true to yourself and to others
  You are intelligent and competitive
  You take chances on anything
  You are magnetic and exciting

Key words for a negative Aries Dragon's Tail

- You are self-centered with no valuable ideas involving others and carry low self-esteem
You are afraid of new people, you are insecure and accident prone to the head
You are too impatient and demanding, you should forget the word me
You will take a chance only if there is something to gain for yourself
You run out of energy of stamina
You are jealous and unsafe
You are dictatorial

Key words for a positive Taurus Dragon's Head

- You have faith in your abilities to make millions of dollars or launch any business
You are a genius with your and other people's money
You are willing to work harder than anyone to get there
You have plenty of great ideas to give away
You give with love and respect
You are creative and beautiful
You are financially secure

Key words for a negative Taurus Dragon's Tail

- You have a bad attitude with money; you would do anything against the law to get it
You loose all you possessions and credit cards a few times
You are financially insecure and won't do a thing about it

You do not want to work and expect others to provide
You want to marry an older wealthy person only
You can't stop shopping no matter what
You will use sex for money

Key words for a positive Gemini Dragon's Head

- You know you are a "Messenger of the Gods," a mental genius, and a proficient writer
You have plenty of mental and physical energy to spare looking for the truth
You are joyful and possess a gift of youth
You tell the truth and joke all the time
You like photography and music
You're versatile and curious
You speak French

Key words for a negative Gemini Dragon's Tail

- You lie, you are continually confused and you don't trust anyone
You avoid any and all direct and honest communication
You talk too much and don't listen to others
You have no opinion of your own
You are a lost "Jack of all trades"
You steal all from anyone
You are indecisive

Key words for a positive Cancer Dragon's Head

- You are a great cook, caring, loving with a great family life
  You are a genius with real estate
  You own a beautiful home(s)
  You spend time your family
  Children love you
  You are a mystic
  You are sensual

Key words for a negative Cancer Dragon's Tail

- You are afraid of a career and responsibility
  You are smothering to all
  You are in trouble with your family
  Your anxiety causes ulcers
  You're often depressed
  You're over emotional
  You are too needy

Key words for a positive Leo Dragon's Head

- You have tons of physical and spiritual energy
  You want to be world famous or a leader
  You are honorable and true to yourself
  You'll travel far to get opportunities
  You have an incredible self esteem
  You are gifted and competitive
  You're shining and magnetic

Key words for a negative Leo Dragon's Tail

- You'll not travel anywhere for opportunities
  You are lazy asking for heart trouble
  You have a self-destructive attitude
  You have dependency problems
  You refuse all responsibilities
  You love shocking people
  You are an egocentric

Key words for a positive Virgo Dragon's Head

- You are a genius with organization, a researcher
  You are a very valuable Public Relations person
  You are a real master in communication
  You regenerate with plants and nature
  You are health conscious
  You are very spiritual
  You are an artist

Key words for a negative Virgo Dragon's Tail

- You disclaim the values of the metaphysical
  You are a traditionally educated mental snob
  You know better than everyone around you
  You are a fussy and picky perfectionist
  You are extremely critical of others
  You are a fanatic about diet
  You are a vegetarian

Key words for a positive Libra Dragon's Head

- You have "Savoir Faire" and are at ease with others
  You attract an honorable and wealthy crowd
  You are loving, refined and magnetic
  You have a positive self-image
  You are lucky with the law
  You are good with words
  You are a true diplomat

Key words for a negative Libra Dragon's Tail

- You feel you have no real strengths with groups
  You provide too much aid to the wrong partner
  You allow yourself to be manipulated
  You have been married a few times
  You attract ineffectual people
  You can't say no without guilt
  You have no regard for the law

Key words for a positive Scorpio Dragon's Head

- You work for the law or medicine and achieve a high position
  You are deep, mystical, refined and magnetic
  You have a wealth of residual inner power
  You have a will of steel and artistic ability
  You know you are the eagle of the Zodiac
  You are lucky with corporate endeavors
  You are an incredible investigator

Key words for a negative Scorpio Dragon's Tail

- You are a masochist with a lust for death and drama
  You use your metaphysical power the wrong way
  You enjoy the night and attract the wrong crowd
  You can't let go of people and you are secretive
  You are often jealous, resentful and dangerous
  You hate the cops and you have gone to jail
  You reject life

Key words for positive Sagittarius Dragon's Head

- You are a great teacher and you travel the globe around
  You use your inner knowledge of Indian philosophy
  You are a philosopher with a great love of animals
  You are lucky in gambling and with foreigners
  You know you are a real "Truth Seeker"
  You are independent and courageous
  Your great works are published

- **Key words for negative Sagittarius Dragon's Tail**

- Your philosophy, religion or your guru is the only right one
  You won't change your mind, your views or your beliefs
  You believe that animals are better than humans
  You won't challenge what has been written
  You are afraid of pursuing real education
  You have been religiously poisoned
  You think you are above the law

Key words for positive Capricorn Dragon's Head

- You run your own business or you are a great architect
  You are practical, honest, down to earth and spiritually elevated
  You have a position of power and respect in your career
  You are wise, organized and your attract responsibilities
  You have been working for Uncle Sam all your life
  You are gifted with politics in all it's facets
  You make time for your home life

Key words for negative Capricorn Dragon's Tail

- You are a snob, cold and calculated
  You have trouble with government
  Your knees and stomach hurt
  You use and abuse others
  Your career is a mess
  You're often depressed
  You're self-serving

Key words for a positive Aquarius Dragon's Head

- You have a great interest in UFO's as well as science and investigation
  You work for television, radio promoting the new age
  You service the world with an important mission in your heart
  You are a gifted communicator, speaker, and you

write unusual books
You travel the world with a considerable message
You are an inventor, a computer genius
You are born an astrologer or a pilot

- **Key words for a negative Aquarius Dragon's Tail**
  You only dream about your wishes
  You can't make a commitment with love
  You attract wrong friends and weird people
  You are afraid of flying and enclosed places
  You are afraid of success and responsibilities
  You are too independent or pursue lost causes.

- **Key words for a positive Pisces Dragon's Head**
  You are a successful actor or artist
  You find yourself in your psychic power
  You are involved to protect the environment
  You understand mankind's experiences and their differences
  You are a great caretaker of the world (Edgar Cayce)
  You are gifted in astral projection (like Nostradamus)
  You are compassionate, spiritual, and active in charity work

- **Key words for a negative Pisces Dragon's Tail**
  You are addicted to chemicals including prescriptions
  You read too much negative material and fear the "end times" are near
  You can't stop complaining and you are afraid of everything
  You are a religious fanatic or deceived by a "guru"
  You spend life in your own dream world
  You use sickness to avoid responsibility
  You waste your precious talents and gifts

CHINESE HOROSCOPE

There are twelve different animals, beginning with the "Rat," referring to the 12 energies found in occidental astrology. Chinese Astrology uses only animals, while Divine Astrology uses animals and human figures and symbols.

Rat or Sagittarius involves the same energy: There is a strong sense of justice, aggressiveness, and an inner knowledge of philosophy. Interestingly enough, the Chinese consider the Rat a domestic animal. So those born within the year of the Rat are domestic, protective, and are family orientated. A Rat's enemy is the Horse.

Bull or Capricorn involves the same energy: The Bull has staying power and will not stop until all is said and done. The soul is strong, steady, hard worker, very domestic, and will not change its mind once it is made up. A Bull's enemy is the Lamb and particularly the Tiger.

Tiger or Aquarius is the same energy: This is not a domestic animal and is somewhat dangerous and dignified. The soul is independent and like the Tiger fearless in front of danger. The Tiger is endowed with magnetism, freedom and courage. The enemies of the Tiger are the Monkey and Bull.

Rabbit or Pisces is the same energy: This is a domestic sign. The Rabbit is sensitive, creative, spiritual, and needs to help other people. The Rooster is the enemy of the Rabbit.

Dragon or Aries is the same energy: In Chinese Astrology, the Dragon is wise unlike Aries who is a "hothead" and learns by making lots of mistakes. The soul has presence, strengths, stature, and people will respect its true power. The Dog is the enemy of the Dragon.

Snake or Scorpio is the same energy: The snake is not domestic and prefers to stay clear of man. Many fear the Snake, but the Snake has a lot to offer. The Snake's world is magical and sensual. The Snake's poison is deadly and his eyes very hypnotic. The Snake will not have many friends but if you are a lucky one, the snake will protect you at all times. The enemy of the Snake is the Boar.

Horse or Gemini is the same energy: The horse is a domestic animal and he is fast, he is used by man for speed and work. The horse loves to parade and will always be in the front, ready to shine and run. The enemy of the Horse is the Rat.

Sheep or Cancer is the same energy: The Sheep is domestic and is a loving, soft and domestic animal that lives with man. The soul is given the power to get everything it seeks due to an annoying disposition to whine for its wants and needs. Home, family, security, food, and being taken care of by humans are given to this Chinese sign. The Lamb uses his artistic talent, the power of diplomacy and sensitivity to get what it wants. The enemy of the Sheep is the Ox or Bull.

Monkey or Leo is the same energy: A Monkey always lands on its feet. This is a domestic sign and will do all the faces he can to get what he needs from you. Among the best actors you will often find the monkey. To be a real actor you have to be a great liar and make the people watching you believe the part you play is real. The monkey is warned to beware of the deadly Tiger, as this sign's honorable traits cannot stand lies.

Rooster or Virgo is the same energy: The Rooster is domestic, clean, fussy and organized. The rooster is talkative and will make sure all listen to the fist call of dawn. They need to sanitize every thing and they are critical to those who will not listen to them. The enemy of the Rooster is the Rabbit.

Dog or Libra is the same energy: The dog is very domestic and lives with man. The soul needs and can provide true love, justice, fairness and honesty. The Dog will be your best friend for ever and will never let you down. The Dog is endowed with powerful fangs to protect the home of those they love, and will fight to the death for you. The best friend of a dog is the magnificent and loyal Tiger because they both enjoy honesty and courage. But the Dog has to be careful of the Dragon and rely on the powerful and invincible Tiger to take on this dangerous task.

Boar or Taurus is the same energy: This is a domestic sign and is protected by man. They are very lucky in business and easily attract money and power. They are endowed with great business sense, but usually end up consumed by other frugal signs. The enemy of the Boar is the Snake.

ASTRO-TAROT

The ASTRO-TAROT is a part of the advanced Astropsychology course. Visit www.drturi.com for the next class in your area or contact madrose@europa.com to schedule a class in your city.

Madeline Rosenstein Copyright 2001

ASTROLOGICAL WHEEL

This is where we put Divine Astrology and the Tarot together; it reads your present state of mind and the outcome within the next few months. The client to pick the cards must use the left hand. The "French Tarot De Marseille" or US, Swiss Tarot is used, and only the 22 major arcana. This customized table is available for the students upon request, email Madeline at madrose@europa.com.

MEANINGS TO HOUSES

House 1: Outward appearance, Personality, How other people see you.

House 2: Money, Personal possessions, Self-Esteem.

House 3: Brothers and sisters, Short trips, Private thoughts, Studies.

House 4: Foundation, Home, Father, Real estate, Mother.

House 5: Love affairs, Children, Entertainment.

House 6: Health, Service to the World, Working environment, Co-workers.

House 7: Partnerships, Marriage, Public, Known enemies, Facing the world.

House 8: Legacy, Talent, Debts, Taxes, Insurance, Mortgages, Other's money.

House 9: Philosophies, Long distance travel, Teaching, Publishing, Lecturing.

House 10: Career, Superiors, Public Standing, Honors, Accomplishments.

House 11: Friends, Hopes, Wishes, Traveling, Original Experiences.

House 12: Secret: Occult, Subconscious, Self-undoing, Unknown enemies.

Take the time to learn to visualize the wheel. Take the time to master each house and all the appropriate key words.

LAYING OF CARDS

The Reader shuffles the card and concentrates on self. He has the client cut the deck and put the bottom half on top. The reader opens the cards into a fan face down.

1) Astropsychologist shuffles the cards, concentrates on self. He has the client cut the deck and put the other cards back on the deck.

2.) Client picks the cards; the Astropsychologist puts the cards face down, one card at the time in each house beginning with the first house of the zodiac (the client's month of birth), and continues counter clockwise until he fills each house with a card.

3.) Soft background music and burning candles is recommended in this ritual.

4.) Your telephone must be turned off with no disturbances.

5.) Recording equipment must also be used.

6.) If you own a dog or a cat (as do I), keep your pet close or inside your office as they are sensitive to subtle nuances and pick up psychic vibrations.

0. The Fool (Le Mat)

Passive, negative. Submission to external influences. Impulsiveness, madness. Lack of knowledge. This is the only card that has no number, and so a substitute card is then picked.

I. The Magician (Le Bateleur)

Active, positive. Initiative, in control of oneself. Wisdom, reason, good use of the tools learned.

II. The High Priestess (Junon)

Intuition, divination. The spirit of penetrating the unknown. Hypnotic sciences of hidden things.

III. The Empress (L'Imperatrice)

Observation, comprehension, conception, study. Wisdom, reason behind the generating of ideas.

IIII. The Emperor (L'Empereur)

Inner Light. The word made flesh. Concentration of thought and will. Spiritual energy, positivism.

V. The Pope (Jupiter)

Abstract. Speculative reality, metaphysics, Religion. Spirituality. Transcendental knowledge. Morality.

VI. The Lovers (L'Amoureux)

Freedom, choice, tests. Doubt. Anxious battle against the difficulties of life. Sentiment, affections, dual.

VII. The Chariot (Le Chariot)

Domination, triumph. Talent, ability. New road. The master who commands obedience. Progress.

VIII. Justice (La Justice)

Law, order, equilibrium. Stability. Logic. Placidity, calm, regularity. Discernment. Legal paperwork.

VIIII. The Hermit (L'Ermite)

Abstention, isolation. Prudence, discretion. Reservation, avarice. Meticulous scholar. A doctor.

X. Wheel of Fortune (La Roue De Fortune)

Luck, ambition, inventions, discoveries. Life-giving seed. Maintenance of individual existence. Growth.

XI. Strength (La Force)

Strength, power, feasible ideas. Practical spirit, intelligence ruling matter. Energy, courage, magnetism.

XII. Hanged Man (Le Pendu)

Impotence, utopia. Dreamer, spirit escaping from matter. An apostle, a martyr, waiting period, lost.

XIII. Death (La Mort)

Fatality, disillusion. Decomposition, putrefaction. The end, new life, rebirthing, transformation.

XIIII. Temperance

Participation, communion. Carefreeness, frankness. Circulation, prodigality. Adept of occult medicine.

XV. The Devil (Le Diable)

Confusion, instinct. New knowledge, real power, metaphysician, true light, religious poisoning. Blindness.

XVI. The Tower (La Maison De Dieu)

Presumption, fall. Infatuation, inability. The victim of forces in revolt. Explosion, catastrophe.

XVII. The Star (L'Etoile)

Predestination, hopefulness. Surrender to the faith of immortality. Cosmic consciousness, Universal love.

XVIII. The Moon (La Lune)

Concrete. Moody, tears with the mother. Illusion of the senses. Superstition. Materialism, mistakes.

XVIIII. The Sun (Le Soleil)

Universal light. The Eternal World. Expansion, illumination which gives genius. Serenity, arts, idealism.

XX. Judgement (Le Judgement)

Inspiration, exaltation. Enthusiasm, prophecy. Protection, opportunity, end or start of karma.

XXI. The World (Le Monde)

Ecstasy, clairvoyance. The unknown revealing itself to the soul. Integral sciences of the absolute.

Note - Always remember that your client is responding to your suggestions and that his own future is based upon his own thought process. Your are entering the reality of the Superconsciousness and you are responsible for the positive or negative spiritual legacy imprinted in his own Superconscious in time and space. Always counteract a negative card with a positive comment, such as explaining that the Death card does not mean death but a re-birth of some sort and that the devil means a must higher knowledge is imposed upon the self. Never leave your client with uncertainty, as he needs direction and spiritual support. Always counsel with honesty but remain diplomatic and insist on teaching the Cabalistic candle ritual to clean up the thought process of your client.

Cabalistic Candle Ritual

This ritual may be done to purify a space or the thoughts or spirits of a person. If the Temperance card (angel) is drawn during the Tarot, this ritual can be done with a guardian angel, to strengthen the energy of the house it was in.

Purchase a white, green, and blue candle during the new moon period, and always perform this ritual for the very first time during a new moon and for best results on the first day of the New Moon. Arrange the candles in a triangle. At the tip of the triangle (farthest away from you), place the white candle. The green will be to your left and the blue to your right. The green and blue are the base of the pyramid where you stand. A small bit of incense is placed in the center. Before anything is started, grab a full hand of salt with the left hand, and turn around in a circle, dropping the salt around the entire area where the ritual will be performed. Do the candle ritual inside the circle of protection. If you wish, you may buy a small guardian angel and place it in front of the white candle (inside the triangle).

First the incense is lit, then the white candle, the green candle, and the blue candle. The prayer or meditation is made for the length of time the incense is burning. The candles, the color's mixture and the incense's smoke, create a vacuum funnel in time and space and reach the entity, guardian angel, protective spirit which will grant your wishes. When the incense is burnt, the ritual is over and the candles extinguished. You may repeat this ritual anytime you choose before or after a new moon thereafter.

What is God?

This is a question many have asked throughout the ages, and it is up to each and every one of us to find this answer for himself. I would like to share with you a couple of letters some students have written about this subject.

Dear Dr. Louis Turi,

You're right, I am into astrology now. I even planned my trip next week in accordance to the New Moon coming up on 1/13/02. And my traditional outlook on religion and spirituality has shifted into a whole new paradigm. Astrology (and the re-incarnation theory) has brought to the table - many legitimate questions that need to be asked concerning God and the nature of who he really is and how we relate to him and the universe....I've developed my 'own' theory thus far which I never would have been able to do if not for your reading. I feel my journey from this point forward will only get more exciting and rewarding. And I have to say that for the first time in my life, I feel a feeling of liberation. I feel like I just took off an old pair of trousers (traditional religion) which I have worn for 34 years and now slipped into a nice satin robe (freedom to ask questions and seek the truth).

I appreciate the gift.

P////

And another from one of my best students, a magnificent Leo –

Dr. Turi,

My reality of God. There is one God, and every person has a different interpretation of what this God is. For example, some people worship an elephant, and others Buddha, and others Jesus etc. The reality is semantics; what do you mean when you worship your god? It is the same intangible God, but different tangible meanings to what their God is. This is where all the confusion plays a role. In the end, all the tangible Gods want Universal Love and that is the bottom line.

Love. Lisa the Lion LL

And finally another student has written:

Dr. Dr. Turi,

God I cannot see. But I see his creation in all forms everywhere I look. He is the Creator of all that is, was, or shall be, the Creator of all that is both seen and unseen. But this is evident. I think a more pertinent question is, "How do I relate to this Creator?" One can study the sciences and find God's intelligence in the thought patterns of mathematics and ordered systems which hold this great universe together. And to find the answer to "Who am I?" a careful psychology has been planned in the ordered system of the stars. It is through this system which is called "Astropsychology," that one can see a divine blueprint for one's life. Nevertheless, it is the intention and growth of the soul which inhabits the body, that makes the best or worst use of these stars. Let us determine to use the stars we were given to uncover our best talents and become the highest beings, closest to the light of that almighty Creator.

Thank you for showing us the way,
M///////

Student feedback

Dr. Turi:
I wanted to let you know the Astropsychology class in Portland has changed my life! You are an amazing speaker and have incredible POWER. You are too generous to share 30 years of information in 5 days. I am happy you are apart of my life, to help me with my spiritual awareness and to help others learn the stars. Thank you for flying to Portland, and your time. I am forever grateful, Love and Light,

Lisa //

Hello Dr. Turi;

I have just returned from the July Astropsychology class. What a unique and enlightening experience! Besides the valuable knowledge given, Dr. Turi himself makes the class challenging and entertaining. By the end of the week, I could see the reflex action of intuition beginning to form in everyone who was there. I did not think such a thing could be possible. It is a life changing experience, and one can never view the world in quite the same way. When Dr. Turi says, "you will be given the keys to the Universal Mind", he really means it! I encourage anyone who is thinking of attending, to go, as I guarantee they will be raised in spirit. My blessings to all who attend this course in the future.

M///////

Dear Dr. Turi,
We are thankful for the profound blessing of enlightenment shared with our July Astropsychology class. With your guidance, we - reunited old souls in the Arizona desert - rededicated ourselves to the vision of sharing Astropsychology with the children of the world, who will carry it forward as the only practical spiritual philosophy of the emerging Aquarian cycle. The highest

of spiritual world is now in our hands. Together we are changing the human world into a world of light and awareness. With much love,
Chief Sonne and Claudine

Dear Dr. Turi;
Definitely Divine Astrology for me, I have never been exposed to any Astrology before hearing Dr. Turi on Jeff Rense's national program, but if modern Astrology is littered with mathematical jargon then it is more of a hand down Win for Divine Astrology. The favorite part for me was Dr. Turi's great humor through out the tapes, I of course need to practice the reflex and know it will get more interesting when I receive my computer program and plug in people I know birth dates to practice with the housing system.

Thank you, Joyce

To Dr. Turi;
I have just return from the July Astropsychology class, and it was the greatest class I ever attended. Dr. Turi is the one of the best teachers I have ever known. I have learnt so much from this man. This class is a must for every one. If you want to soar with the eagles and be number one in your field as an astrologer and to help every one that will be in your life take the class. For it is truly enlightenment. Thank you once again Dr. Turi for all that you have taught me. Love & light

Alice //////

To all prospective Astropsychology students;
It has now been one week since I have completed Dr. Turi's advanced astrology course in Phoenix AZ. It has been about five months since I passed his basic astrology class by mail. I am here to state that I absorbed so much more information and reflex in five days of hands on schooling, than I could ever imagine getting in months of home study. Don't get me wrong, the home course I hold

very dearly, and It was an excellent prerequisite, and I highly recommend it, but it only put me on the runway, where as traveling to AZ. to get hands on schooling, placed me in the air. I guess it depends on what you want to do with the knowledge, and how fast you want to do it. Myself I planned to make a career out of it, and I knew that the home course would eventually produce those results. Now having completed the advanced course, I now face that reality. My new career has now sprouted, and I owe it all to one incredible man, Dr. Louis Turi. There are not enough kind words to describe this incredibly gifted, spiritual pioneer. To be taught by him is a great honor, and pure enlightenment. There is no doubt that you will notice that he has a little something different to offer, something you won't find anywhere else. With that I leave it up to you, the prospective student to find that answer.
Thank You, Charles

Hi Dr. Turi,
There is a driving force of energy that moves and propels us in our quest for the truth, and the truth does not lie in any one area. This truth that the seeker seeks, lays scattered through out our planet. So we as we seek must be patient and discerning when we come across the path of others speaking the truth. And from my discernment and the trust of my heart, I feel very fortunate and blessed to have crossed paths with Dr. Turi in this time of life. Dr. Turi's wisdom and understanding is a vast as the stars he speaks of. I am thankful that we taped the seminar! Thank You again for sharing your wisdom of the stars! Many Blessings,

James

Thanks Dr. Turi you are the greatest. Learning to do astrology the way you do it has made such a difference in my life. I use it all day long every day. My birthday is ///, I have the stars to teach astrology and that is what I want to do, I do it all day long for everyone around me I can't help myself, I see it in the news, the weather, everything everywhere, my cats and dogs, it's wonderful. It is nice to know who you are dealing with, where is Neptune? What will you lie about. Where is Pluto. What part of your life do you rearrange all of the time. Where is Jupiter? What do you want to learn and teach, where will you expand and be lucky. I have Jupt in the 1st house I want to teach. It is all so wonderful. One of these days I am going to call Jeff Rense when you are on the air and ask some general questions, so people can see how powerful it is. Wind heat and fires for the next two years. With the DT in Sag. and Pl. in Sag the list is long for what this will bring.

Thank you so much Dr. Turi.
Barbara

Dear Dr. Turi,

After finishing your Advanced Astropsychology class, my dream state has been enhanced. I've always journeyed my dreams, and I can see a change of consciousness in myself. The Universal Mind has certainly come to new life. It's exciting to meet new people and see the qualities that the stars have influenced in their lives. It helps one to have a more open mind to personality traits that would normally be unpleasant, to understanding what makes people tick. For me, it has made me a more compassionate, understanding person. With the help of your teachings, I've learned the future is the reincarnation of thoughts today. I'm thinking and planning my future with light and love for a beautiful new life. It is just the beginning of great things to come. Thank you for all you've done for me. Thank you for being such a beautiful channel of light in this world.
Your student,

Kiki //

John /// here. I just wanted to take a moment and thank you for your excellent work in the Portland

Astropsychology class. What memories you gave me! I will be smiling for many years to come.
All the best,
John /////

Here is an amazing story from a Scorpio student of mine.....

Let me tell you that I had a dream of Dr. Turi back in mid-March of 2001. I didn't know who he was then, nor his information, as I had never seen or heard of him.
Two weeks later I had fallen asleep while listening to my local public radio station, and at three in the morning awoke to a man talking real fast and speaking of astrological symbolism. I still didn't know it was Dr. Turi, until I went to his web site two days later—and there was the individual I had dreamt of two weeks earlier— Dr. Louis Turi.
I knew that the Universe had guided me to him. That culminated with the unique and undeniably accurate method he rekindled from the Great Seer, Nostradamus. Long gone are the nights of confusion and frustration because now I have the tools to decipher the messages from the Universe.
May you all find your way to the place of your souls origin,

Salvador//

Phoenix Class July 2001 (Dr. Turi on far left)

Portland Class December 2001

Astropsychology Classes

Welcome to the world of Astropsychology. Let me take this opportunity to thank you for your trust in my work and welcome you to our growing family of Astropsychologists . Take the time to watch the video and read the book "The Power Of The Dragon" before starting to listen to the audiotapes. As you watch the video again, after the completion of your course, you will see how much more knowledge you gained in your study. Take your time in listening to all your tapes, and don't be afraid to ask as many questions as you can to those close to you. You will have to build a "reflex" in which your wisdom will allow you to gain answers where traditional psychology has failed. As you gain confidence over the few months ahead of you, apply your knowledge to reinforce your own. If you take the time to study properly, sooner or later you will enjoy the results, as the people around will be astonished at your insights. Keep in mind that you will not build up your cosmic consciousness overnight, but with time and patience I assure you that you will.

Don't give up in your study, please help me to further true knowledge and the great therapeutic values found in the old science of Divine Astrology. Send your first exam when you're ready then the second one to graduate. Soon my infomercial will be aired, and you will gain from my national exposure. Once you pass both of your exams and graduate as an Astropsychologist, a special Divine Astrology program that I designed with the help of Halloran software is available to those willing to use it when turning professional. This basic program is available for $210.00. To set it up to show the monthly housing system and the Dragon's Head/Tail, follow this procedure. Once you have installed it, go to "customization" and click on "Housing System." Click on "Monthly." Then go to "Chart Center Image" and check "Moon Nodes Dragons," then the dragon should appear in your wheel. The children of tomorrow as all the people born before you will be able to regenerate and find in your newfound knowledge the golden keys of what it mean to human. Keep in mind that famous author John Gray "Men are from Mars, women from Venus," also took my course, and surely has made a good use of the knowledge. Please get in touch with Madeline at madrose@europa.com. She is my Promotional Manager; I intend to have all my students' names and addresses inserted on my site so they can all communicate and participate in our future endeavors and Astropsychology Schools and Universities. In case you need more than the starting software, you can also obtain more as you go along in your study. I also have the Personal Path Natal Interpretations, the Star Match Compatibility Interpretations, the Life Trends Transits interpretations, the Journey Interpretations, or the Career Path Interpretations. The discounted price for those five professional (cd's/disks) programs (includes the basic program) is $ 587.00. You may also start only with the basic $150.00 software program (PC) and upgrade as you wish. You may use those programs immediately to generate an income from your home on your computer as you perfect your knowledge in your Astropsychology practice. Dear Student, welcome to the light, master the light and promote the light.

--Dr. Turi

If you have any questions about certain parts of the tuition do not hesitate to contact me at: dr.turi@cox.net , or Madeline atmadrose@europa.com and let us know if you are ready for the advanced Astropsychology course in your area or by mail.

True Celestial Knowledge and Astropsychology

Dr. Turi

Startheme Publications Ltd.
4411 North 23rd St. Phoenix, Arizona 85016

Tel: (602) 265-7667 Fax: (602) 265-8668

web Page: http://www.drturi.com

Email dr.turi@cox.net

For bulk or wholesale purchases please contact:
info@reevolutionpress.com Phone 818-774-0054

The celebrated French Astrologer Dr. Turi is offering a 7-day crash course (see website www.drturi.com). You will enjoy Nostradamus' 16th century Divine Astrology method and become an Astropsychologist in a single week. Master the golden key to the universe and congregate with spiritually advanced people. You will enjoy mental stimulation and meet exceptional new friends. Gain true cosmic consciousness, open your 3rd eye, and develop your celestial affiliation with infinity. Ultimately you will realize your direct relationship with God and the Universe. Start your own career, become financially independent while bringing the light to the children of tomorrow. No complicated math involved and a 98% graduation rate. Certainly the most advanced spiritual experience of your life. Call Dr. Turi at (602) 265-7667 or visit www.drturi.com for all information and a yearly schedule.

Fee for 7 full day live class: $2.175.00

TRUE KNOWLEDGE IS PRICELESS

Dr. Turi also offers his classes in taped versions and they can be studied at home.

(DEAL! save $550) Advanced Astropsychology album course # 1 by mail or $1,050.00 + S&H (original $1600). Included - 16 - 90MN tapes, 1 exam, 2 books, 2 videos and course materials. You must call Madeline for your safe credit card transaction at (503)-671-9072. You may also call me for any information about my courses or services at (602) 265-7667.

Advanced Astropsychology album course # 2 by mail: $1600.00 + S&H. Included - 13 - 90MN tapes, 1 exam, 3 books, 2 videos and course materials. This course will also be available on video soon. You must call Madeline for your safe credit card transaction at (503)-671-9072. You may also call me for any information about my courses or services at (602) 265-7667.

Software is available and is separate from the class fees.

Full Seven Programs with 10% discount, $690.10 Credit card or check accepted (additional conditions for a Mac)

The Basic Program Astro Deluxe costs $210.00 for a PC, Mac users need to adapt with a virtual pc.

Pre-Registration: If you decide to take the live Astropsychology class, you need to confirm with Dr.Turi ASAP (dr.turi@cox.net) or 602-265-7667 and send your payment to reserve a seat for you. Paid in full - Credit card or check accepted.

Thank you,
--Dr. Turi

****

Dr. Turi runs his practice in Phoenix, Arizona. You may call (602) 265-7667 or go to his website www.drturi.com to order any of the following services:

- Taped full life readings--progressed and comparison readings--weekly, monthly and yearly transits--astro-cartography.

- Books: "The Power of the Dragon" -- "I Know All About You"-- "And God Created the Stars"--and his two yearly publications, "Moon Power Starguide" and "Nostradamus Forecast for all Signs"

Note: What was your favorite part of this tuition? What do you think needs improvement in this tuition? I will appreciate any comments you would like to make. All the new information received could shape the future students knowledge to a much higher level.

I will now take this opportunity to thank you for reading my book and congratulate you for your effort and desire to become an Astropsychologist. Many of the children of today and tomorrow will gain from your knowledge and the legacy left by your efforts to promote the light. This will help to make the world a much better place to live for us all.

The ones that will really benefit from your research for the truth are the children, and the signature of your high deed is forever writing in light, in the heavens. In this process you will inherit a much better set of stars in your next reincarnation as "for every action, spiritual or physical, an equal reaction is to be expected". And finally, as you are looking for your higher self, you are simply looking for God. When you find God, you find yourself, thus when you find yourself you have finally found God, All is that and that is all.

Thank You,

~Dr. Turi

Cover design, zodiac wheel on page 141, the Tarot poster on page 182, and the dragon below, were all created by Madeline Rosenstein. Madeline is a graduate of the University of California Berkeley, and received her Master's at San Diego State University. She has applied her unique style of artwork to many facets, including teaching college art, sign painting, designing wine labels, illustration, logo and product design, book covers, and web art. She has a penchant for the unusual. Visit her website at www.madroseart.com. Let her creative design fit your individualized needs.

Lightning Source UK Ltd.
Milton Keynes UK
UKHW011823300322
400846UK00001B/137